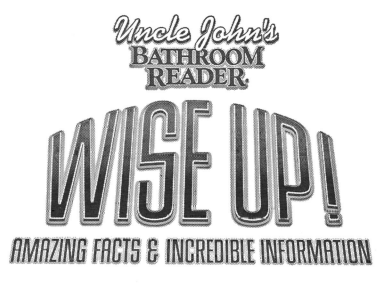

Uncle John's BATHROOM READER

WISE UP!

AMAZING FACTS & INCREDIBLE INFORMATION

The Bathroom Readers' Institute
Ashland, Oregon, and San Diego, California

UNCLE JOHN'S BATHROOM READER WISE UP!

ISBN 13: 978-1-60710-037-9

For information, write...The Bathroom Readers' Institute
P.O. Box 1117, Ashland, OR 97520
www.bathroomreader.com
e-mail: mail@bathroomreader.com

Library of Congress Cataloging-in-Publication Data
Uncle John's bathroom reader wise up.
p. cm.
Includes bibliographical references.
ISBN 978-1-60710-037-9 (pbk.)
1. American wit and humor. 2. Curiosities and wonders.
I. Bathroom Readers' Institute (Ashland, Or.)
PN6165.U5287 2009
081.02'07—dc22
2009022956

Printed in the United States of America
09 10 11 12 13   5 4 3 2 1

Thank You!

The Bathroom Readers' Institute thanks the following people
whose advice and assistance made this book possible:

Gordon Javna

JoAnn Padgett

Melinda Allman

Amy Miller

Jay Newman

Michael Brunsfeld

Jeff Altemus

Angie Kern

J. Carroll

Dan Mansfield

Chris Stuart

Scot A. McKibbin

Maggie McLaughlin

Stephanie Spadaccini

John Dollison

Sydney Stanley

David Cully

Monica Maestas

Amy L. and Lisa M.

Ginger Winters

Jennifer Frederick

Brian, Thom, and Julia

David Calder

Karen Malchow

Sophie, J.J., and Bea

Porter the Wonderdog

Uncle John's Bathroom Reader Wise Up! is a compilation of running feet and
selected articles from the following previously published Bathroom Reader titles:
Uncle John's Bathroom Reader Golden Plunger Awards © 2008, *Uncle John's Bathroom
Reader Plunges Into Great Lives* © 2003, *Uncle John's Bathroom Reader Plunges Into
History* © 2001, *Uncle John's Bathroom Reader Plunges Into History Again* © 2004,
Uncle John's Bathroom Reader Plunges Into Hollywood © 2005, *Uncle John's Bathroom
Reader Plunges Into Music* © 2007, *Uncle John's Bathroom Reader Plunges Into
National Parks* © 2007, *Uncle John's Bathroom Reader Plunges Into the Presidency*
© 2004, *Uncle John's Bathroom Reader Plunges Into Texas* © 2004, *Uncle John's
Bathroom Reader Takes a Swing at Baseball* © 2008, *Uncle John's Bathroom Reader
Tees Off on Golf* © 2005, *Uncle John's Bathroom Reader Wonderful World of Odd* ©
2006, *Uncle John's Curiously Compelling Bathroom Reader* © 2006, *Uncle John's Fast-
Acting Long-Lasting Bathroom Reader* © 2005, *Uncle John's Great Big Bathroom Reader*
© 1998, *Uncle John's Slightly Irregular Bathroom Reader* © 2004, *Uncle John's
Triumphant 20th Bathroom Reader* © 2007.

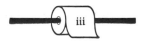

Contents

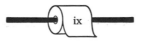

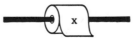

The Intro-duck-tion

Here at the Bathroom Readers' Institute, we're suckers for cool facts, and we're constantly quizzing each other: How many gallons of peanut oil does it take to deep-fry a turkey? What cartoon character is prohibited from running for elected office in Texas? Why did the game of bingo used to be called beano?

So a few years ago, when Uncle John noticed that many of the letters we received from fans were asking for the same thing—an entire book of running feet (those fun factoids at the bottom of *Bathroom Reader* pages)—he called in a team of bathroom-reading writers and sent them on a fact-finding mission: search old *Bathroom Readers* for running feet and then organize the facts into interesting lists. The finished product turned out so great that even more readers wrote in asking us to do it again.

We got right to work...diving into a whole new batch of *Bathroom Readers* and pulling out the running feet. We sorted the facts, organized them, argued (gently) about how best to arrange them, and then organized them again. We also came up with 50 *new* pages of facts.

The end result is *Uncle John's Bathroom Reader Wise Up!*, more than 380 pages packed with useful—and sometimes useless—but always interesting information.

If you're joining us for the first time, welcome! And if you're on your second *Bathroom Reader* book of facts, welcome back! We're really glad you're here. And as always, go with the flow...

—Uncle John and the BRI Staff

P.S. We're already gathering new running feet for the next *Bathroom Reader*. So email your favorite obscure bits of trivia and fun facts to *mail@bathroomreader.com*!

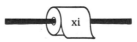

It Would Take...

...630 silkworm cocoons to make one silk blouse.

...a chicken-plucking machine 14 seconds to pluck a whole chicken.

...a drop of ocean water more than 1,000 years to circulate around the world.

...a manned rocket ship 70,000 years to reach the next closest solar system.

...about 540 peanuts to make a 12-ounce jar of peanut butter.

...a combine harvester nine seconds to harvest enough wheat to make 70 loaves of bread.

...a car traveling at 75 mph 258 days to drive around one of Saturn's rings.

...a year's worth of corks from all the wine bottled in France to circle the world three times.

...Pluto 248.53 years to travel around the Sun.

...every star in the Milky Way to fill an Olympic-size swimming pool (if each star were the size of a grain of salt).

...the Milky Way about 200 million years to make one revolution.

...about 600 grapes to make a bottle of wine.

...70 separate pieces of wood to make a violin.

...up to six gallons of peanut oil to deep-fry a turkey.

...only one steer to yield enough ground beef for 1,000 McDonald's Quarter Pounders.

...the average American 40 days to earn enough money to pay for a year's worth of food.

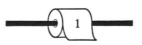

One & Only

Colorado is the only state to have turned down the opportunity to host the Olympics, in 1976.

The only player in the Los Angeles Dodgers' starting lineup with a batting average of .300 or better going into the 1965 World Series was pitcher Don Drysdale.

Only cats born with no tail: the Manx. The breed carries a genetic mutation that causes the abnormality.

Only all-female African American military unit to deploy to Europe during World War II: the 888th Central Postal Directory Battalion, out of Georgia. They sorted and delivered mail to soldiers.

Frank Zappa's only Top-40 song: "Valley Girl," in 1982 (it reached #32).

Only player to get caught stealing to end the World Series: Babe Ruth, in 1926.

According to *Billboard*, only two songs with the word "summer" in the title have reached number one: "Summer in the City" and "Theme from a Summer Place."

Only Norwegian band with international success: a-ha. Biggest hit: "Take on Me."

Michelangelo signed only one of his sculptures—the *Pietà*.

Only golfer to spend 30 minutes on a single hole in the U.S. Open: Ray Ainsley (1938).

The only member of Pink Floyd to play on every one of the band's albums: drummer Nick Mason.

Shirley Bassey is the only artist to have recorded songs for more than one James Bond movie (*Goldfinger*, *Diamonds Are Forever*, and *Moonraker*).

The only horse to defeat Man o' War was named Upset.

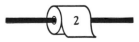

Canada

In the 1940s, the Canadian government advised mothers to begin toilet-training babies at one month old.

Of Canada's 36 "Fathers of Confederation," two of them were named John Hamilton Gray.

One in ten Canadians say they'd support a law that encouraged people in major cities to wear name tags.

During World War II, German U-boats sank 23 vessels in Canada's St. Lawrence River.

The United States has invaded Canada twice—once during the American Revolution and once during the War of 1812.

One of Canada's founding fathers was an American: William P. Howland of Pawling, New York.

In 1943, Fred Rose became the only Communist ever elected to the Canadian parliament.

Despite their good-guy image, Canada's Mounties have been caught spying on people illegally.

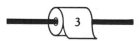

Talk Like a Pirate

THREATS

Your sands are run!
(*I'm going to kill you!*)

I'll slit a couple of feet of steel
into your vitals!
(*I'll stab you with my sword!*)

I come from hell, and I'll carry
you there presently.
(*How all good pirates answer the
question "Where are you
from?"*)

INSULTS

You're a dung-souled knuckle
brain.
(*You're an incapable idiot.*)

You've got a split tongue.
(*You're a liar.*)

You should be fed on pap
and suckets.
(*You're acting like a baby. Pap
and suckets were soft foods often
served to babies.*)

The smell of you alone is
enough to wrinkle the noses
of pigs.
(*You stink.*)

GENERAL DIRECTIONS

"Scupper your hide out of
here."
(*Go away.*)

Clap a stopper on your eyes.
(*Quit crying.*)

Put a name on what you're at.
(*What do you mean?*)

Bestir yourself!
(*Move it!*)

Cough up your tale.
(*Tell us your story.*)

Keep your tongue behind
your teeth.
(*Don't say anything.*)

Shiver your timbers.
(*Wait a minute.*)

Stay your claws.
(*Keep your hands to yourself.*)

Strike your colors.
(*Surrender.*)

Cock your piece.
(*Get your gun ready.*)

Too Cool for School

Chuck Berry has a degree from a beauty school.

Tony Blair's schoolmaster called him "the most difficult boy I ever had to deal with."

Singer Huey Lewis scored a perfect 800 on the math portion of his SAT.

Philosopher and author Eric Hoffer (*The True Believer*, published in 1951) was self-educated. He was homeless for many years, and then worked as a dishwasher and longshoreman.

Gene Simmons of KISS was once an elementary school teacher.

Garth Brooks's college major: advertising.

Al Capone dropped out of school when he was 14.

Jack Nicholson spent every day of an entire school year in detention.

In high school, Mariah Carey's nickname was "Mirage" because she was absent so often.

Monica Lewinsky's classmates voted her "Most Likely to Get Her Name in Lights."

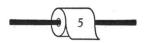

The Blues

The term "feeling blue" has its roots in nautical traditions. In the old days, when a captain or officer died, the ship flew a blue flag.

People sitting in the first few rows of a Blue Man Group concert get plastic ponchos before the show to protect them from the mess created as the performers bang on the liquid-filled tops of drums.

In many languages, people use the same word for the colors blue and green.

The sky is blue because of the way the human eye perceives color. On sunny days, light scatters in such a way that the eye "sees" only the blue part of the spectrum.

First official blues record: Hart A. Wand's "Dallas Blues," in 1912.

In 2002's *Die Another Day*, James Bond sliced Thomas Gainsborough's painting "The Blue Boy" with a sword.

The Toronto Blue Jays are the only Major League Baseball team located outside the United States.

World's largest blue sapphire: the Blue Giant of the Orient, at 466 carats.

Canada's largest fruit crop: blueberries.

The term "blue jeans" comes from the French *bleu de Gênes*, meaning "blue of Genoa." Why? Some of the first denim pants were manufactured in Italy and were shipped out of the port of Genoa.

Bluebirds were considered a rare species until 1996.

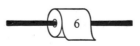

10 Strange Bands

1. THE FIRST VIENNESE VEGETABLE ORCHESTRA

This nine-member Austrian group plays instruments made completely out of fresh vegetables, including carrot flutes, eggplant drums, and a "gurkaphone" (a hollow cucumber with a carrot mouthpiece and green-pepper bell). At the conclusion of live performances, the Orchestra chops up its instruments and makes a soup, which is shared with the audience.

2. MAX Q

It's the world's only soft-rock band made up entirely of former astronauts. All six members flew on the U.S. space shuttle in the 1980s and 1990s. They play mostly love songs about space and alienation. "Max Q" refers to the maximum air pressure experienced in the shuttle moments after blastoff.

3. HORSE THE BAND

This American group plays fast, heavy versions of the instrumental music from 1980s Nintendo video games, such as Super Mario Brothers and The Legend of Zelda.

4. GWAR

The band dresses in elaborate rubber ogre and monster costumes and takes stage names like "Oderus Urungus," "Flattus Maximus," and "Beefcake the Mighty." GWAR plays hard-driving heavy metal songs (such as "Maggots" and "Death Pod"). Their show includes staged deaths and buckets of fake vomit and blood that they throw at the audience.

5. MUSCLE FACTORY

First, the tank-top-and-spandex-shorts-clad sextet performs songs about weightlifting, such as "Pump to Failure" and "The Spotter." Then they lift weights—onstage.

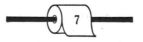

6. QNTAL

Qntal is a German trio that sings, in Latin and ancient German dialects, haunting, medieval-style ballads about all sorts of historical events. They're backed with a thumping drum machine. The name Qntal came to a group member in a dream.

7. TRACHTENBERG FAMILY SLIDESHOW PLAYERS

This is an old-fashioned family band. Dad Jason plays guitar and sings lead, teenage daughter Rachel plays drums and sings backing vocals, and mom Tina operates the slide projector. Why slides? Their songs are based on picture slides, bought at garage sales and thrift stores, which are projected along with the songs.

8. THE CANDY BAND

Four former Detroit rock musicians who became stay-at-home moms started this band to entertain their children. Their songs are punk-rock covers of nursery rhymes, classic children's songs, and TV show theme songs. (The Candy Band has also performed on *The Today Show*.)

9. SUPER FURRY ANIMALS (SFA)

Playing psychedelic/electronic pop, with many songs sung in Welsh, SFA is extremely popular in England. What makes them so weird? During live shows, the band members—using secret special-effects technology—slowly morph into furry, hulking Sasquatches.

10. ARNOCORPS

Heavily inspired by Arnold Schwarzenegger, the "pioneers of action-adventure hardcore rock and roll" pretend to be action-adventure movie heroes from the mountains of Austria.

* * *

"I don't know anything about music. In my line, you don't have to."
—**Elvis Presley**

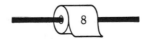

Ancient Eating

In ancient Rome, it was considered a sin to eat a woodpecker.

The first volume of published recipes dates to AD 62. Titled *De re coquinaria* ("On the Subject of Cooking"), it described the feasts enjoyed by the Roman emperor Claudius.

The first archaeological evidence of soup dates back to 6000 BC. The main ingredient was hippopotamus.

Romans did not eat sitting up—that was considered extremely bad manners. They ate lying down on couches around the table.

The oldest known sample of a chewing gum was found in Sweden in 1993. The 9,000-year-old gob of honey-sweetened resin still contained tooth marks.

In the 13th century, quality standards for pasta were set by the pope.

Romans flavored food with garum, a paste made by leaving fish to rot for several weeks.

Pepper was so valuable during Elizabethan times that it was sold by the individual grain.

The ancient Romans had soft drinks of root juices and water.

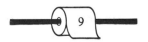

Trash Talk

The average American throws away about 10 pounds of trash per day.

Newspapers take up the most space in landfills.

Almost 7 million tons of clothing and fabric are thrown away every year. Just 12 percent of that is reused or recycled.

It takes 80 to 100 years for an aluminum can to degrade.

In 2007, Americans threw out twice as much trash as they did in 1960.

By the year 2020, the city of San Francisco plans to recycle all of its trash.

In 2002, astronauts removed 4,000 pounds of trash from the International Space Station. Some of it was brought back to Earth in the space shuttle, but the rest was stuffed into an unmanned Russian rocket and burned up in Earth's atmosphere.

Most common litter: cigarette butts. Smokers toss 4.5 trillion butts a year.

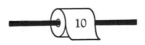

Everyday Inventions

Who invented the coat hanger? Historians say Thomas Jefferson.

Hungarian László Bíró, who patented the ballpoint pen, was also a sculptor and hypnotist.

Pizza was invented in 1889 by Raffaele Esposito in Naples, Italy.

The Countess du Barry, mistress of France's King Louis XV, invented the fishbowl.

Bette Nesmith Graham, mother of Monkee Mike Nesmith, invented Liquid Paper in the 1950s.

Jack Johnson, the first African American world heavyweight boxing champion, invented the common household wrench.

Band-Aid is the trademarked name for the 1921 invention of Earle Dickson.

William Blackstone of Indiana invented the washing machine in 1874 as a birthday gift for his wife.

Marion Donovan made the first diaper cover out of a shower curtain.

Coca-Cola, invented by Dr. John S. Pemberton in 1885, was originally sold as a "brain tonic."

The first pencil with an attached eraser was invented in 1858 by Hymen L. Lipman of Philadelphia.

A cigar-smoking lawyer from Lima, Pennsylvania, named Joshua Pusey invented book matches in 1889.

The pop-top can was invented by Ermal Fraze of Kettering, Ohio, in 1959.

Thor Bjørklund, a Norwegian, came up with the first cheese slicer in 1925.

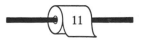

Death...

Mark Twain was born in 1835, a year that Halley's Comet was visible from Earth. As an adult, he predicted he would also die in a year that the comet made an appearance. He did, in 1910.

Hair and fingernails do not grow after death. Skin recedes, making them appear longer.

In 1995, inmates on death row in Texas protested because the state had banned smoking in prisons.

"Old age" hasn't been allowed on death certificates in the United States as an official cause of death since 1951.

Thorton's Mortuary in Atlanta, Georgia, opened the first drive-through funeral parlor in 1968. Mourners drove past a large window, through which they could see the deceased.

After her husband Albert died in 1861, Queen Victoria slept with a portrait of him on the pillow next to her.

...and Taxes

The simplest U.S. tax form (the 1040EZ) has more than 30 pages of instructions.

The U.S. tax code contains more than 7 million words.

Many states require people to pay taxes on illegal drug sales.

In 1798, the United States instituted its first property tax on land, homes...and slaves.

There are twice as many U.S. tax preparers as police officers.

In Alabama, there's a 10¢ tax on playing cards.

Random Thirteens

The number 13 is considered lucky in China because its symbol resembles one that means "must be alive."

In 1941, Joe DiMaggio struck out only 13 times. (In contrast, Phillies first baseman Ryan Howard struck out 199 times in 2007, the most on record.)

Napoléon Bonaparte, Herbert Hoover, and Franklin Delano Roosevelt all feared the number 13.

In 1959, Harvey Haddix became the first pitcher to throw 12 perfect innings—and then he lost the game in the 13th.

Apollo 13 was launched at 13:13, military time. The astronauts aborted the mission and turned back to Earth on Friday, April 13.

Black Sabbath released its self-titled first album in February 1970...on Friday the 13th.

Cost to U.S. economy when superstitious people stay home on Friday the 13th: $800 million.

Although DVDs are the same size as CDs, a DVD can store 13 times as much data.

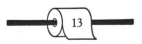

Sports Milestones

Most strikeouts thrown in one baseball game: 21, by the Washington Senators' Tom Cheney, in 16 innings (1962).

In 1954, Roger Bannister was the first person to run a mile in under four minutes, with a time of 3:59.4.

Ray Harroun was the first winner of the Indianapolis 500, in 1911.

In 1986, American Greg LeMond became the first non-European to win the Tour de France.

Tallest golfer to play on the PGA Tour: Phil Blackmar (6'7").

In 1981, John Henry was the first Thoroughbred to win a million-dollar race.

In 1926, Gertrude Ederle became the first woman to swim the English Channel. Only five men had done it before her.

Most seasons as a major-league baseball umpire: Bill Klem and Bruce Froemming, each with 37 years.

First Asian American woman to win an Olympic gold medal: figure skater Kristi Yamaguchi, in 1992.

The winner of the first Kentucky Derby was Aristides, ridden by Oliver Lewis, on May 17, 1875.

First basketball player to enter the NBA directly from high school: Moses Malone, in 1974.

The first Ironman Triathlon was held in Hawaii in 1978.

The New York Yankees have won 26 championships, more than any other professional sports team.

Late 19th-century boxer John L. Sullivan was the first American sports figure to become a national celebrity.

Winter Facts

In the United States, the first day of winter is on the 21st or 22nd of December. But in Australia, it's between June 20 and June 23.

On average, winters in Europe were colder just a few hundred years ago. In fact, London's river Thames sometimes froze completely during the winter, and between the 1400s and 1800s, Londoners held festivals called "frost fairs" on the ice.

So much snow falls in the Japanese Alps during the winter that most buildings have entrances on their second stories.

People have been building snowmen since the Middle Ages.

Largest ice-sculpting festival in the world: the World Ice Art Championships, held every March in Fairbanks, Alaska.

The legend of Jack Frost probably originated with the Vikings.

Symptoms of SAD (seasonal affective disorder): excessive sleeping, tiredness, depression, and physical aches.

Winter skating rinks in Moscow, Russia, cover more than 26,000 square feet.

* * *

MOTHER IN MOURNING

According to ancient Greek mythology, winter began because Hades, god of the underworld, kidnapped Persephone, the daughter of the earth goddess Demeter. Eventually, Hades and Demeter worked out a deal where Persephone spent six months aboveground with her mother and six months below with Hades. But during the six months Persephone was away, Demeter became so depressed that she prevented plants and crops from growing, thus causing winter.

Transportation

On average, a commercial airplane in the United States gets struck by lightning at least once a year.

The first car manufacturer to introduce seat belts: Saab, in 1958.

China's Shanghai Maglev Train is the world's fastest passenger train. It reaches speeds of more than 250 mph.

There are about 600 million passenger cars in the world, one for every 11 people.

First monorail in the United States: the Disneyland Monorail System, which opened in 1959.

Motorola's first products were car radios. The company's name is a combination of "motor" and "Victrola."

Germany was the first nation to develop rocket-powered aircraft, during World War II.

First member of the British royal family to fly in a jet: the Queen Mother, in 1952.

The word "train" comes from the Latin *trahere*, meaning to pull or draw.

Very early automobile models didn't have steering wheels. Drivers used a lever to control the car's direction.

The first commercial jet—the de Havilland Comet—made its inaugural flight in 1952.

The first flying device: the Pigeon, invented around 400 BC, looked like a bird and was propelled by steam.

World's steepest railroad: Switzerland's Pilatus Railway. It climbs 7,000 feet to the top of Mt. Pilatus at a grade of 48 percent.

Most car horns in the United States beep in the key of F.

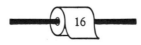

Fighting Women

First women's boxing match in the United States: 1876 in New York City. The prize was a silver butter dish.

First female boxing star: Barbara Buttrick, from England. She was 5'0" and weighed 100 pounds. In 1954, in a match in Canada, she fought in the first female boxing bout broadcast on the radio.

In 1987, former world women's lightweight champion Marion "Lady Tyger" Trimiar staged a hunger strike outside promoter Don King's New York office. She wanted more money and better promotion for female boxers. (It worked.)

Three female boxers have famous prizefighters for dads: Laila Ali (daughter of Muhammad Ali), Jacqui Frazier-Lyde (daughter of Joe Frazier), and Freeda Foreman (daughter of George Foreman).

During her boxing training for *Million Dollar Baby*, actress Hillary Swank gained about 20 pounds...most of it pure muscle.

Three rules that make women's boxing different from men's: 1) Women have to wear breast protectors; 2) They must prove they aren't pregnant; and 3) Rounds last two minutes instead of three.

Under the Sea

Bottlenose dolphins don't sleep at all until they're one month old. And when they do nap, they always keep one eye open.

The blue whale's tongue weighs as much as an adult female brown bear.

Sea otters sometimes tie themselves together with kelp to avoid being separated while they sleep.

Humans are responsible for the deaths of as many as 73 million sharks every year.

Sea slugs can have as many as 25,000 teeth.

Dolphins can recognize themselves in a mirror.

There are at least 34 shark species in the Gulf of Mexico.

Orcas (killer whales) live in every ocean on Earth.

Mudskippers are fish that live in tide pools and can breathe through their skin. As long as they stay moist, they can climb out of the ocean and walk around on land.

Found in a shark's belly in 1941: 3 belts, 9 shoes, 14 stockings, and 43 buttons.

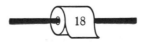

The Senses

On average, human taste buds live only 7 to 10 days before they die and are replaced with new ones.

A cricket's hearing organ is located in its front legs.

Your tongue can detect sweetness in a solution of 1 part sugar to 200 parts water.

Snakes have no ears, but they can still "hear." Their tongues sense sound vibrations.

The human eye can tell the difference between about 500 shades of gray.

If you lost an eye, you would lose only about 20 percent of your vision.

Women tend to have wider peripheral vision than men do.

Animal and fish brains devote more space to the sense of smell than human brains do.

The cornea is the only body part with no blood supply. It gets oxygen directly from the air.

First sense to develop in human infants: touch.

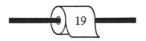

Music Men

Ted Nugent has been a Michigan sheriff's deputy since 1978.

Marilyn Manson's real name: Brian Hugh Warner.

When Elvis Presley was three years old, his father altered a check from his employer (raising his pay from $3 to $8). The punishment: the King's dad spent eight months in the Mississippi State Penitentiary.

Rob Zombie's first job in entertainment: as a production assistant on the 1980s TV show *Pee-wee's Playhouse.*

Michael Jackson's first onstage moonwalk: 1983.

What does LL Cool J's name stand for? "Ladies Love Cool James." (His real name is James Todd Smith.)

B. B King was playing a concert in 1949 when two men fighting over a woman named Lucille accidentally set fire to the club he was playing in. King risked his life to save his $30 guitar, and when the ordeal was over, he named it—and all his future guitars—after the woman at the center of the ruckus.

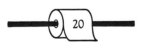

Bathroom Break

According to one study, a toilet has 49 germs per square inch. A desktop has 20,961.

Toilet paper was first produced on rolls in the 1870s, but they didn't become popular until the 1900s.

King Louis XIV had more than 250 personal chamber pots in and around the Palace of Versailles.

Britain's Prince Charles owns a collection of toilet seats.

Emperor Vespasian introduced pay toilets to Rome in the first century AD.

Golfers Walter Hagen and Joe Kirkwood once played a round in downtown Tijuana, Mexico, using the toilet in their hotel room as the 18th hole.

British government toilet paper used to be stamped with "Govt. Property, Now Wash Your Hands."

In Australia, outhouses are called "dunnies."

The Spike Jones Orchestra used an instrument called the latrinophone—a toilet seat with strings.

Montana's Cow Pasture Open golf tournament includes a toilet-seat hole.

Liberace owned a retracting toilet that sank into the bathroom floor.

Jack Nicholson has a rattlesnake embedded in his toilet seat.

During the 1790s, the White House lavatory consisted of an outdoor wooden privy. In 1801, Thomas Jefferson had two outhouses installed, one at each end of the house.

Thirty-three percent of Americans flush the toilet while still sitting on it.

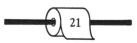

Why's It Called That?

Canned herring are called sardines because the canning process was developed in Sardinia.

Producer Terry Melcher wrote "(untitled)" as a placeholder for the name of the Byrds' ninth album. It mistakenly went to press with the title (*Untitled*).

In the 1920s, the nickname "the Big Apple" was popularized by New York newspaper columnist John J. FitzGerald.

Pink Floyd got its name from two Georgia bluesmen, "Pink" Anderson and Floyd Council.

The original "quisling" (traitor) was Norwegian fascist Vidkun Quisling, who helped the Nazis invade his own country.

The word "maverick" came into common use in 1845. It referred to unbranded cattle owned by Texas rancher Samuel Maverick.

The term "ritzy" comes from the posh European hotels run by Swiss innkeeper César Ritz.

Billboard magazine was founded in 1894 as a trade publication for people who manufactured and used billboards.

Bingo was originally called "beano" because players used beans to mark their cards.

In golf, the word "green" once meant the entire course.

The Pet Shop Boys claim they titled their album *Please* so people would have to ask for it politely.

The word "aftermath" was originally "aftermowth," and it referred to the new growth of grass after mowing.

"Acid rock," "country rock," and "hard rock" were all geological terms before they were musical genres.

Loony

Loons are aquatic birds that look like small ducks with black and white spots and red eyes.

There are five species of loons: common, red-throated, Pacific, arctic, and yellow-billed.

Loons get their name from their high-pitched yodeling cry. Many people say that it sounds like maniacal laughter.

Minnesota's state bird: the common loon.

The birds have sharp beaks that they use to stab prey.

Loons are clumsy on land, and typically leave the water only to nest. They're much faster and more agile when swimming.

Unlike most birds whose bones are hollow, loons' bones are solid.

Loons can fly as fast as 75 mph.

A swimming loon appears on Canada's one-dollar coin, nicknamed the "loonie."

In England, loons are also called "divers" because they can dive as deep as 250 feet to look for fish, and can stay underwater for five minutes.

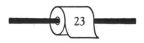

Food!

Gerber once tried to market premade foods for adults.

Until about 200 years ago, people in many Asian countries used bricks of tea as money.

Huey Lewis's grandfather invented the red wax sealant used on some varieties of cheese.

Most widely used herb in the world: parsley.

Throughout *The Big Lebowski*, the Dude (Jeff Bridges) drinks nine White Russians.

There are more than 20,000 brands of beer worldwide.

Seventeenth-century Italian cardinal Jules Mazarin took his personal chocolate-maker with him everywhere.

Before he made it big in films, actor Alan Ladd operated a hot-dog stand called Tiny's.

The world's most expensive spice: Spanish saffron. It can cost more than $1,000 a pound.

In the 1600s, thermometers were often filled with brandy instead of mercury.

When dropped in water, a fresh egg will sink; a stale one won't.

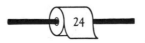

Around the World

Thirteen percent of the world's population lives in deserts.

World's largest urban national park: Golden Gate National Recreation Area (74,820 acres).

Fifty-one countries were involved in World War II, the most of any war in human history.

Sweetwater, Texas, boasts the world's largest rattlesnake roundup. The annual festival began in 1958 as a way for local farmers to get rid of rattlesnakes on their property. In the years since, it's grown to include a parade, a snake-charmer competition, and a cook-off. (And they still collect snakes. More than 120 tons' worth have been caught over the years.)

More people have seen magician David Copperfield perform live than any other entertainer in the world.

The *Saturday Night Fever* soundtrack has sold more than 30 million copies worldwide.

World's biggest army: China's People's Liberation Army, with 2.2 million active troops.

Since 1495, the world has never seen 25 consecutive years without at least one war.

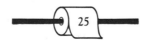

What's in a Name?

Most popular names for U.S. high school sports teams: Eagles and Tigers.

The troll dolls of the 1960s were also known as Dam Dolls, after their creator, Thomas Dam.

The first Atlantic storm to carry a man's name was Hurricane Bob (1979). (Before that, they were all named after women.)

The O' prefix in Irish surnames means "grandson of."

Babe Ruth's residence in Sudbury, Massachusetts, was named Home Plate Farm.

There are approximately 600 different surnames in China but more than a million in the United States.

Author Douglas Adams (*The Hitchhiker's Guide to the Galaxy*) chose the name of Pink Floyd's 1994 album *The Division Bell*.

To enter the Bob Jones Open golf tournament, you must be named Bob Jones.

The world's most common name: Muhammad.

According to some studies, the surname Baer has the most spelling variations—36. Snyder is second with 29, and Bailey has 22. (But these are the most common spellings.)

Malcolm X named his first daughter, Attalah, after Attila the Hun.

Miss Ima Hogg, the "First Lady of Texas," was a beloved philanthropist and patron of the arts.

Pete Townshend and John Entwistle of the Who played in a Dixieland band called the Confederates.

According to legend, Paul Bunyan's cook was named Hot Biscuit Slim.

Hail to the Chief

To date, every U.S. president with a beard has been a Republican.

Only one person in ten is left-handed, but three of the past six presidents have been.

The first president to be impeached was Andrew Johnson.

Midnight Cowboy was the only X-rated movie shown to a U.S. president (Jimmy Carter) in office.

All U.S. presidents have worn glasses, though some didn't like wearing them in public.

William Henry Harrison is one of two presidents to have double letters in both his first and last names. The other: Millard Fillmore.

Presidential film screenings began in 1915, when Woodrow Wilson watched *The Birth of a Nation*.

Most common presidential religious affiliation: Episcopalian, followed by Presbyterian.

Presidential candidate who ran the most times: Socialist Norman Thomas, six times.

Candidate with the most electoral and popular votes: Ronald Reagan, in 1984.

The film Lyndon B. Johnson most often requested be shown in the White House while he was in office: a 10-minute short about himself.

Herbert Hoover was the last president whose term ended on March 3. They now end on January 20.

Last U.S. president with a mustache: William Howard Taft.

In 1963, Lyndon B. Johnson became the first Southerner to hold the office since Andrew Johnson in 1869.

Women's Fashion

Go-go boots, popular in the 1960s, got their start in the collection of André Courreges, a Parisian designer.

Most costume changes in a movie: 85, by Madonna in *Evita*.

In 1968, the Ladies Professional Golf Association officially sanctioned miniskirts for tournament play.

After Faye Dunaway wore a beret in the 1967 film *Bonnie and Clyde*, thousands of the hats were sold in the United States.

Chinese brides traditionally wear red wedding dresses.

Cleopatra's eye makeup was blue-black (upper lid) and green (lower).

Mae West was only 5'1". To compensate in films, she wore platform shoes.

Vivien Leigh often wore gloves because she thought her hands were too large.

Hot pants, all the rage in the early 1970s, were worn years earlier by European prostitutes.

Science

A paleoscatologist is an archaeologist who studies ancient poop.

Every minute, there are two minor earthquakes somewhere in the world.

The first U.S. patent was issued in 1790 for a process to make potash (potassium carbonate).

Liquid air (below –310°F) looks like water with a bluish tint.

French physicist Jean-Antoine Nollet did some incredible experiments during the 1700s. In one demonstration, an electric jolt tossed 200 monks into the air.

During a total solar eclipse, the local temperature can drop as much as 20°F.

Hydrofluoric acid will dissolve glass—but can be stored safely in plastic containers.

The "Armstrong limit" is the altitude at which blood begins to boil (63,000 feet above sea level).

A typical hurricane lasts nine days.

Kevlar is five times stronger than steel.

Scientists have revived bacteria that were 250 million years old.

Forest fires move faster uphill than downhill.

Glow sticks contain an ingredient called luciferin.

In 2005, scientists found fossilized blood vessels from a T. rex.

The human eye blinks more than 4 million times a year.

Botulism bacteria are so toxic that one pound of it could kill every human on earth.

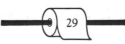

Famous Siblings

3 DUCKS
1. Huey
2. Dewey
3. Louie

9 KENNEDYS
1. Joe Jr.
2. John
3. Rosemary
4. Kathleen
5. Eunice
6. Patricia
7. Robert
8. Jean
9. Edward (Ted)

3 BARRYMORES
1. Lionel
2. Ethel
3. John

6 BRADYS
1. Greg
2. Marsha
3. Peter
4. Jan
5. Bobby
6. Cindy

5 ROMANOVS
1. Olga
2. Tatiana
3. Maria
4. Anastasia
5. Alexei

4 CAMERONS
1. Kirk
2. Bridget
3. Melissa
4. Candace

2 MOZARTS
1. Marianne
2. Wolfgang

6 JOLIE-PITTS
1. Maddox
2. Pax
3. Zahara
4. Shiloh
5. Knox
6. Vivienne

3 REDGRAVES
1. Vanessa
2. Lynn
3. Corin

9 JACKSONS
1. Rebbie
2. Jackie
3. Tito
4. Jermaine
5. La Toya
6. Marlon
7. Michael
8. Randy
9. Janet

4 TUDORS
1. Arthur
2. Margaret
3. Mary
4. Henry VIII

4 JONAS
1. Kevin
2. Joe
3. Nick
4. Frankie

5 TRUMPS
1. Donald Jr.
2. Ivanka
3. Eric
4. Tiffany
5. Barron

Inspired By...

Pink plastic lawn flamingos were inspired by a photo of real flamingos in a 1957 *National Geographic* magazine.

The polka is thought to have been the inspiration for polka dots, which, in turn, were the inspiration for the game Twister.

According to Jude Law, he was named after the Beatles song "Hey, Jude."

Crooner Michael Feinstein named his production company, Bing Clawsby Music, after his cat.

The film *Stand by Me* (1986) is based on Stephen King's short story *The Body*.

Orson Welles admired John Ford's film *Stagecoach* (1939) so much that he watched it about 40 times while making *Citizen Kane* (1941).

In *A Few Good Men*, Tom Cruise's Jack Nicholson impersonation was ad-libbed.

Author Anne Rice's real name is Howard O'Brien. (She was named after her father.)

Young Albert Einstein became interested in science when he was given a magnetic compass.

The villain in *Scream* was based on a Florida serial killer known as "the Gainesville Ripper."

In 1946, Henrietta Radner saw the movie *Gilda*. She liked the film so much that she named her daughter Gilda.

Jeremiah Johnson (1972) was based on the story of real-life trapper John Johnson.

Star Wars creators modeled Yoda's face on Albert Einstein's.

In 2003, thousands of Russian citizens wrote angry letters to Warner Bros., claiming that the character of Dobby the house-elf was based on their president, Vladimir Putin. (It wasn't.)

Impressive Feats

Former Doobie Brother Jeff "Skunk" Baxter now advises Congress on missile defense.

Chevy Chase was an original member of Steely Dan.

TV handyman Bob Vila was a Peace Corps volunteer.

Composer Franz Liszt's first piano concerto includes a triangle solo.

Switch-hitter Pete Rose, who got most of his 4,256 hits left-handed, plays golf right-handed.

Keith Richards sang in the choir at Queen Elizabeth II's coronation.

Rowan Atkinson (Mr. Bean) studied electrical engineering.

Jimi Hendrix never took a formal music lesson.

Composer Philip Glass once played in a new-wave band called Polyrock.

Actor Tom Hulce practiced piano for four hours a day for his role in *Amadeus*.

KISS front man Gene Simmons speaks four languages and has a bachelor's degree in education.

After his victory in the Roman civil war, Julius Caesar proclaimed that every poor family in the Roman Empire would live rent-free for one year.

Before becoming an actor, Peter Falk worked at the Connecticut State Budget Bureau.

When she got the lead role in the film *Whale Rider*, actress Keisha Castle-Hughes claimed she could swim—but she couldn't. After the film, she said her whale-riding scene was "terrifying."

The left arm of golfer Ed Furgol is six inches shorter than his right arm.

Flower Power

National flower of the United States: the rose, officially adopted in 1986.

Hydrangeas produce pink and white flowers in alkaline soil, and blue ones in acidic soil.

Bucket orchids release a chemical that can make bees drunk.

More than 200 kinds of wildflowers bloom in the Mojave Desert.

Texas sage, often called "barometer bush," tends to bloom when rain is coming.

The tallest sunflower plant on record: 25 feet, 5.4 inches.

Sixty-nine percent of the roses purchased on Valentine's Day are red.

Apples are part of the rose family.

The first wildflower of the year in the eastern United States: usually the eastern skunk cabbage, which starts blooming in February.

Garlic is a member of the lily family. So are onions.

Brand Names & Logos

The term "brand name" originated among American alcohol distillers, who branded their names onto their kegs.

Actors who portray Ronald McDonald are forbidden to reveal their true identities.

"PEZ" is short for *pfefferminz*— German for "peppermint."

What do the initials stand for in the company name of Maine retailer L. L. Bean? Leon Leonwood.

Hello Kitty has appeared on more than 15,000 different products, including an AR-15 assault rifle.

The motto of Mary Kay Cosmetics: "Fake it till you make it."

Ex-Lax was originally called Bo-Bo's.

In 1907, two teenagers in Seattle started United Parcel Service (UPS).

The initials in B. F. Goodrich stand for Benjamin Franklin.

Tokyo Telecommunications Engineering was founded in 1946. It later got a shorter name: Sony.

World's largest maker of musical instruments: Yamaha. Their logo is three interlocking tuning forks.

In 1971, Carolyn Davidson, a student at Portland State University, created the Nike swoosh logo.

Professional golfer Howard Twitty agreed to display Burger King's logo on his golf bag. His price: 500 Whoppers.

Three men named Brandley, Voorhees, and Day opened an underwear company in 1856 that's now known by their initials: BVD. (Their first names remain a secret.)

First trademark: the Bass Beer symbol, a red triangle.

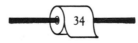

Rhode Island

THE SMALLEST STATE. Rhode Island covers 1,212 square miles...about one-third the size of Yellowstone National Park.

NAME ORIGIN. In the 1520s, Italian explorer Giovanni da Verrazzano sailed up the east coast of New England. North of New York, he noticed a group of islands, one of which he thought looked like the Isle of Rhodes in Greece. What he saw was actually modern-day Block Island, but the colonists who moved into the area 100 years later thought he'd been talking about Aquidneck Island, the largest in Narragansett Bay. So they started calling their settlement there "Rhode Island." Later, the name was used for the larger mainland colony, and the island went back to its American Indian name, Aquidneck.

THE OCEAN STATE. Rhode Island got its official nickname, "the Ocean State," from two sources: 1) About one-tenth of its inland area is covered with salt water, and 2) Most residents live within 30 minutes of the ocean. It's not actually an island, though. Most of the state's land is connected to the U.S. mainland.

FIRSTS. Rhode Island was the first state to...

- Prohibit slavery in North America (1652).
- Have a newspaper with a female editor, Ann Smith Franklin of the *Newport Mercury* (1762).
- Declare itself independent from Great Britain (1776).
- Patent a motion-picture machine (1867). The small box showed a movie of animals.
- Host a polo game in the United States, in Newport (1876).
- Hold an automobile race on a track (1896).

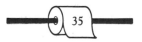

Sports & Games

Polo is the only game that requires participants to play right-handed. (Left-handed play was banned in 1975 for safety reasons.)

In 2001, Marco Siffredi of France became the first person to snowboard down Mt. Everest. It took 2 hours and 30 minutes.

With the development of strong, lightweight fabrics and ultralight rods, kite flying is now possible indoors. Kite flyers say the key is to keep the kite moving all the time. Running isn't required—small movements are enough to keep an indoor kite airborne. (All you need is a high-ceilinged room.)

The Vasaloppet is the world's oldest, largest, and longest cross-country ski race. The race between the towns of Sälen and Mora, Sweden, a distance of 56 miles, has been held every year since 1922.

A set of nine stone bowling pins was unearthed from the tomb of an Egyptian child buried around 5200 BC.

In the 1930s, some journalists claimed that record-breaking American sprinter Helen Stephens was actually a man because "no woman could run as fast as she does." Olympic officials investigated—Stephens was female. (But Poland's Stella Walsh, whom Stephens outran in the 1936 Olympics, turned out to be a hermaphrodite.)

Numbers

Miss Piggy's measurements are said to be 27-30-32.

There are 20 possible answers on a Magic 8-Ball: 10 positive, five negative, and five neutral.

U.S. Patent #4,429,685 was issued for a "Method of Growing Unicorns."

Average age of male golfers: 50. Females: 42.

Sam Malone's (*Cheers*) baseball jersey number: 16.

The only number that is twice the sum of its digits is 18.

Antarctica's country code: 672.

According to experts, it's about 10 times easier to shoot a hole in one while playing golf than it is to bowl a perfect 300 game.

But the odds against an amateur golfer scoring a hole in one are 12,000 to 1.

From 1950 to 1970, U.S. guitar sales grew from 228,000 to 2.3 million, a 1,000 percent increase.

Life span of a U.S. patent: 17 years.

The first three digits of a 13-digit bar code indicate the product's country of origin.

What's a septillion? 1,000,000,000,000,000,000, 000,000.

When making a peanut-butter and-jelly sandwich, people put the peanut butter on first about 96 percent of the time.

In the 1962 hit song "Duke of Earl," the word "duke" is sung 125 times.

The 40-day pre-Easter period of Lent is actually 46 days long (Sundays aren't counted).

The Four Horsemen of the Apocalypse: Conquest, Death, Slaughter, and Famine.

The Human Condition

When people are asked to pick a number between one and ten, they most often choose seven.

One in eight men snores while sleeping. One in ten grinds his teeth.

The vocabulary of the average adult human consists of 5,000 to 6,000 words.

When choosing bathroom reading, women prefer magazines. Men favor newspapers.

Morology is the study of ridiculous conversation.

In ancient Greece, sick people slept in "medicine temples" to dream about how to get better.

The scientific term for left-handedness is sinistrality. Right-handedness is dextrality.

Male patients fall out of hospital beds twice as often as female patients do.

One in seven adults spends more than 30 minutes a day in the bathroom.

But on average, men spend just 45 seconds in a public restroom stall. Women spend about 80.

Studies show: feeling guilty may damage your immune system.

According to experts, human knowledge is increasing so fast that 90 percent of what we will know 50 years from now hasn't been discovered yet.

The world's population increases by 237,748 every 24 hours.

For most people, honey is easy to digest. Why? Because it's already been digested...by a bee.

Worldwide, there are 4.2 babies born every second and 360,000 born every day.

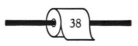

Mating Rituals

Some female cockroaches mate only once and then die as soon as they give birth.

An oyster may change gender several times during its life.

Crocodile babies don't have sex chromosomes—the temperature at which the egg develops determines gender.

Most clams are hermaphrodites.

Rabbits and hares can't mate with each other.

White-fronted parrots kiss before mating by locking beaks and flicking their tongues at each other. Then the male parrot vomits up food and offers it to the female as a token of his affection.

Many alligators "snuggle" for days before mating.

Female sea turtles don't reach sexual maturity until they are about 25 years old.

Elephants show affection for each other by entwining their trunks.

To attract a female hippopotamus, the male poops and pees while spinning his tail to spray it around.

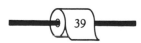

Body Parts

The space between your eyebrows is called the glabella.

What is your buccal cavity? Your mouth.

What makes cheese, sweaty feet, and vomit smelly? Butyric acid.

Your outermost layer of skin is called the stratum corneum (Latin for "horny layer").

What is a natal cleft? The medical term for a butt crack.

The scientific name for stinky armpits: tragomaschalia.

You know that little membrane under your tongue? It's your frenulum.

A "gut feeling" (or hunch) is sometimes called a "splanchnic," referring to the splanchnic nerves of the intestinal area.

The skin that peels off after a sunburn is called blype, and the skin under your fingernails is called the whickflaw.

Do you have a diasthema between your front teeth? (It's a gap.)

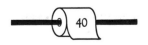

World War I

Ernest Hemingway, Irving Berlin, Winston Churchill, and F. Scott Fitzgerald all served in the military during World War I.

The British royal family renounced its German ties in 1917. By royal proclamation, King George V changed the family's name from Saxe-Coburg-Gotha to Windsor. (He got "Windsor" from the name of one of their castles.)

The Turks killed more than a million Armenians between 1914 and 1918.

Canada's mascot during the war: a live black bear named Winnipeg ("Winnie"). The Canadians ultimately donated the bear to England's London Zoo, where A. A. Milne and his son Christopher often visited. Young Christopher named his teddy bear after Winnie, and it became the inspiration for the Winnie-the-Pooh stories.

World War I saw the first women officially enlisted in the U.S. armed forces. It was also the first war in which tanks, airplanes, blood banks, and X-rays were used.

American fighter ace Eddie Rickenbacker raced cars before he joined the army. After the war, he founded an automobile company.

In 1916, the Germans tried to negotiate peace with the Allies...naming themselves the winners. (The Allies refused.)

Many words and phrases came into common use during World War I, including "chow down," "trench coat," "red tape," "zero hour," "cushy," "ace," "cootie," and "basket case."

During the second half of 1914, the French lost as many men in battle as the United States lost in the entire 20th century.

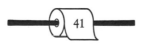

Music on TV

Song that received *American Bandstand*'s lowest rating ever: "The Chipmunk Song" (1958).

The Muppet named Animal was modeled after the Who's drummer, Keith Moon.

MTV's first guest VJ: Adam Ant.

Twilight Zone's well-known theme was composed by an American named Marius Constant. He didn't find out his music was used until after the show aired.

Frank Sinatra's last appearance on a TV show was on the sitcom *Who's the Boss?* in 1989 (though he didn't sing).

MTV aired its millionth video in March 2000.

Vinnie Vincent of KISS was a staff songwriter for TV's *Happy Days* and *Joanie Loves Chachi*.

In 1991, Data (Brent Spiner) of *Star Trek: The Next Generation* released an album titled *Ol' Yellow Eyes Is Back*.

Number 16 on *Billboard*'s Hot 100 for the week of September 26, 1970: "Rubber Duckie" by Ernie (*Sesame Street*).

Dead Ends

Because Spencer Tracy died 17 days after filming *Guess Who's Coming to Dinner*, Katharine Hepburn never watched the completed film—she thought it would make her too sad.

Marlon Brando kept the ashes of his friend, comedian Wally Cox, in his Tahiti home.

Art Scholl, a stunt pilot, was killed during the filming of *Top Gun* (1986).

Singer Tom Jones was on Charles Manson's hit list.

Archaeological studies show that 1 in 25 coffins from the 16th century has scratch marks on the inside.

Swedish confectionery salesman Roland Ohisson was buried in a coffin made of chocolate.

Jimi Hendrix, Janis Joplin, and Jim Morrison all died at 27.

In 1968, Samuel L. Jackson was an usher at Martin Luther King Jr.'s funeral.

Aimee Semple MacPherson, an early 20th-century evangelist, was buried with a working telephone. When she didn't call after seven years, the line was disconnected.

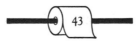

Leading Ladies

In *Cold Mountain*, Nicole Kidman did all of her own piano playing.

Salma Hayek is of Lebanese and Mexican descent.

Country singer Tonya Watts was a body double for Pamela Anderson in the 1996 film *Barb Wire*.

Actress Goldie Hawn worked as a can-can dancer at the 1965 World's Fair in New York.

Before she appeared in *Splash*, Daryl Hannah was in an all-girls band called Psychotic Kindergarten.

Before she became famous, Michelle Pfeiffer worked as a supermarket cashier.

Julia Roberts played clarinet in her Smyrna, Georgia, high school band.

Cyd Charisse had to be taught how to smoke for a dance sequence in *Singin' in the Rain*.

According to one of the dancers on her early films, Joan Crawford loved to tell dirty jokes.

Before she took the role of Roxie Hart in *Chicago*, Renee Zellweger had only sung in public twice.

Kate Winslet didn't win an Oscar until 2008, but she took home a Grammy in 2000 for her performance in the spoken word recording "Listen to the Storyteller."

Linda Fiorentino won her role in *Men in Black* in a poker game with the director, Barry Sonnenfeld. (She also won about $1,200 in cash.)

A newspaper critic on Faye Dunaway's first movie: "[Her] rib cage looks marvelous."

Susan Sarandon is one of only two actresses to win an Oscar for playing a nun. (The other was Jennifer Jones in 1943's *Song of Bernadette*.)

Leading Men

George Clooney campaigned for the lead role in 2004's *Sideways*, but director Alexander Payne thought he was too big a star for the small film.

Before he became famous, Keanu Reeves managed a pasta restaurant in Toronto, Canada.

Christopher Walken has worked as an actor, a catalog model, and a lion tamer.

Tom Hanks collects typewriters from the 1940s.

Robert Redford didn't see *The Sting* (1973) until June 2004.

Before becoming an actor, Humphrey Bogart played chess for money; he usually won about $1 a game.

Clark Gable's birth certificate originally listed him as a girl.

Johnny Depp played slide guitar on the 1997 Oasis album *Be Here Now*.

Harrison Ford played the school principal in *E.T.*, but his back was to the camera.

Jack Nicholson's first job in Hollywood: office boy in MGM's cartoon department.

Denzel Washington's son John David used to be a running back for the NFL's St. Louis Rams.

Al Pacino's grandparents were natives of Corleone, Sicily.

Warren Beatty turned down the role of Bill in the *Kill Bill* movies. He thought they were too violent. (The part went to David Carradine instead.)

Sean Connery competed in 1953's Mr. Universe pageant. He placed third in the "tall man's" category.

Will Smith met his wife Jada Pinkett Smith when she auditioned to be his girlfriend on *The Fresh Prince of Bel Air*. (She didn't get the part.)

The Planets

Each pole of Uranus is dark for 42 years at a time.

The ancient Sumerians were the first to record sightings of the planet Mercury, in about 3000 BC.

Jupiter's Great Red Spot is 25,000 miles wide.

At last count, there were more than 300 known planets outside of our solar system.

There are rocks on Mars named Scooby-Doo, Yogi Bear, and Gumby.

Saturn's rings are made of chunks of ice, ranging from dust- to house-sized.

It's estimated that about half a ton of Martian material falls to Earth each year.

Because of Saturn's tilt and the thinness of its rings, every 14 years the rings seem to disappear.

In 1989, *Voyager 2* (the only spacecraft to visit Neptune) discovered a unique cloud pattern that circles the planet extremely fast. Its name: the Scooter.

On Venus, the sun rises in the west.

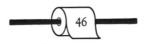

To the Extreme

Most expensive MP3 player: The gold-and-gem-encrusted Douglas J. Presidential costs $44,000. It comes with 1GB of memory, and a "personal escort" will hand-deliver it to your house.

Most expensive concert ticket ever: $1,530. (Front row at Barbra Streisand's 2000 Australia tour.)

Floyd Rood hit a golf ball across the continental United States. (It took him 114,737 strokes.)

Eating champion Mort Hurst once ate 16 double-decker Moon Pies in 10 minutes, and 38 eggs in 29 seconds.

The record for hula-hooping the most hoops simultaneously: 100, held by Kareena Oates.

Jerry Rice has the most career touchdowns in Super Bowl history: eight.

Roger Staubach holds the career record for the most Super Bowl fumbles; he dropped the ball five times.

Students at England's Stockport College built an 896-pound fully operational yo-yo. Diameter: 10 feet 5 inches. It was launched off a crane at a height of 189 feet.

Elaine Davidson of Edinburgh, Scotland, has a world-record 720 body piercings.

World record bubblegum bubble: 23" in diameter, blown by Susan Montgomery Williams.

The pogo-stick jumping world record: 41 hours.

Basketball player with the most points scored in his career: Kareem Abdul-Jabbar, with 38,387.

World's oldest restaurant: Casa Botín in Spain. It's been in operation since 1725.

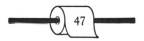

Water

There are almost 800 different brands of bottled water available for sale in the United States.

According to some experts, the world's best-tasting tap water is in Los Angeles.

Every day, the sun's heat evaporates about a trillion tons of water.

With just one gulp of air, a beaver can swim up to half a mile underwater.

Each day, the United States uses 134 billion gallons of water to irrigate crops.

Sunlight can penetrate clear ocean water to a depth of 240 feet.

Eighty percent of a baby's body weight at birth is water.

In the ancient Egyptian language, the word *nile* means "water."

Beethoven often dipped his head in cold water before he began composing.

All sturgeon caught in British waters are legally the property of the queen.

If all the ice in Antarctica melted, sea levels would rise by about 200 feet.

An average golf course uses about 6,000 gallons of water per day. Some desert courses use a million gallons.

It's recommended that we consume eight cups of water a day, but people can actually drink up to three gallons (or 48 cups).

By the time you feel thirsty, you've already lost 1 percent of the water in your body.

An average water droplet contains 100 quintillion molecules of water.

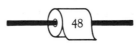

Names

Booker T. Washington's middle name was Taliaferro, which he pronounced "Tolliver."

The "S" in Ulysses S. Grant didn't stand for anything; his real name was Hiram Ulysses Grant.

France had kings named Charles the Fat, Charles the Bold, Charles the Simple, and Charles the Well-Served.

Queen Elizabeth's last name is Mountbatten-Windsor.

Soprano Maria Callas was christened Maria Anna Sofia Cecilia Kalogeropoulou.

Boxer Sugar Ray Leonard's full name: Ray Charles Leonard. (He was named after singer Ray Charles.)

Malcolm X's last name is symbolic of the African names his ancestors lost to slavery.

Before his victory at Hastings, William the Conqueror was called "William the Bastard."

Robert McNamara, U.S. secretary of defense in the 1960s, had a strange middle name: Strange.

Dance, Dance, Dance

Justin Timberlake once won a "Dance Like the New Kids on the Block" contest.

Bobby Pickett titled his song "Monster Mash" to cash in on the 1960s Mashed Potato dance craze.

A typical male ballet dancer lifts about a ton's worth of ballerinas during his dancing career.

A 1909 song called "Uncle Josh in Society" was the first whose lyrics contained the term "jazz." In the song, it referred to a type of dancing known as ragtime.

World record: in August 1983, Peter Stewart of England disco-danced for 408 hours.

"Dance floor dehydration syndrome" (DFDS) can be fatal.

Tap dancing is derived from Irish clogging.

Athlete Jim Thorpe was a national ballroom dance champion.

In his youth, King Louis XIV of France was an avid ballet dancer.

State dance of South Carolina: the shag.

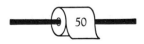

Inventions

Guitarist Les Paul invented the multitrack recording. The first song to use it was his "How High the Moon" (1951).

Henry Ford, father of the Model T, is also the father of the charcoal briquet.

Englishman Sir Humphry Davy created the technology for the lightbulb in 1800, more than 70 years before Thomas Edison did.

Eli Whitney came up with the idea for interchangeable parts to fill a large army order for muskets in 1797.

Jerry Lewis invented and patented a video monitor system in 1956; it's still used throughout the film industry today.

Thomas Edison at first thought his phonograph was "a mere toy, which has no commercial value."

Jacques Cousteau invented the Aqualung (scuba-diving gear) while fighting with the French Resistance in World War II.

Leonardo da Vinci invented an alarm clock that woke him by rubbing his feet.

In 1891, Samuel O'Reilly used a Thomas Edison invention (the electric pen) as a model for the first electric tattoo machine.

Film star and racing enthusiast Steve McQueen patented a type of bucket seat in 1969.

Benjamin Franklin is credited with the invention of the odometer.

Thomas Jefferson invented the dumbwaiter, swivel chair, and lamp heater.

Wilhelm Maybach got the idea for the carburetor after observing a perfume pump spray.

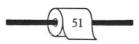

Underwear

Pro golfer Gary McCord split his pants open at the 1984 Memphis Classic—and had no underwear on.

The first boxer shorts appeared in the 1920s as part of the costume for boxers, whose footwork in the ring benefited from the loose shorts.

Lisa Zobian-Lindahl and Hilda Miller of Vermont invented the sports bra in 1978. It was was called the Jogbra.

Michael Jordan always wore the shorts of his North Carolina uniform under his Chicago Bulls uniform.

According to one study, 25 percent of women in Arkansas keep a spare pair of panties in their car's glove compartment.

Average number of days a German man goes without washing his underwear: seven.

A pair of nylons is made from a single filament four miles long, knitted into 3 million loops.

King Tut was buried with 145 pairs of loincloth underwear.

What do Scottish men wear under their kilts? Traditionally, nothing at all.

According to manufacturers, the average bra size today is 36C. In 1980, it was 34B.

Surveys say: about two-thirds of American men prefer boxers to briefs.

Harpo Marx and George Burns enjoyed golfing together in their underwear.

Large-scale production of the modern bra didn't begin until the 1930s, when it began to replace the corset. But bra-like undergarments have been around since 1400 BC.

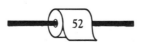

Questionable Behavior

At any point in time, 0.7 percent of the world's population is drunk.

About 1,500 New York residents are bitten every year...by other New Yorkers.

Americans bet $6 billion a year at Internet gambling sites.

Percentage of high-school seniors in 1970 who smoked: 18.4. In 2008: 10 percent.

Two-thirds of Americans say they regularly use the "f-word."

Up to 98 percent of college students have admitted to cheating in school at least once.

Experts say it's harder to tell a convincing lie to someone you find sexually attractive.

According to researchers, the number of public apologies issued by famous figures in the United States doubled between 1990 and 2002.

Odds that one of your party guests will peek into your medicine cabinet: 40 percent.

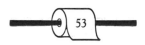

That's the Size of It

How big is home plate on a baseball diamond? It's five-sided: 17" x 8½" x 12" x 12" x 8½".

A cloud measuring one cubic mile weighs about 3.5 million pounds.

The Slinky toy was made of an 87-foot piece of wire, 3" in diameter and 2" high.

Actual dimensions of a record: a 12" disk (LP) is 11.89", and a 7" disk (45 rpm) is 6.89".

An NFL field is 360 feet long (including end zones) by 160 feet wide.

Diameter of the wire in a standard paper clip: about 0.04".

Average length of a coat hanger when straightened: 44".

There are exactly 216 noodles in every can of Campbell's chicken noodle soup.

Average depth of a golf ball dimple: 0.01".

Fattest newspaper ever printed: *The New York Times*, October 17, 1965, at 946 pages. It weighed 7½ pounds.

The average iceberg weighs 20 million tons.

A standard CD is 4.7" in diameter.

A baby grand piano is 5'11" long. Professional grand: 6'. Concert grand: 8'11" or longer.

Plymouth Rock weighs about four tons.

At liftoff, a space shuttle weighs about 4.5 million pounds.

The first Band-Aids ever made were 2½" wide...and 18" long.

If you had $1 million in $100 bills, they would weigh 20.41 pounds.

Simons Say

"If your lifeguard duties were as good as your singing, a lot of people would be drowning."
—Simon Cowell,
American Idol judge

"Discussing personal things in front of an audience creates a release; people recognize something from their own lives. Humor is the optimism, the release."
—Simon Amstell, comedian

"The whole point in forming a band: Girls. Absolutely gorgeous girls."
—Simon Le Bon, lead singer of Duran Duran

"Judgment comes from experience, and experience comes from bad judgment."
—Simón Bolívar

"What I want to do and what I do are two separate things. If we all went around doing what we wanted all the time, there'd be chaos."
—Simon Birch,
from the film *Simon Birch*

"I used to lie in bed in my flat and imagine what would happen if there was a zombie attack."
—Simon Pegg, British writer and actor

"I miss meat pies. They don't have them in L.A. Actually, all I think about the whole time I'm in America is what I'm missing out on in Australia."
—Simon Baker, actor

"Violence is like a weed—it does not die even in the greatest drought."
—Simon Wiesenthal

"I think I have a superior brain and an inferior stature, if you really want to get brutal about it."
—Paul Simon

"I remember being onstage once when I didn't have fear: I got so scared I didn't have fear that it brought on an anxiety attack."
—Carly Simon

Celebrity Contracts

Van Halen created the famous "M&M rider" clause (which prohibited brown M&Ms backstage) to test whether concert promoters had read the entire contract.

Per his contract, Oakland A's relief pitcher Rollie Fingers got $300 extra in 1973 for growing the longest mustache on his team, and $100 more to pay for mustache wax.

Diana Ross once had a contract that said no one backstage was allowed to make eye contact with her.

Fox Television forbids actor Dan Castellaneta from doing his Homer Simpson voice in public.

Bollywood actor Shahid Kapoor had to spend several months under house arrest in 2009. Why? His contract stipulated that he couldn't go out in public and reveal his "tough-guy" look for a movie he was filming.

In 1987, Charlie Kerfeld signed a contract to pitch for the Houston Astros...with two stipulations: he wanted to be paid a salary of $110,037.37 (to honor his #37 jersey), and he wanted 37 boxes of orange Jell-O.

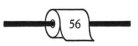

Pollution

The average car releases one pound of pollutants for every 25 miles it drives. But...

...A midsize car in the 1960s emitted 20 times more pollution than a brand-new midsize car emits today.

Colorado has traffic cones with sensors that can measure the amount of air pollution cars give off.

It takes just one gallon of used motor oil to pollute a million gallons of fresh water—an entire year's supply of drinking water for 50 people.

A house produces twice as many polluting greenhouse gases as the average car.

The Amazon rain forest produces more than 20 percent of the world's oxygen.

Tasmania, an island state off the coast of Australia, has the world's cleanest air.

Bad news: indoor pollution can be 25 times more toxic than outdoor pollution. Worse news: most people spend nearly 90 percent of their time inside.

In just one Coastal Cleanup Day, beach lovers collected 338,876 cigarette butts from California beaches.

According to the World Health Organization, the air in Cairo, Egypt, is so polluted that breathing it is like smoking 20 cigarettes a day.

Every month, Americans throw away enough aluminum cans to rebuild every commercial airplane in the country.

Disposable diapers take up about 1 percent of the space in U.S. landfills, and require at least 250 years to decompose.

Americans use more than 2 million plastic bottles an hour.

Canadian Firsts

First person to walk across Canada: John Hugh Gillis, in 1906. It took him nine months to walk from Halifax, Nova Scotia, to Vancouver, British Columbia.

Martin Frobisher, an English explorer, held Canada's first Thanksgiving in 1578 to celebrate surviving the long trip from England to Newfoundland.

Canada received the world's first transatlantic wireless message. In 1901, using a kite as an antenna, an operator in Cornwall, England, sent a message to inventor Guglielmo Marconi in Newfoundland.

In 1922, 14-year-old Leonard Thompson of Toronto was the first person to be treated successfully for diabetes. His doctors, Frederick Banting and Charles Best, invented insulin the year before.

Auyuittuq National Park in Nunavut is the oldest park in the world to lie inside the Arctic Circle.

First city in North America to be put on the UNESCO World Heritage list: Quebec City.

World's first surviving (and only identical female) quintuplets: Annette, Cecile, Emilie, Marie, and Yvonne Dionne, born in Ontario in 1934.

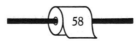

Patron Saint Of...

Mad Dogs...Domingo of Silos
Dumbness...Drogo
Editors...John Bosco
Blackbirds...Kevin of Glendalough
Country girls...Germaine Cousin
Air crews...Joseph of Cupertino
Arm pain...Amalburga
Eczema...Anthony the Abbot
Holy wafer bakers...Honorius of Amiens
Button makers...Louis IX
Children learning to talk...Zeno of Verona
Demonic possession...Amabilis
Disappointing children...Louise de Marillac
Dentists...Apollonia
Murderers...Caedwalla
Relief from pestilence...Roch
Grave diggers...Barbara
Wandering musicians...Julian the Hospitaller
Hairdressers...Cosmas
Race relations...Martin de Porres
Lions...Mark the Apostle
Old maids...Catherine of Alexandria
School principals...John Baptist de La Salle
Rope braiders...Paul the Apostle
Unjustly lost lawsuits...Nicholas of Myra
Actresses...Pelagia the Penitent (The Beardless Hermit)

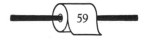

Welcome to California

California boasts the highest (Mount Whitney) and lowest (Death Valley) points in the continental United States.

The state's vineyards produce more than 17 million gallons of wine a year.

About 8 percent of all Californians are vegetarians.

Raisin capital of the world: Fresno. Date capital of the world: Coachella Valley.

More than 1,200 people have committed suicide by jumping off the Golden Gate Bridge.

In the town of Pacific Grove, near Monterey, you can be fined $500 for "molesting" butterflies.

Many of California's redwoods are more than 2,000 years old.

During the gold rush (1848–52), California's population grew from 14,000 to more than 200,000.

Hearst Castle in San Simeon has the most expensive swimming pool in the world—its 1 million tiles are all inlaid with gold.

World's largest outdoor ampitheatre: the Hollywood Bowl in Los Angeles.

Willow Creek calls itself the "Bigfoot Capital," and claims more Bigfoot sightings than anywhere else in the United States.

California's economy ranks 10th in the world.

In 1947, the Castroville Fair's first Artichoke Queen was a young Marilyn Monroe.

California's largest state park (and the second largest in the United States) is the 600,000-acre Anza-Borrego Desert, 90 miles east of San Diego.

The world's first movie theater opened in Los Angeles in 1902.

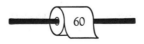

That's Rich

Billionaire Warren Buffett once paid $100,000 to caddy for Tiger Woods in a charity event.

The NFL buys up to 150 Super Bowl rings per year, at a cost of $5,000 each. (Losers also get rings.)

In 2005, Napoléon Bonaparte's tooth sold at an auction for $19,400. In 2006, William Shatner's kidney stone sold for $25,000.

Estimated earnings of the Rolling Stones' 2006–7 concert tour: $500 million.

The Pentagon's 2008 budget was about $439 billion...which amounts to spending $13,920 per second.

In 1987, Charlie Chaplin's bowler hat and cane sold for $150,000.

First pro golfer to earn over $100,000 in a single year: Arnold Palmer, in 1963.

In 1965, CEOs earned about 44 times as much as their factory workers did. In 1999: 419 times more.

Undefeated world heavy-weight boxing champ Gene Tunney made more money in one match in the 1920s than baseball player Babe Ruth made in 14 seasons combined.

America's first billionaire: John D. Rockefeller, founder of Standard Oil.

On her 2006 Confessions tour, Madonna used a two-ton disco ball with $2 million worth of Swarovski crystals.

In 1988, Mike Tyson won $20 million in 91 seconds when he defeated Michael Spinks.

Pablo Picasso's artworks have fetched more than $1.2 billion at auction houses.

Bill Gates is richer than the poorest 114 million people in the United States combined.

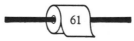

Trees

One tree gives off about 260 pounds of oxygen annually, a year's supply for two people.

Myrrh is made from dried tree sap.

Average growing time for Christmas trees to reach proper height: seven years.

World's oldest tree: Methuselah, a 4,800-year-old bristlecone pine in California's White Mountains.

A mature birch tree makes about a million seeds every year.

If every reader recycled a single day's run of the *New York Times*, it would save about 75,000 trees.

A mature oak tree can have as many as 400,000 caterpillars living in it.

Cypress trees have "knees," mysterious growths on their roots.

In Florida, gumbo limbo trees are nicknamed "tourist trees"...because they stand in the sun, turn red, and peel.

Studies show: people in hospitals heal faster if their room's window looks out on trees.

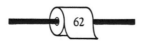

Ups & Downs

Fats Domino had 18 songs that sold a million copies each, but he never had a #1 record.

Tina Turner won a Grammy in 1971, was on food stamps in 1976, and won another Grammy in 1985.

W. W. Clements started as a delivery-truck driver in 1935 and later became CEO of the Dr. Pepper Company.

Composer Jan Paderewski was told he'd never be a good pianist because his middle finger was too short.

As a 5' 11" sophomore, Michael Jordan was cut from his high school's varsity basketball team.

In 1983, *Billboard* magazine declared Madonna a "flash in the pan."

In 1977, Ben (Cohen) and Jerry (Greenfield) took a $5 correspondence course in ice-cream making.

The Spice Girls had a #1 hit in 53 countries within six months of their debut.

Artist with the most singles on the *Billboard* Hot 100 without a #1 hit: James Brown.

In 1980, Seattle Mariners starting pitcher Mike Parrott won on opening day. His record that season: 1–16.

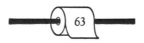

Female Flyers

First licensed female pilot in the United States:
Harriet Quimby, in 1911. She died a year later
when her plane pitched forward and ejected
her during an air show in Massachusetts.

During World War II, the Soviet army had
three female air divisions.

Record-breaking pilot Jackie Cochran (the first
woman to break the sound barrier and to fly a
jet across an ocean) was one of the founders of
the WASP, the Women Airforce Service Pilots,
during World War II.

Beginning in 1976, women could train to be
U.S. military pilots. But they weren't allowed
to fly combat missions until 1993.

A women pilots' club, the Ninety-Nines, began
in 1929 with 99 members (hence the name).
Today, the group lists more than 5,000 female
pilots on its roster.

Today, women make up about 6 percent of all
U.S. pilots.

Amelia Earhart's reason for making her
(doomed) 1937 trip around the world: "I want
to do it because I must do it. Women must try
to do things as men have tried. When they fail,
their failure must be a challenge to others."

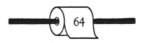

World Records

World's longest hot dog: a 1,996-foot wiener made by the Sara Lee Corporation for the 1996 Olympics.

Largest art museum: the Hermitage in St. Petersburg, Russia (322 galleries, nearly 3 million works of art).

The world record for the most golf balls balanced on top of each other is seven.

World's largest baseball card collection: the Metropolitan Museum of Art (200,000 cards).

Largest mass yodel: 1,795 people, participating in the 2004 Yahoo! Yodel Challenge.

The world's largest jazz festival took place in Quebec in 2004; more than a million jazz fans turned out.

World's largest playable electric guitar is 43' 7 ½" long and weighs 2,244 pounds.

Largest free concert ever: Rod Stewart in Brazil, 1994. More than 3.5 million people attended.

Minute Maid Park in Houston, Texas, has a 50,000-square-foot sliding glass door, the world's largest.

The world's longest golf course: the 8,450-yard Jade Dragon Snow Mountain Golf Club in Lijiang, China.

The world's oldest rock band that's still together is the Dutch group Golden Earring, which formed in 1961.

Pink Floyd's *Dark Side of the Moon* was on the charts longer than any other album in history (741 weeks).

Largest group with a hit single: "Battle Hymn of the Republic" by the 375-member Mormon Tabernacle Choir (1959).

Technology Bytes

In computer lingo, a nybble is four bits, or half of a byte.

E-mail was introduced into the White House in 1992.

The Vatican has named Saint Isadore the patron saint of computers and the Internet.

At its height, Elwood Edwards's AOL "You've Got Mail" greeting was heard 18,000 times a minute.

One survey showed that, of 25,500 standard English words, 93 percent had been registered as dot-coms.

Sixty-three percent of online music suppliers are based in Europe.

In 2004, the first "robot conductor" led the Tokyo Philharmonic. They played Beethoven's Fifth.

The patent name for the first computer mouse was "X/Y position indicator for a display system."

The iCarta is a combination iPod and toilet-paper holder.

The South Korean government has promised to put a robot in every home by 2013.

First downloadable single to sell more than a million copies: Gwen Stefani's "Hollaback Girl" (2005).

The billionth song downloaded from iTunes: Coldplay's "Speed of Sound."

Computer equipment gets dusty faster than furniture.

First nonhuman to be named *Time* magazine's Person of the Year: the personal computer (1982).

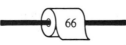

People in the Bible

ISREALITES. The word "Israelite" is an English translation of a term found in the ancient texts that make up the Jewish Torah and the Old Testament of the Christian Bible. It means "Children of Israel" and refers to an ancient nomadic people who were enslaved by the Egyptians around 1585 BC. Their language, Hebrew, is still in use today and is the world's oldest. It's a Semitic language, like Arabic, and comes from a word that means "one who traverses." Today, Hebrew is one of two official languages of Israel. (Arabic is the other.)

CANAANITES. When the Israelites arrived in "the promised land" of Canaan (which took up most of modern-day Israel), they discovered a group of people already living there...the Canaanites. The civilization was protected by walled cities and included a thriving merchant class. One of Canaan's most-traded goods was a purple dye made from the secretions of indigenous snails. In cuneiform, an ancient type of picture writing, the word for "Canaan" looked like the symbol that meant "reddish purple." So the Israelites' promised land was known to locals as the "Land of the Purple Dye."

PHILISTINES. This seafaring culture invaded and occupied modern-day Israel and Lebanon around 1200 BC. There's a lot of debate among historians about what region the Philistines called home, but today, many people believe that they originally hailed from Greece.

BEDOUINS. Desert-dwelling Arabs, the Bedouins have been around for thousands of years and consist of dozens of different communities throughout the Middle East. They typically herd sheep and goats and are known for being polite, hospitable hosts who regularly invite other travelers into their homes. Today, as during biblical times, many Bedouins live in handwoven tents

called *beit al-sha'ar*, or "houses of goat hair." The tents are so durable that they keep out the cold in winter, the heat in summer, and shrink in the rain to become waterproof.

ZEALOTS. In the Bible, "zealots" were Jewish rebels who plotted to overthrow the Roman government. The word comes from the Greek *zelotes*, which means "emulator" or "follower." One zealot, Simon, was a disciple of Jesus.

* * *

SHAKESPEAREAN INSULTS

"You should be women, and yet your beards forbid me to interpret that you are so." —*Macbeth*

"[Thou art] a most notable coward, an infinite and endless liar, an hourly promise breaker, the owner of no one good quality."
—*All's Well That Ends Well*

"Thou stale old mouse-eaten dry cheese!" —*Troilus and Cressida*

"I scorn you, scurvy companion. What, you poor, base, rascally, cheating, lack-linen mate! Away, you moldy rogue, away!"
—*Henry IV, Part II*

"Go prick thy face and over-red thy fear, thou lily-liver'd boy."
—*Macbeth*

"Thou art like the toad, ugly and venomous."
—*As You Like It*

"If thou wilt needs marry, marry a fool; for wise men know well enough what monsters you make of them." —*Hamlet*

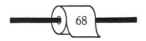

TV Trivia

The name originally considered for the TV show *Friends* was *Insomnia Café*.

The Lone Ranger was the first TV show ever to be shown in reruns.

Eighty percent of Hollywood executives believe there's a link between TV violence and real violence.

Families who turn off the TV during meals tend to eat healthier.

Jerry Seinfeld turned down $5 million per episode to continue *Seinfeld* past 1998.

Billy Graham broke his strict rule against watching TV on Sunday for the Beatles' first appearance on *The Ed Sullivan Show*.

There are more than 80 different games on *The Price is Right*.

Most popular TV show in the world in 2008: *CSI*.

The Emmy Award was originally called the Immy. It's named after TV camera "imaging" tubes.

Most-watched series finale of a TV drama: *Magnum, P.I.* (1988).

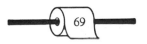

Place Names

The town of Notrees, Texas, founded in 1946, was named for its lack of vegetation.

Three most common U.S. town names: Midway, Fairview, and Oak Grove.

The state of Georgia was named for England's King George II. Louisiana was named for King Louis XIV of France.

Shortest place name in the United States: Y, Alaska.

Portland, Oregon, got its name in a coin toss...tails, and it would have been Boston, Oregon.

Marfa, Texas, took its name from a character in Dostoyevsky's *The Brothers Karamazov*. The town was used as a locale for the movie *Giant* and other films.

In 1916, Berlin, Ontario, changed its name to Kitchener due to anti-German sentiment during World War I.

Whiskeytown, California, got its name when donkeys lost their footing on a local trail and spilled a load of whiskey into a nearby ravine.

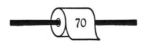

Legal Roots

Around 2100 BC, the Sumerians were the first to write down official legal codes. Their first law: a ban against witchcraft.

Red hand—which means being caught "red handed," or with blood on your hands—is a Scottish legal term that dates to 1432.

Historians believe that the American 12-person jury system came from the Vikings, who used committees of 12 "law men" to hear crimes.

The first U.S. Supreme Court case: *West v. Barnes*, tried in 1791. The court upheld a law saying a plaintiff had to file his case in person in Washington, D.C., to get a hearing.

Louisiana still refers to the Napoleonic Code in its state law.

American police officers were first required to read suspects their Miranda rights in 1966, but those rights are required only if the police want to interrogate someone they've detained. Police can arrest and hold people without issuing a Miranda warning, as long as they don't subject the person to questioning.

Until President John F. Kennedy was killed in 1963, it wasn't a federal crime to assassinate the president.

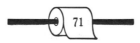

The Noble Nobel

First Nobel Peace Prize winner: Jean Henri Dunant, founder of the Swiss Red Cross (1901).

Wangari Maathai of Kenya was the first African woman to win the Nobel Peace Prize (2004).

John Enders cultivated polio in a test tube, and in 1954, he—not Jonas Salk—got a Nobel Prize for his work.

Dr. Martin Luther King Jr., at age 35, was the youngest person to win the Nobel Peace Prize.

António Egas Moniz won the Nobel Prize in Medicine for developing the lobotomy (1949).

There is no Nobel Prize for mathematics.

Pearl S. Buck was the first American woman to win the Nobel Prize in Literature, in 1938.

To date, there are no female Nobel laureates in economics.

Winston Churchill won a Nobel Prize—not for peace, but for literature.

Marie Curie was the first person to win two Nobel Prizes.

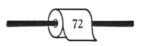

Facts About the Famous

At last count, Ozzy Osbourne has been in rehab 14 times.

Princess Diana's favorite band was Duran Duran.

For the band Emerson, Lake, and Palmer's 1977 tour, they took 63 roadies...including a karate instructor.

On waking from a diabetic coma, Jerry Garcia's first words were, "I'm not Beethoven."

Angus Young of AC/DC performed in a gorilla suit before settling on his schoolboy look.

Merle Haggard was born in a converted train car.

Mark Twain called the accordion the "stomach Steinway."

Jimi Hendrix played a comb and wax paper "kazoo" on his 1968 recording of "Crosstown Traffic."

Vincent van Gogh's self-portrait shows a bandaged right ear—he painted a mirror image. (He actually cut off the left one.)

Steven Tyler of Aerosmith insists that no one call him Steve.

Mick Fleetwood of Fleetwood Mac estimates that he spent $8 million on cocaine.

Vivien Leigh hated kissing Clark Gable while filming *Gone With the Wind*. She said he had bad breath.

Tom Cruise writes with his right hand, but does almost everything else left-handed.

In 1966, singer Joan Baez sued cartoonist Al Capp for parodying her in one of his comic strips. She lost.

Al Capone's business card said that he was a used furniture dealer.

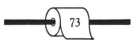

Circus, Circus

The flying trapeze was invented in late 19th-century France by Jules Léotard, namesake of the leotard.

Diameter of a standard circus ring: 42 feet...the size needed for a horse to circle comfortably at full gallop while a standing performer rides on its back.

In 1793, George Washington attended one of the first circus performances in America.

On September 13, 1916, an elephant named Mary was hanged for murder in Erwin, Tennessee. The crime: killing a circus worker.

The shout "Hey, Rube!" can be used either as a rallying call or as a cry for help for circus people involved in a fight.

Actor Burt Lancaster worked as a circus acrobat from 1932 to 1939...and did his own stunts in the 1956 movie *Trapeze*.

"Equilibristics" is an act that combines juggling and gymnastics.

The Emmett Kelly Museum in Sedan, Kansas, honors Kelly, a circus performer who created the now-famous sad-faced clown in the 1930s. He modeled it after Depression-era hoboes.

Human cannonballs aren't blasted from the cannon with gunpowder—they're propelled by a catapult. The flash, smoke, and boom are supplied by fireworks.

Most famous little person act: the Doll family, made up of four siblings (three sisters and a brother). The group performed with the Ringling Brothers and Barnum and Bailey Circus from the 1920s to the 1950s.

Technically, knife throwing falls under the heading of "impalement arts."

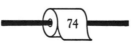

Animal Parts

The triangular soft part on the underside of a horse's hoof is called a frog.

A group of hares is a down. (A group of hairs is called a wig.)

In Sweden, cockroaches are called *kackerlacka*.

The swollen, light-colored section seen on earthworms: the clitellum.

What do you call a cross between a Tibetan yak and a buffalo? A yakalo.

A female lobster is called a hen or a chicken.

A cow's first stomach is the rumen.

The sound made by ferrets during play is called dooking.

When a male horse and female donkey mate, the offspring is a hinny.

Bears live in dens, badgers live in setts, and squirrels live in dreys.

Crepuscular animals (from the Latin *crepusculum*, meaning "twilight") are most active at dawn and dusk. Examples: dogs, deer, mice, and some birds.

Flour Power

The words "flour" and "flower" are related. Both come from French terms that mean "blossom."

A five-pound bag of flour yields about 17 ½ cups.

Bread made from flour is one of the oldest prepared foods in the world. As far back as the Neolithic period (around 9500 BC), people were using flour to make bread.

The primary difference among cake, bread, and all-purpose flour is the amount of gluten (a type of protein that comes from wheat) that each contains. Bread flour has the most, cake flour the least.

The inner part of a loaf of bread is called the crumb.

Whole-wheat flour has fives times more fiber and 25 percent more protein that white flour.

Flour particles suspended in the air are highly flammable and have caused many mill explosions throughout history.

Want to kill weevils or insect eggs in your flour? Freeze it for 48 hours.

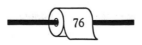

I'll Fly Away

Hummingbirds rarely walk, and when they do, they usually do it for just an inch or two.

Buzzards are legally classified as songbirds in Ohio.

Bats, like cats, groom themselves.

Some birds, such as gulls and cormorants, can drink salt water.

Some grizzly bears eat as many as 40,000 moths in one day.

Storks use their long bills (some can be more than a foot long) to fight off predators.

A male bird of paradise needs several years to develop his extravagant, flower-shaped plumage.

Yellow canaries that are fed red pepper will turn bright orange.

Pigeons can't walk without bobbing their heads.

Owls cannot move their eyes. They have to move their heads, which they can swivel 270 degrees.

A pelican's pouch can hold three gallons of water...more than twice what will fit in its stomach.

Standing on one leg is a flamingo's most comfortable position.

World's most ancient bird: New Zealand's Kiwis. The species has been around for about 30 million years.

The ostrich has the biggest eyes of any land animal—two inches in diameter.

To make sure it doesn't lose its balance, a bald eagle will drop a feather from one wing if it loses one from the other.

Bats aren't birds or rodents; they're mammals. They also aren't blind. Bats see very well, but mostly in shades of gray.

Eleanor Roosevelt

The town of Eleanor, West Virginia, was established in 1934 and named for Eleanor Roosevelt.

According to some stories, Roosevelt ate three pieces of chocolate-covered garlic every morning. Supposedly, it was to improve her memory.

When she married Franklin D. Roosevelt in 1905, Eleanor's uncle—President Theodore Roosevelt—gave her away.

Eleanor and Franklin Roosevelt got so many death threats that she started carrying a concealed revolver during his years as a New York senator. Members of the state police force taught her how to shoot it.

When King George VI and the future Queen Elizabeth II visited the White House in 1939, Roosevelt arranged a meal of smoked turkey, Virginia ham, green salad, strawberry shortcake...and hot dogs.

*　　*　　*

"Campaign behavior for wives: Always be on time. Do as little talking as humanly possible. Lean back in the parade car so everybody can see the president."
　　　　　　　　　　　—Eleanor Roosevelt

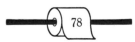

Tough Guys

Pro golfer Frank Nobilo's ancestors were Italian pirates.

Richard Pryor was raised in a brothel.

To prepare for his role in *Down and Out in Beverly Hills* (1986), Nick Nolte spent five weeks as a homeless person.

Robert De Niro accidentally broke Joe Pesci's rib during a sparring scene in *Raging Bull*.

Tom Cruise spent two years preparing for *The Last Samurai* (2003), learning how to use swords and speak Japanese.

Gene Kelly had a fever of 103 degrees when he danced the title song in *Singin' in the Rain*.

Western hero most often portrayed on film: William "Buffalo Bill" Cody.

Humphrey Bogart appeared in only one horror film: *The Return of Dr. X* (1939). He played a zombie.

Al Pacino was once arrested for carrying a concealed weapon.

John Wayne was a star college football player, but a bodysurfing accident at Newport Beach, California, cost him his athletic scholarship and ended his football career.

Robert Mitchum once served time on a chain gang.

Sylvester Stallone grew up in foster homes until he was five years old.

Who played Robert De Niro's homicidal passenger in *Taxi Driver*? Martin Scorsese.

Actor Mark Wahlberg has three nipples.

Woody Harrelson claims that he had more than 17 jobs one year—and was fired from most of them.

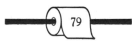

Toys & Games

The game of marbles dates back to the Stone Age and is found in almost every culture.

The three most-landed-on Monopoly squares: Illinois Avenue, Go, and the B&O Railroad.

And Monopoly's Boardwalk is called Mayfair in England, Schlossallee in Germany, and Rue de la Paix in France.

The soundtrack for the video game Onimusha includes a 203-piece orchestra.

World's largest toy distributor: McDonald's.

Best-selling video games of all time: Super Mario Bros. (40 million) and Tetris (33 million).

If you divided the world's Legos among the world's humans, every man, woman, and child would get 75.

The answer cube inside a Magic 8-Ball is a 20-sided icosahedron.

There are 324 possible solutions in the game of Clue.

Three thousand years ago, Egyptian children played with hoops of dried grapevines.

There are 255,168 possible outcomes in tic-tac-toe.

Billiards was introduced to America by the Spanish in 1565.

Chess is a descendant of an Indian game known as Chatur-Anga, played in the seventh century.

Top-selling toys of 1929: American Flyer model trains and the Popeye Paddle and Ball.

Number of white dots in the Pac-Man arcade game? 240.

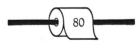

Motherhood

In 17th-century America, the average married woman gave birth to 13 children.

The birth-control pill was invented by three men.

Disposable diapers are five times more likely to cause diaper rash than cotton ones.

Queen Victoria was one of the first women to use chloroform as anesthesia during childbirth.

The American Birth Control League's founder, Margaret Sanger, was against changing the group's name to Planned Parenthood.

According to folklore, an axe or knife placed under a woman's bed will "cut the pain" of childbirth.

The frequency of twin births has almost doubled since 1980.

Animals that give birth to live young are "viviparous."

Tammie Green participated in the 1998 Solheim Cup golf tournament...while six months pregnant.

In nearly every language, the word for "mother" begins with the "m" sound.

The original birth-control pill contained five times as much estrogen as today's pills.

Of Queen Anne's 18 children, 13 were stillborn. The only one that survived infancy died at age 11.

No babies have ever been born within the border of Vatican City.

*   *   *

Gulp! Many old English gambling dens employed someone to swallow the dice in case of a raid.

Speed Demons

An adult pig can run a mile in 7.5 minutes—about the same speed as the average human.

Sailfish, which live in the warmer parts of the Pacific Ocean, are the fastest fish in the world. They can swim at speeds of more than 60 mph.

Bad news: polar bears can smell you from 20 miles away. Good news: their top speed is only 25 mph.

How fast does a bumblebee flap its wings? 160 beats per second.

A hummingbird's heart beats about 615 times per minute.

Fastest land animal in North America: the pronghorn antelope can run up to 53 mph.

Research has shown that dogs can locate the source of a sound in six hundreths of a second.

A three-toed sloth can move twice as fast in water as on land, but he's fastest when climbing trees.

A school of piranhas can devour a 400-pound hog in just a few minutes.

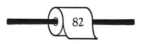

Global Gourmets

The people of the United Kingdom eat more cans of baked beans than the rest of the world combined.

Country with the highest per-capita consumption of soft drinks in the world: Iran.

Popular meal in Russia: *mockba* pizza—topped with sardines, tuna, mackerel, salmon, and onions.

Cubans eat more sugar than any other nation in the world. The Irish eat the most corn flakes.

Italy imports most of its pasta from the United States and Canada.

On average, the French eat 200 million frogs per year.

In Japan, there are vending machines that dispense fresh-cooked spaghetti.

Germany produces more than 1,200 varieties of sausage.

In the United Kingdom, about eight servings of fish and chips are sold every second.

In China, pancakes are often served as side dishes.

In India, pickled ginger and minced mutton are popular pizza toppings.

Middle Eastern Dunkin' Donuts shops sell fig-filled doughnuts.

Favorite pizza toppings in Germany: sauerkraut and onions.

In Sweden, horse meat is more popular than lamb.

The ancient Greeks ate cheesecake.

China consumes an average of 135 million tons of rice every year.

Favorite pizza toppings in Japan: eel and squid.

The Queen's Titles

At her coronation in 1953, Queen Elizabeth II took on 27 titles:

Her Majesty
Elizabeth II

By the Grace
of God, of Great
Britain, Ireland
and the British
Dominions beyond
the Seas Queen,
Defender of the
Faith

Duchess of
Edinburgh

Countess of
Merioneth

Baroness Greenwich

Duke of Lancaster

Lord of Mann

Duke of Normandy

Sovereign of the
Most Distinguished
Order of Saint
Michael and Saint
George

Sovereign of the
Order of Mercy

Sovereign of the
Most Honourable
Order of the Bath

Sovereign of the
Most Ancient and
Most Noble Order
of the Thistle

Sovereign of the
Most Illustrious
Order of Saint
Patrick

Sovereign of the
Most Excellent
Order of the
British Empire

Sovereign of the
Distinguished
Service Order

Sovereign of the
Imperial Service
Order

Sovereign of the
Most Exalted Order
of the Star of India

Sovereign of the
Order of Burma

Sovereign of the
Order of Merit

Sovereign of the
Most Eminent
Order of the Indian
Empire

Sovereign of the
Order of British
India

Sovereign of the
Indian Order of
Merit

Sovereign of the
Royal Order of
Victoria and Albert

Sovereign of the
Royal Family Order
of King Edward VII

Sovereign of the
Order of the
Companions of
Honour

Sovereign of the
Royal Victorian
Order

Sovereign of the
Most Venerable
Order of the
Hospital of Saint
John of Jerusalem

Special Occasions

Most popular reason for eating out: birthdays.

More babies are born on Tuesday than on any other day of the week.

Every year, the U.S. Postal Service delivers 20 billion cards, letters, and packages between Thanksgiving and Christmas.

New Year's Eve and July 4th are the two deadliest holidays for car travelers. Reason: drunk drivers.

Three percent of pet owners give Valentine's Day gifts to their pets.

An average Super Bowl party has 18 people.

How much do Americans spend on Easter candy each year? $1.9 billion.

What month do most couples get engaged? According to studies: December.

Eight percent of pet owners dress up their dogs and cats for Halloween.

Among Americans, 45 percent of women and 25 percent of men say they cried at their wedding.

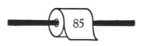

Earth News

The average American uses about 57 squares of toilet paper per day.

The light put out by the sun is equal to that of 4 trillion trillion lightbulbs.

The 10 hottest years on record have all occurred in the last two decades.

Scientists believe a 1 percent drop in the atmosphere's ozone levels causes up to a 6 percent rise in skin cancer cases.

In a year, most elevators travel the equivalent of nearly halfway around the equator.

About 27 percent of the food in developed countries is wasted each year.

Acid rain was first identified and named in 1852.

Every year, one ton of concrete is poured for every person on earth.

Rachel Carson's book *Silent Spring* inspired measures to curb the use of the insecticide DDT.

Every year, the average American uses paper and wood equivalent to one 100-foot-tall tree.

Since the mid-18th century, 1.7 million species have been identified and described.

From the fields to your fork, the average American dinner travels 1,500 miles.

Americans consume nine pounds of food additives every year.

If you yelled for eight years, seven months, and six days, you'd create enough energy to heat one cup of coffee.

The average American household wastes 14 percent of the food it buys.

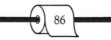

Name Changes

The band Blondie was originally called Angel and the Snakes.

Basketball star Kareem Abdul-Jabbar's given name: Ferdinand Lewis Alcindor Jr.

Writer Truman Capote's real name was Truman Streckfus Persons.

Crooner Bing Crosby's first group, in 1925, was called Two Boys and a Piano.

Ayn Rand's own working title for her second book was *Second-Hand Lives*. Her editor suggested changing it to *The Fountainhead*.

Producer Robert Stigwood came up with the name "Bee Gees." The band preferred "Rupert's World."

Neil Diamond once considered the stage name Neil Kaminsky.

Charles Dickens's character Tiny Tim was originally called Small Sam.

Gene Simmons of KISS (real name: Chaim Witz) financed Van Halen's first demo tape. He suggested that the band change its name to Daddy Longlegs. (They declined.)

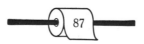

Communications

In the United States, more than 18 billion text messages are sent every month.

American soldiers in Vietnam sometimes used Slinkies as radio antennae.

Roman emperor Claudius was signaled to join his army by a chain of bonfires from Britain to Rome.

James K. Polk's 1845 presidential inauguration was the first reported by telegraph.

The last Western Union Singing Telegram was delivered in 1974.

In 2004, *Billboard* magazine added a "Hot Ringtones" chart.

In 1929, Herbert Hoover was the first president to put a phone in the Oval Office.

In 1871, five years before Alexander Graham Bell was granted a patent for the telephone, inventor Antonio Meucci filed a patent for a similar device, but could not afford the $10 fee.

Third-most-used language in the United States: American Sign Language. (English and Spanish are first and second.)

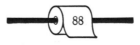

Kid Stuff

National Park WebRangers are kids who learn about the parks by solving mysteries and puzzles, playing games, and gathering secret words online.

Most common name in nursery rhymes: Jack.

In 21 states, spanking is still a legal form of punishment in schools.

Igor Stravinsky said his music was "best understood by children and animals."

The melody to "Twinkle, Twinkle, Little Star" is from a 1761 French song. (The lyrics date to 1806.)

Early European jesters made balloons out of animal bladders and intestines.

All-time best-selling lunch box: the Walt Disney School Bus (9 million sold between 1961 and 1973).

Sesame Street's Big Bird has a teddy bear named Radar.

First lunch box character from a TV show: Hopalong Cassidy (1950). The design sold 600,000 in its first year.

The first merry-go-round appeared at a fair in Philippa-polis, Turkey, in 1620.

In one episode of their TV show, Batman and Robin traveled through time to save Marco Polo.

Comic superhero Captain Marvel's appearance was modeled after actor Fred MacMurray.

The comic strip *Peanuts* was originally called *Li'l Folks*.

Who are the Springfield Isotopes, Shelbyville Shelbyvillains, and Salem Boulevardiers? Minor-league baseball teams on *The Simpsons*.

Since 1959, more than 105 million yards of fabric have been used to create Barbie clothes.

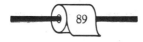

Comic Relief

In the 1960s, DC Comics and Marvel Comics jointly trademarked the term "Super Hero."

Donald Duck was Mussolini's favorite cartoon character.

World's most valuable comic: *Action Comics* #1 (1938), which introduced Superman. Cover price: 10¢. Present-day value for a copy in mint condition: $600,000.

Superman's full Earth name: Clark Joseph Kent.

The 1960s comic book character Eclipso was called "The Genius Who Fought Himself."

First published drawing by Charles Schulz: a 1937 cartoon for *Ripley's Believe It or Not*.

Spider-Man's first appearance came in Marvel Comics' *Amazing Fantasy* #15 (1962).

Salvador Dalí and Walt Disney once collaborated on a cartoon called *Destino*. They never finished it.

First female superhero to have her own comic book: Wonder Woman (1942).

Who was Hoyt Curtin? He wrote the theme songs for *The Flintstones*, *The Jetsons*, and *The Yogi Bear Show*.

Popeye began as a comic strip in 1929.

Shaquille O'Neal's favorite superhero: Superman. (He even has a Superman tattoo.)

Editorial cartoonist Pat Oliphant founded the Bad Golfers Association in 1994.

Superman once gave Batman a ring of green kryptonite so that if Superman ever lost his mind and became a danger to humans, Batman could use the ring to defeat him.

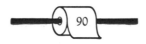

Food Bites

Swedish golfer Jesper Parnevik once ate volcanic sand "to cleanse his system."

Ted Nugent makes and sells his own line of beef jerky called Gonzo Meat Biltong.

Actor Vincent Price was also an author and a gourmet cook. In 1965, he published his own cookbook, A *Treasury of Great Recipes*.

Fletcher Davis, who once owned a diner in Athens, Texas, claimed he invented the hamburger in the 1880s.

Pro golfer Amy Alcott's day job: short-order cook.

Alexander Graham Bell preferred to sip his soup through a glass straw.

Napoléon Bonaparte carried chocolate with him on all of his military campaigns.

Both Hitler and Mussolini were vegetarians.

Orville Wright numbered his chickens' eggs so he could eat them in the order they were laid.

The Joy of Cooking was first self-published by Irma Rombauer in 1931.

Singer Chaka Khan once came out with a line of chocolates called "Chakalates."

Charles Lindbergh's only food on his transatlantic flight: Four sandwiches.

Ernest Hemingway's favorite food while writing: peanut butter and onion sandwiches.

In 1954, Alice B. Toklas (longtime partner of writer Gertrude Stein) published a cookbook and memoir called *The Alice B. Toklas Cookbook*. Its most famous recipe was for "Hashisch Fudge," which included a mixture of fruit, nuts, spices, and "canibus sativa," or marijuana.

Creatures Great & Small

The largest dinosaur was probably the Argentinosaurus. It grew to be 120 feet long and weighed 110 tons.

Some prehistoric dragonflies had wingspans as big as a hawk's.

A hummingbird egg is the size of a Tic-Tac breath mint. A hummingbird nest can be the size of a walnut shell.

The world's largest goldfish is 15 inches long. (He lives in Hong Kong and is named Bruce.)

The largest American alligator measured 19.8 feet in length.

Largest land invertebrate: the coconut crab. It can grow to be three feet across and cracks open coconuts with its pincers.

Longest snake in the world: the royal python, which can grow to be 35 feet long.

The annual Banana Slug Derby at California's Prairie Creek Redwoods State Park is held on a course that's 18 inches long.

World's heaviest carnivore: the southern elephant seal. Males can weigh 8,000 pounds and grow to be 16 feet long.

The largest bacterium can grow to the size of the period at the end of this sentence.

Smallest mammal on earth: the Etruscan shrew. It weighs less than a penny.

Largest rodent in North America and second-largest in the world: the beaver. (The world's largest is the South American capybara, which looks like a big guinea pig.)

The tentacles of the giant arctic jellyfish can grow to be 120 feet long.

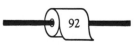

Space Facts

In space, fish swim in loops, rather than straight lines.

First Canadian in space: Marc Garneau (1984).

Animals that have flown in space: dogs, chimps, mice, spiders, frogs, and jellyfish.

The *Apollo 11* lunar module had only 30 seconds of fuel left when it landed safely on the Moon.

According to NASA, the foods astronauts miss the most are pizza, ice cream, and soda.

To date, only one man-made satellite has been destroyed by a meteor: the European Space Agency's *Olympus* (1993).

Outer space officially begins 62 miles up.

Astronauts gave Walter Cronkite an "honorary astronaut" title for his 24 hour coverage of *Apollo 11*.

Nineteen years elapsed between the first and second women in space. Both were Russians.

First African American woman in space: Mae Jemison on the space shuttle *Endeavour*.

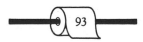

Foreign Flora

The mango is the world's most popular fruit, but the most harvested are grapes, followed by bananas, apples, coconuts, and plantains.

For 3,000 years, hemp was the world's largest agricultural crop.

There were more than 300 banana-related accidents in Britain in 2001. (Most people slipped on peels.)

A coffee tree yields about one pound of coffee in a year.

China grows more pears than any other country in the world.

China also grows the most sweet potatoes worldwide.

A company in Lancashire, England, grew the world's tallest tomato plant—it reached a height of 65 feet.

The national symbol of Wales is the leek.

World's smallest tree: the dwarf willow of the arctic tundra, which reaches only about two inches high.

The jungle's most pest-ridden tree: the cacao, the source of chocolate's main ingredient.

Cacao trees grow only in tropical climates, 20 degrees north or south of the equator.

The largest (and possibly smelliest) flower on earth is the *Rafflesia arnoldii*, which grows in the rain forests of Borneo and Sumatra. It's nicknamed the "stinking corpse lily" and smells like a dead body.

Just 2 percent of Antarctica's soil is free of ice, so only hardy plants grow there, including lichens, mosses, fungi, and liverwort.

Every second, the world's rain forests lose about two football fields' worth of area.

Scientific Numbers

This page is about 500,000 atoms thick.

You have to process 88,000 pounds of liquefied air to get a single pound of neon gas.

At –90°F, your breath will freeze in midair...and drop to the ground.

Quick! Convert –40°C into Fahrenheit! Answer: –40°F. (It's the one temperature that's the same in both systems.)

A hundred calories will propel a bicycle three miles or drive a car 280 feet.

A gallon of water weighs 8.34 pounds.

The sun converts more than 4 million tons of matter into energy every second.

Only 5 percent of the stars in our galaxy are bigger than our sun.

Earthquakes travel at speeds of up to 4.8 miles per second.

The Milky Way galaxy moves through space at 170 miles per second.

Gallons of beer in a standard U.S. barrel: three.

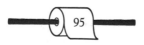

Tips & Advice

Housing prices are usually lowest in winter and highest in summer.

Buy a new car at month's end; that's when dealers focus on volume of sales instead of commissions.

The best time to teach a dog new tricks is shortly after its first birthday.

Buy shoes in the afternoon, after you've walked around for a while. Feet tend to swell after you've walked, and you'll get a better fit.

Most fish are delivered to stores on Mondays and Thursdays, so the freshest are usually available on Tuesdays and Fridays.

Best time to visit the emergency room: between 8:00 a.m. and noon on Wednesdays, Thursdays, or Fridays. Mondays and Tuesdays are the most crowded.

If you want to achieve the best workout, hit the gym in the morning. Your metabolism slows during sleep, so morning exercise jump-starts it.

Placing a bet? If it is on an underdog, wait until game time. But if you're betting on a favorite, do it as soon as possible. Most amateurs bet on favorites close to game time, so bookies change the point spread to attract bets on the underdog.

Best time to have your photo taken: midday. In the morning, your face is puffy from sleeping, and by late afternoon, your face and eyes start to show fatigue.

Taking a trip and hoping to depart on time? Book the second flight of the day. Statistics show that an airline's first departure is often delayed because so many other carriers are trying to send flights out at the same time.

Have a Ball

A regulation baseball has 108 stitches.

In the 17th and 18th centuries, it took four years of apprenticeship to become a featherie golf ball maker.

A good pitcher can make a baseball curve as much as 17½ inches from a straight path.

There are 122 bumps per square inch on a Spalding basketball.

Glitter (disco) balls were first used in nightclubs in the 1920s.

When pitched, the average major league baseball rotates 15 times before it's hit by the batter.

In 1935, the L.A. Young Golf Company introduced a ball with a honey-filled center.

The rubber used to make SuperBalls is called Zectron.

Average life span of an NBA basketball: 10,000 bounces.

Early tennis balls were leather pouches stuffed with wool or animal hair.

American inventor Charles Goodyear manufactured the first rubber soccer ball in 1855. Before that, soccer balls were usually made from pigs' bladders.

Golf balls begin to lose their resilience after about a year.

In 2008, representatives from the Carnival Cruise Line (which created the ball) bounced a 36-foot-wide beach ball—the world's largest—down Elm Street in Dallas, Texas. On its first day out, the ball hit a car antenna and popped, but it was later repaired.

Billiard balls used to be made of ivory. One tusk usually yielded about four balls.

BIG News

Studies show: There are 7,500,000,000,000,000,000 grains of sand on the world's beaches.

Song on *Billboard*'s Top 40 with the longest title: "Jeremiah Peabody's Poly Unsaturated Quick Dissolving Fast Acting Pleasant Tasting Green and Purple Pills," by Ray Stevens.

A googol is the mathematical term for 1 followed by 100 zeros.

The full title of Fiona Apple's *When the Pawn* album is 90 words long—the longest album title ever.

It took Michelangelo four years to paint the ceiling of the Sistine Chapel.

As of 2008, the largest known prime number is 12,978,189 digits long.

Diameter of Mars: 22,290,026 feet.

Floccinaucinihilipilification is a long word meaning "the action of estimating something as worthless."

But James Joyce's "Klikkakla-kkaklaskaklopatzklatschabat-tacreppycrottygraddaghsem-mihsammihnouithappluddyap-pladdypkonpkot" from *Finnegan's Wake* is even longer. (It means "an act of God.")

Supposedly, King Arthur's Round Table seated 150.

An estimate of the diameter of the universe: 620,000,000,000,000,000,000,000 miles.

Victor Hugo's *Les Misérables* contains one of the longest sentences in French literature—823 words.

Rodin's statue *The Thinker* was originally intended to be part of a pair of large doors.

You can fit 600,000,000,000,000,000,000,000 atoms in a thimble.

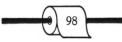
98

Spring Facts

In the United States, flooding is most common in the spring.

Daylight Saving Time, which takes place in March, saves the nation about 1 percent a day on electricity costs.

Led Zeppelin, Nina Simone, Van Morrison, Frank Sinatra, and Billie Holiday all sang songs about spring.

Spring astrological signs: Aries, Taurus, and Gemini.

Children grow faster in the spring.

In modern times, May Day is celebrated on May 1. But the Celts, who originated the pagan holiday, typically celebrated it on or around May 15.

In Afghanistan and Iran, the first day of spring is also the start of the new year.

* * *

"Every year, back comes Spring, with nasty little birds yapping their fool heads off and the ground all mucked up with plants."
—Dorothy Parker

1980s Milestones

1980: Mount Saint Helens erupted in Washington State.

1980: Quebec tried to secede from Canada...and failed.

1981: Sandra Day O'Connor became the first female Supreme Court justice.

1982: Canada finally became officially independent from Great Britain.

1983: Top-selling toy: Cabbage Patch Kids.

1984: Apple launched its first Macintosh computer.

1984: New York was the first state to require that people wear a seat belt in a moving car.

1984: The PG-13 movie rating was introduced.

1985: Bob Geldof and Midge Ure organized Live Aid, the largest television broadcast ever.

1985: Mikhail Gorbachev became the leader of the Soviet Union, introducing policies that would lead to the fall of communism there and in Eastern Europe.

1986: Martin Luther King Jr. Day became a national holiday.

1986: The Hands Across America benefit—in which 7 million people held hands in chains across the United States—raised $20 million for charity.

1987: *The Simpsons* first appeared on television as a short cartoon on *The Tracy Ullman Show*.

1988: Japan's Great Seto Bridge, the world's longest two-tiered bridge, opened to traffic.

1989: Actress Kim Basinger bought the town of Braselton, Georgia, for $20 million. (She sold it in 1993.)

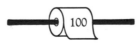

The 7 Chakras

Chakra (pronounced SHOCK-ruh) is Sanskrit word that means "wheel" or "disc." According to traditional Indian medicine, chakras are centers of energy, and every human body has seven:

1. The Root chakra at the base of your spine is all about security. It's associated with basic survival needs like food (real and spiritual), water, and shelter.

2. The Sacral chakra in your lower abdomen controls emotions, pleasure, and finding balance in life.

3. The Navel chakra is located in the solar plexus and has to do with self-esteem and personal power. "Gut instincts" are centered here.

4. The Heart chakra, in the middle of the chest, is the love center of the human energy system, governing circulation, fluent thought, and a sense of security and peacefulness.

5. The Throat chakra at the base of the throat controls metabolism and is all about creativity, expressing yourself, and telling the truth.

6. The Third Eye chakra is located between and slightly above your eyebrows, and governs your powers of insight and intuition.

7. The Crown chakra at the very top of the head is the pinnacle of the chakras. It has to do with wisdom and being at one with the world.

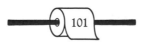

World Politics

The first English Parliament was called into session on January 20, 1265.

Australian prime minister Harold Holt vanished while swimming in Port Phillip Bay in 1967.

The so-called Roman salute (an arm held out straight with the palm down) used by Italy's Benito Mussolini was once common in the United States when reciting the Pledge of Allegiance.

There has never been a United Nations Secretary-General from the United States.

The longest-serving UK party leader was David "Screaming Lord" Sutch of the Monster Raving Loony Party.

Lionel Nathan de Rothschild of the British House of Commons was the first Jewish member of Parliament (1858).

Women in Switzerland didn't get the right to vote until 1971.

An American, William Walker, became president of Nicaragua in 1856.

There has never been a left-handed pope.

Benjamin Disraeli (1804–81) was the only British prime minister of Jewish ancestry.

According to legend, Harald Fairhair united Norway in AD 872 to impress a girl.

Mickey Mouse is prohibited from running for office in Comal County, Texas.

Spencer Perceval (1762–1812) is the only British prime minister to have been assassinated.

Longest speech delivered to the United Nations: Fidel Castro, in 1960. It lasted four hours and 29 minutes.

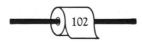

Man's Best Friend

Only one dog appears in Shakespeare's plays: Crab, in *The Two Gentlemen of Verona*.

King Henry III of France often walked the streets with a basket of puppies around his neck.

When Anne Boleyn was beheaded, so was her wolfhound.

John Steinbeck's dog ate the first draft of his classic novel *Of Mice and Men*.

At the end of the Beatles' song "A Day in the Life," there's an ultrasonic whistle audible only to dogs.

Actor William H. Macy once told a reporter that he believed he was a golden retriever in a past life.

In the 1950s, the dog that played Lassie made $5,000 a week.

Movie theater owners' pick for 1926 "Actor of the Year": Rin Tin Tin.

Paul McCartney wrote the Beatles song "Martha My Dear" for his sheepdog, Martha.

Walt Disney owned a poodle named Lady.

Name of Batman's dog: Ace the Bat-Hound.

Although foxes are members of the dog (canid) family, they cannot mate and reproduce with any other canid.

Zeppo Marx helped to establish the Afghan hound as a breed in the United States.

Mamie Stuyvesant Fish (wife of a railroad millionaire) once threw a dinner party for her dog...who arrived wearing a $15,000 diamond collar.

J. Edgar Hoover's dog was named Spee-De-Bozo.

Kings & Queens

There really was a King Macbeth. He ruled Scotland from 1040 to 1057.

Alfred, king of England from 871 to 899, is the only English king called "the Great."

Edward IV—at 6' 3"—was the tallest English monarch.

From 1918 to 1944, Denmark's Christian X was also king of Iceland.

Lady Jane Grey ruled England for only nine days, from July 10 to July 19, 1553.

Before Louis-Philippe I became king of France in 1830, he lived above a Philadelphia bar.

Good King Wenceslas was a real king—of Bohemia.

Between 1978 and 1999, American-born Lisa Halaby was queen of Jordan. She's better known as Queen Noor.

Marie Antoinette liked to entertain herself by dressing up as a shepherdess and milk-maid.

So far, the longest reign of any British monarch was Queen Victoria's—63 years, 7 months.

Dieu et Mon Droit ("God and My Right") is Queen Elizabeth II's motto.

England's Queen Anne became so heavy that she needed to be moved with pulleys.

Queen Lili'uokalani was the last Hawaiian monarch. She abdicated in 1893 in the face of an American-backed coup d'état.

England's King Henry VIII did have a male heir (Edward VI) who was crowned king of England at the age of nine. But the boy died at 15, probably of tuberculosis.

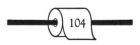

Jailbirds

Miguel de Cervantes wrote *Don Quixote* while in prison.

One of London's best-known jails was located on Clink Street. That's why jails are referred to as "clinks."

Marco Polo dictated his *Travels of Marco Polo* to a fellow inmate in a Genoa prison.

When English author Geoffrey Chaucer was taken prisoner by the French in the Hundred Years' War, his ransom was 16 pounds. The English refused to pay.

For four days in 1941, Nazi Rudolf Hess was the last state prisoner to be held in the Tower of London.

Later, Hess was the only occupant of Spandau Prison in Berlin.

Merle Haggard was in San Quentin State Prison in 1958 when Johnny Cash performed there.

Author Hunter S. Thompson (*Fear and Loathing in Las Vegas*) missed his high school graduation ceremony because he was in jail.

Mobster Charles "Lucky" Luciano was arrested 25 times but convicted only once.

Marie Antoinette took her bidet to prison with her.

Jazz legend Louis Armstrong was sent to reform school for firing a shot into a New Year's Day parade.

The first sponsored fundraising "walk" inside a prison occurred in an Oregon prison in 1988. The prisoners were raising money for organ transplants and walked a combined 3,400 miles.

The first indicted bank robber in the United States: Edward Smith, in 1831. He was sentenced to five years' hard labor on the rock pile at Sing Sing Prison in New York.

Travel Abroad

Kyoto was the capital of Japan from 794 to 1868. Today, the capital is Tokyo.

Sweden was a major European military power until 1709, when it lost the Battle of Poltava to Russia's Peter the Great.

In Asia, a black cat is considered lucky.

Most sparsely populated country in the world: Mongolia, with 4.5 people per square mile. Most crowded country: Monaco, with an average of 42,649 people per square mile.

Sixteen percent of all Africans live in Nigeria.

Switzerland hasn't gone to war with another country since 1515.

The University of Bologna in Italy, founded in 1088, is the oldest still-operating university in the world.

Coal miners in Wales once believed that washing coal dust from their backs weakened their spines.

Before joining Canada, Newfoundland was technically an independent country.

The border between Italy and Vatican City is marked by a painted white line.

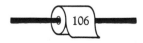

Star Trek & Star Wars

The crew of the *Enterprise* under Captain Kirk's command: 430. Under Captain Jean-Luc Picard: 1,012.

The word "Jedi" in *Star Wars* is derived from the Japanese words *jidai geki*, which means "period drama."

In the original draft of *Star Trek*, the *Enterprise* was called the USS *Yorktown*.

Nick Nolte was originally considered for the role of Han Solo in *Star Wars*.

Before he played Mr. Spock, Leonard Nimoy owned a pet store.

David Lynch turned down the chance to direct *Return of the Jedi*.

After the death of James "Scotty" Doohan at age 84 in July 2005, William Shatner, 74, became the oldest surviving cast member of the original *Star Trek*.

Only one shot in *The Phantom Menace* included no digital effects: the moment where gas blows out of a vent into one of the meeting rooms.

Captain Jean-Luc Picard's fish was named Livingston.

Before the original *Star Trek* series aired, publicity for the new show included photos in which Mr. Spock's eyebrows and ears were airbrushed to be more rounded. NBC, the network that was producing the series, was afraid his pointed ears and eyebrows would offend viewers because they made Spock look like the devil.

The character of Luke Skywalker in *Star Wars* (1977) was originally written as a girl.

Only person to appear as himself in the *Star Trek* franchise: Stephen Hawking on *Star Trek: The Next Generation* in 1993. (He beat Data at poker.)

Shopping

Minnesota's Mall of America has more visitors every year than Disney World, Graceland, and the Grand Canyon combined.

Sixty-seven percent of consumers say they would switch to a different brand if it supported a cause they believed in.

First major coupon campaign: Coca-Cola in 1887.

The average supermarket shopper makes 14 impulse decisions on each visit.

Every week, about a third of all Americans shop at a Wal-Mart store.

If you're average, you'll look around a store for about 15 minutes before you buy anything.

The most frequent "strange" customer request, according to supermarket managers: asking for a refund on food the customer bought and ate, but didn't like.

A new shopping mall opens somewhere in the United States every 7 hours.

What does "100% Natural" signify on food labels? Absolutely nothing official.

Everyday Origins

The first commercial typewriter was produced by gun manufacturer E. Remington and Sons in 1874.

The @ symbol is about 500 years old.

When and where was the wheel invented? Around 4000 BC, in Mesopotamia (now Iraq).

Stilts were invented by French shepherds who needed a way to get around in wet marshes.

The first ballpoint pen cost $12.50 in 1945...and sold out on its first day.

The degree sign (°) is an ancient symbol representing the sun.

The tape measure was patented in 1868.

The people of India and the Mayans were the only ancient people who used the number zero in their mathematics.

The first telephone book ever issued (in New Haven, Connecticut, in 1878) contained only 50 names.

Eyeglasses were invented in Europe in 1286.

What is businessman Oliver Pollock's claim to fame? He invented the dollar sign in 1778.

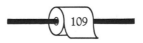

Espresso Yourself

Dark-roasted coffee is "weaker" than medium roast. Roasting burns off caffeine.

Prussia's Frederick the Great liked his coffee made with champagne and mustard.

Until 2004, caffeine was on the International Olympic Committee's list of prohibited substances.

King Louis XIV is credited with being the first person to add sugar to coffee, in 1715.

Beethoven counted out 60 beans for each cup of coffee.

Nationwide, 7-Eleven sells 10,000 pots of coffee per hour, every day of the year.

You can absorb only 300 mg of caffeine (the amount in four cups of coffee) at a time—any more goes right through you.

Technically speaking, coffee is a fruit juice.

In the 1700s, people added butter to their coffee.

A single serving of espresso has less caffeine than a cup of coffee.

Voltaire drank between 50 and 70 cups of coffee every day.

Coffee is the second most traded product in the world. The first: petroleum.

The average American consumes enough caffeine in one year to kill a horse.

Historians believe author Honoré de Balzac died of caffeine poisoning.

One pound of coffee makes about 50 cups of coffee. But one pound of tea leaves makes about 300 cups of tea.

The first coffee pot with a sieve to strain the grounds was invented in 1806.

BIG Debuts

James Earl Jones's film debut: Lieutenant Lothar Zogg in *Dr. Strangelove* (1964).

Richard Gere's first three big films: *Days of Heaven, American Gigolo,* and *An Officer and a Gentleman.* All had been turned down by John Travolta.

Comedian Bill Maher costarred with Mr. T in *D.C. Cab* (1983).

Quentin Tarantino's first screenplay: *Captain Peachfuzz and the Anchovy Bandit.*

On his first night hosting *The Tonight Show* in 1962, Johnny Carson was introduced by Groucho Marx.

Jack Nicholson's first role: Jimmy Walker in *The Cry Baby Killer* (1958).

Leonardo DiCaprio's first TV appearance was on *Romper Room.*

James Dean made his first television appearance in a 1950 Pepsi commercial.

What presidential daughter appeared in the 1964 Elvis Presley film *Kissin' Cousins?* Maureen Reagan.

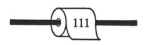

About Pitchers

"Poets are like baseball pitchers. Both have their moments. The intervals are the tough things."
—**Robert Frost**

"You don't save a pitcher for tomorrow. Tomorrow it may rain."
—**Leo Durocher**

"My pitching philosophy is simple—keep the ball away from the bat."
—**Satchel Paige**

"Hitting is timing. Pitching is upsetting timing."
—**Warren Spahn**

"The dumber a pitcher is, the better. When he gets smart and begins to experiment with a lot of different pitches, he's in trouble. All I ever had was a fastball, a curve, and a change-up, and I did pretty good."
—**Dizzy Dean**

"Good pitching will always stop good hitting, and vice versa."
—**Casey Stengel**

"The pitcher has to find out if the hitter is timid. And if the hitter is timid, [the pitcher] has to remind the hitter he's timid."
—**Don Drysdale**

"I hated to bat against Drysdale. After he hit you, he'd come around, look at the bruise on your arm, and say, 'Do you want me to sign it?'"
—**Mickey Mantle**

"I became a good pitcher when I stopped trying to make them miss the ball and started trying to make them hit it."
—**Sandy Koufax**

"[Sandy Koufax's] fastball was so fast, some batters would start to swing as he was on his way to the mound."
—**Jim Murray**

"You know you're pitching well when the batters look as bad as you do at the plate."
—**Duke Snider**

"Pitchers, like poets, are born, not made."
—**Cy Young**

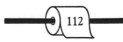

112

Counting Costs

In 1941, a gallon of regular gas cost 19.2¢.

Cost to renovate the Statue of Liberty in 1984: $62 million. Yankee Stadium's 1976 renovations: $167 million.

If your dog lives to age 11, you will probably have spent more than $13,000 on it.

It costs a zoo five times more to keep a panda than to keep an elephant.

Cost of the 13-year Apollo program to put a man on the Moon: $23 billion.

It costs 3¢ to make a dollar bill—and 7.8¢ to make a half-dollar coin.

Cost of a cellular phone in 1984: $4,195.

Estimated cost for having your whole body tattooed: $30,000 to $50,000.

A fifth of the world's population earns just $425 a year—the cost of a day's golf at Pebble Beach.

The Louisiana Purchase cost the United States just 3¢ an acre.

World Leaders

Alec Douglas-Home, former prime minister of the United Kingdom (1963–64), was a world-class cricket player.

From 1951 to 1960, future Ugandan dictator Idi Amin was the country's light heavyweight boxing champion.

Richard the Lionheart (1157–99) was a member of the brotherhood of troubadours and wrote song lyrics.

The CIA once considered killing Fidel Castro by dousing his scuba gear with LSD.

Lester Pearson, Canada's prime minister from 1963 to 1968, was asked to play for Britain's Olympic hockey team.

Hirohito, Japan's 124th emperor, was an internationally respected marine biologist.

Former British prime minister Tony Blair was once in a rock band called Ugly Rumours.

Adolf Hitler personally saved one Jew from the death camps—the daughter-in-law of composer Richard Strauss.

Until World War II, Winston Churchill was known mostly for disastrous political failures.

After he lost the Battle of Waterloo, Napoléon Bonaparte tried to escape to the United States but was captured by a British warship.

U.S. statesman Alexander Hamilton wasn't born in the United States but on the Caribbean island of Nevis.

Beethoven originally dedicated his Symphony No. 3 (titled *Eroica*, or "heroic" in Italian) to Napoléon because he thought the leader embodied the democratic ideals of the French Revolution. But when Napoléon took on the undemocratic title of "emperor," Beethoven scratched out the dedication with a knife.

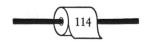

Law & Disorder

Most common reason for hiring a private detective in the United States: tracking down someone who owes you money.

In 1976, Bruce Springsteen got arrested for trying to climb over the gates of Graceland.

John Dillinger was the first criminal designated "Public Enemy Number One" by the FBI.

Pro wrestler and actor Dwayne "the Rock" Johnson has a degree in criminology.

Confucius's day job: he became China's minister of crime in 501 BC.

Like they do with movies and TV today, in 19th-century London, many people blamed the growing crime rate on violence in the theaters.

In 1969, Neil Young and Jimi Hendrix stole a truck to get to Woodstock in time to perform.

The first law school in the United States: the Litchfield Law School in Connecticut, established in 1773. Its graduates included Aaron Burr, Horace Mann, and John C. Calhoun.

Alibi means "elsewhere" in Latin.

The original Draconian (someone who's extremely harsh or cruel), Draco of Athens, executed people for stealing cabbage.

Mary Jenkins Surratt was the first woman executed by the U.S. government. She was hanged in 1865 for conspiracy in the assassination of President Abraham Lincoln.

What crime led to Billy the Kid's first run-in with the law? Stealing cheese. He was 15.

Singer Eddie Money (who had hits in the 1970s and 1980s) is a graduate of the New York City Police Academy.

The Women's Room

The tambourine was traditionally a "woman's instrument." In many Islamic countries, it still is.

Twelve girls have played in a Little League World Series game.

As a high school senior, Nancy Reagan had a part in her school's production of the comedy *First Lady of the Land*.

Actress Charlize Theron and her mother have matching fish tattoos.

Most Grand Slam tennis singles titles won by any player, male or female: Australian Margaret Court with 24.

In ancient Greece, if a woman attended an Olympic event, she could be executed.

Longest-running play in history: *The Mousetrap*, by Agatha Christie.

In 1980, Sherry Lansing became the first woman president of a movie studio: 20th Century Fox.

Women earn about half of the bachelor of science degrees in the United States.

Only winner of a Golden Globe award for "Most Glamorous Actress": Zsa Zsa Gabor, in 1958.

Unlike the word Mr. (Mister), the word "Mrs." cannot be spelled out.

Violet Jessup—a stewardess and ship's nurse—survived three major ocean-liner disasters: the *Olympic*, the *Britannic*, and the *Titanic*.

Most popular jukebox song of all time: "Crazy," by Patsy Cline (1962).

Before the year 1000, the word "she" didn't exist in the English language.

Reds

RED LIGHTS. Some darkrooms are lit with red bulbs, or "safe-lights," because red light doesn't expose black-and-white film.

ERIK THE RED. He was most famous as the Viking explorer who established the first settlement in Greenland in 985. But Erik the Red is also a pseudonym used by three characters in the *X-Men* comic series: Magneto, Cyclops, and alien agent Davan Shakari.

RED POPPIES. One of the most famous literary references to these flowers appears in the poem "In Flanders Fields," written in 1915. Canadian soldier John McCrae composed the poem after seeing his friend Alexis Helmer killed during World War I's Second Battle of Ypres, the first time Germany used chemical weapons. McCrae presided over Helmer's funeral at a cemetery in Flanders (because the military chaplain was unavailable) and scribbled the poem in his notebook the next day while watching fields of poppies in the cemetery. McCrae didn't think much of his poem; in fact, he threw it away. But one of his fellow soldiers rescued it and submitted it to a British newspaper. Today, "In Flanders Fields" is one of the most famous symbols of World War I and an important part of Canada's culture. Its first verse is even printed on the Canadian $10 bill.

RED CARDS. The first penalty cards in soccer were used during the 1970 World Cup in Mexico. The sport's penalty card system (red for expulsion, yellow for a warning) was modeled after traffic lights (red for stop, yellow for caution).

RED-LIGHT DISTRICT. The first use of this term appeared in the Milwaukee *Sentinel* in 1894. It probably comes from the red lanterns that railroad brakemen used to carry to brothels (or bars). They then left the lanterns outside. That way, if there were an emergency with their trains, their colleagues could find them easily and summon them back to the tracks.

First Americans

Three largest Native American tribes in the United States: Navajo, Cherokee, Choctaw.

Oldest continuously inhabited U.S. town: the 1,000-year-old Hopi village of Oraibi, Arizona.

Sitting Bull's Teton Sioux Indian group was known as the Hunkpapa band.

Twenty-eight U.S. states and four Canadian provinces have names with Native American origins.

Charles Curtis, vice president of the United States under Herbert Hoover, was part Kaw Indian.

Many Western movies make it seem like more, but only 0.1 percent of all people on wagon trains were killed by American Indians.

Why "Badlands"? The Sioux thought the South Dakota territory was "bad" because of its rugged terrain and lack of water. They called it Mako Sica, or "land-bad."

Canadian Indians couldn't vote in national elections until 1960. American Indians got the right to vote in 1924.

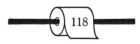

Presidential Dining

Dwight D. Eisenhower liked to watch Westerns while he ate TV dinners.

James Madison's favorite snack: gingerbread. Richard Nixon's favorite: cottage cheese and ketchup.

Lyndon B. Johnson was the first president to host a barbecue on the White House lawn.

Thomas Jefferson thought that sitting around a circular table was "democratic."

Franklin D. Roosevelt's three favorite foods: frog legs, pig knuckles, and scrambled eggs.

To help curb his appetite, John Adams ate boiled cornmeal pudding before a meal.

James Buchanan liked to host parties featuring sauerkraut and mashed potatoes.

Lyndon B. Johnson's favorite foods were canned green peas and tapioca.

Guests at Ronald Reagan's 1980 inaugural parties consumed 40 million jelly beans.

Thomas Jefferson ate meat only "as a condiment to the vegetables which constitute my principal diet."

George Washington loved cream of peanut soup and crabmeat soup. His favorite drink was eggnog.

For lunch, George W. Bush liked to eat grilled cheese sandwiches made with white bread and American cheese.

Dwight D. Eisenhower was a skilled chef, famous for his vegetable soup, steaks, and cornmeal pancakes.

Franklin D. Roosevelt created a cocktail of rum, brown sugar, and orange juice. He called it "my Haitian libation."

Thomas Jefferson once ate a tomato in public to prove it wasn't poisonous.

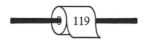

119

Ewww...Insects

There are 2 million insects for every human being on earth.

Statistically, you're more likely to be killed by a champagne cork than by a spider bite.

At an exhibition golf match in South Africa, a swarm of killer bees chased Jack Nicklaus and Gary Player off the green.

The network logo lurking in the corner of your TV screen is called a "bug."

Honeybees kill more people every year than all the world's poisonous snakes combined.

World's biggest bug: the Goliath beetle can grow to be 4 ½ inches long.

Ladybugs aren't bugs—they're beetles. Their official name: ladybird beetles.

The Volkswagen Beetle was first developed in Germany in 1933. Adolf Hitler wanted a cheap car that regular people could afford. In German, *Volkswagen* means "people's car."

The body of a cockroach can live for nine days without its head. (That's the same amount of time a cockroach can live without eating.)

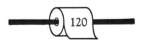

Censored

Released in 1965, *Doctor Zhivago* wasn't shown in Russia until 1994.

"Sweetheart of the Month" in the December 1953 debut issue of *Playboy*: Marilyn Monroe. (A "Sweetheart" is better known today as a "Playmate.")

First R-rated film made by the Disney-owned Touchstone studio: *Down and Out in Beverly Hills.*

A 1946 FBI memo denounced the movie *It's a Wonderful Life* as communist propaganda.

Ronnie James Dio popularized the "devil horns" hand gesture now associated with heavy metal. It was originally an ancient Greek vulgarity called the *mano cornuta.*

William Randolph Hearst wouldn't allow any of his newspapers to run ads for *Citizen Kane.*

In 1945, the liquor industry offered director Billy Wilder $5 million not to release *The Lost Weekend*, which mentions alcoholism and a possible affair between two men. Wilder refused.

In 1967, *The Ed Sullivan Show* made the Rolling Stones change "Let's Spend the Night Together" to "Let's Spend Some Time Together."

Buster Keaton's MGM contract stipulated that he was not to smile in public.

P. T. Barnum was once jailed for libel when he was a newspaper editor.

*　　*　　*

Making Faces: There are six universally recognized facial expressions: happiness, disgust, fear, sadness, anger, and surprise.

121

Soap

The first soap makers appeared in Babylon around 2800 BC.

The pumice in Lava soap was originally imported from the Italian island of Lipari.

1n 1933, Procter & Gamble debuted its first radio serial, a 15-minute daytime drama called *Oxydol's Own Ma Perkins*, about the life and trials of a woman who owned a lumberyard in the South. (Oxydol was a popular laundry detergent of the day.) The show was so successful that, by 1939, Procter & Gamble's soap products were sponsoring 21 daytime dramas for radio. These shows came to be known as "soap operas."

Most stylists don't recommend using soap to shampoo hair. Why? Soaps are made with an alkaline solution that damages hair over time. Soap can also react with other hair products and produce a layer of "scum" that makes hair look dull.

In Europe during the 19th century, taxes on soap were very high—it was considered a luxury item, and average people couldn't afford it.

An Ohio company called the Stinky Bomb makes a soap in the shape of a hand grenade. It comes in three colors: black, army green, and pale pink.

Words & Language

The word "dream" didn't come to mean "sleep images" until the 13th century. In Old English, it meant "music," "joy," or "noise."

The Epic of Gilgamesh, the world's oldest known poem, dates to around the third century BC.

The Sumerians invented cuneiform (picture writing) around 3500 BC.

René Descartes introduced the terms "real number" and "imaginary number" to mathematics.

The word "electric" was first used in 1600 by William Gilbert, Queen Elizabeth I's doctor.

"Booby prize" comes from the German *bubenpreis*, which means "boy's prize."

Italic type dates back to 1500.

In poker, a flush in the suit of clubs is called a "golf bag."

Sports announcer Halsey Hall was the first to say "Holy cow!" during a broadcast.

The ampersand (&) was once considered a letter of the English alphabet.

According to some scholars there was no punctuation in the English language until the 15th century

The Chinese character for "money" originally meant "cowric shell."

The first typewriters typed only in capital letters. The shift key wasn't invented until 1878.

Kamikaze, the name adopted by World War II Japanese suicide pilots, means "divine wind."

The word *tejas*, which became Texas, is the Spanish spelling of *taysha*, an American Indian word that means "friend" or "ally."

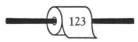

123

Dear Dairy

Milk is used to manufacture glue, paint, and some plastics.

According to experts, the food that people are most likely to crave is cheese.

Number-one consumer of cow's milk worldwide (besides cows): Finland.

For the Beatles' first U.S. tour, Baskin-Robbins created an ice cream flavor called Beatle Nut.

Holy Roman Emperor Charlemagne's favorite cheese: Roquefort.

You can make edible cheese from the milk of 24 different mammals.

Ben and Jerry's mourned Jerry Garcia's death by putting black cherries in their Cherry Garcia ice cream.

The word "galaxy" comes from the Greek *gala*, meaning "milk."

People on the U.S. eastern seaboard consume almost 50 percent of all ice cream sandwiches worldwide.

People who really, really love cheese are called turophiles.

In England, it was once a custom to pass a newborn baby through a cheese rind.

In Spain, many people pour chocolate milk on breakfast cereal.

In 1957, Americans ate more margarine than butter for the first time.

Robert Frost used to milk cows on his farm late at night to avoid having to do it early in the morning.

Hanson, Billy Ray Cyrus, and Tony Bennett have all worn "mustaches" in "Got Milk?" ads.

Baskin-Robbins once made a ketchup-flavored ice cream.

Instruments

Earliest keyboard instruments: the pipe organ, the clavichord, and the harpsichord.

The United States has more bagpipe bands than Scotland does.

According to violin bow makers, white horsehair produces a smoother sound than black horsehair.

Up until the 1800s, the triangle had jingling rings strung on it.

The predecessor to the trombone was called the sackbut.

What are the qanun, nay, mijwiz, buzuq, and daff? They're all Middle Eastern musical instruments.

What instrument has a head, a flange, a tension hoop, and an armrest? The banjo.

A concert harp has 47 strings.

The heckelphone, musette, and piffaro are all rare members of the oboe family.

Saxophones, invented in 1840, did not become popular until the rise of jazz in the 1920s.

BIG Business

First company to earn
$1 billion in one year:
General Motors, in 1955.

Largest industry in Nashville:
health care, at $18.3 billion
annually. Music is second, at
$6.1 billion.

Worldwide, enough Coca-Cola
is consumed every year to fill
3.5 million bathtubs.

The Ford Motor Company was
the first to offer a rebate...$50
cash back on a new Model T.

Nabisco produces about
16 billion Oreo cookies a year
at its Chicago factory alone.

Pop-Tarts are the most popular
product made by Kellogg's,
with more than two billion
sold each year.

Number of Starbucks
in Chicago's O'Hare
International Airport as
of 2009: 15.

Pizza Hut uses 525 million
pounds of tomatoes every year.

Popular items at McDonald's
in India: the Maharaja Mac
and the McAloo Tikki.

There are more than 300
different types of fast-food
chains in the United States.

Mississippi's largest industry
is catfish; 150,000 tons are
produced each year.

Wal-Mart's annual income
is nearly equal to that of
Russia.

Loch Ness Monster tourism
adds $40 million a year to
Scotland's economy.

The busiest Pizza Hut in the
world is in Paris, France.

Fantasy sports is a $3.5-billion-
a-year industry in the United
States.

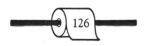

Say It in Quotes

Thomas Jefferson read in seven languages and made it a rule "never to read translations where I can read the original."

Harry S. Truman didn't think much of polls. He once said, "I wonder how far Moses would have gotten if he'd taken a poll in Egypt?"

George W. Bush said, "I never dreamed about being president...when I was growing up, I wanted to be Willie Mays."

During World War II, sauerkraut was renamed "liberty cabbage."

When told that General Ulysses S. Grant drank too much whiskey, President Abraham Lincoln reportedly replied, "Find out the name of the brand so I can give it to my other generals."

Andrew Jackson once described the presidency as "dignified slavery."

The phrase "weapons of mass destruction" was coined in 1937 during the Spanish Civil War in reference to air bombing.

Thomas Jefferson said that, over a 50-year period, the sun "never caught him in bed."

There is no record of Patrick Henry actually saying, "Give me liberty or give me death."

In 1988, former baseball player Bill "Spaceman" Lee ran for president. Slogan: "No guns. No butter. Both can kill."

"No two men can differ on a principle of trigonometry," said Thomas Jefferson.

Harry S. Truman on religious differences: "It has caused more wars and feuds than money."

Morphine addiction became known as the "soldier's disease" after the Civil War.

Kid Stats

On average, kids touch their mouths with their hands once every three minutes.

Fifty-four percent of American kids ride the bus to school.

Sixty-five percent of children have an imaginary friend before the age of seven.

Eighty-four percent of American children read with their parents every day.

U.S. parents spend about 38 minutes a week in "meaningful conversation" with their kids.

Sixty-three percent of American teenagers have their own cell phone.

A typical American kid spends 18 percent of his or her day in front of a TV or computer screen.

Sixty-one percent of American parents of children over eight do not establish TV-watching rules.

Seventy-one percent of kids who play Internet games say the virtual worlds they visit online are "very important" to them.

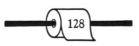

Hair It Is

The ancient Assyrians cut their hair into the shape of a pyramid.

What does author Bram Stoker's title character in *Dracula* have that most movie Draculas don't? A mustache.

The amount of lather shampoo produces has little to do with its cleaning ability.

Famous redhead Lucille Ball actually had brown hair.

Most wig changes in a movie: 35, by Angela Bassett in *What's Love Got to Do with It?*

The ancient Romans thought unibrows were sexy.

Some shampoos contain formaldehyde.

Walt Disney first started drawing cartoons in exchange for free haircuts.

The tall wigs worn by British judges are called *perukes*.

Cleopatra used a mixture of horse teeth, bear grease, burned mice, and deer marrow in an attempt to cure Julius Caesar's baldness.

Doubles

Eighty Eight, Kentucky, was named by a man who had 88 cents in his pocket on the day he founded the town.

What do 11 and 88 have in common? They both read the same upside down.

Baseball player Bill Voiselle, who was from a South Carolina town called Ninety Six, wore the number 96 on his uniform.

The right-field wall at PNC Park in Pittsburgh is 21 feet high...a tribute to Roberto Clemente, who wore number 21.

From 1971 to 1974, the UCLA men's basketball team won 88 straight games.

The novel Catch-22 was originally titled Catch-18.

Prince's song "7" made it to number 7 on the pop charts.

Real headline on a newspaper article about a golf tournament: "Shot Off Woman's Leg Helps Nicklaus to 66."

Stephen Foster, composer of "Camptown Races," died with 38 cents in his pocket...when he was 38.

First tabloid: The Illustrated Daily News (now the Daily News), published in New York City in 1919.

Matthew Webb was the first person to swim the English Channel in 1875. It took about 22 hours.

Early in his career, Babe Ruth wore the number 3 on his jersey because he batted third.

It takes Mercury 88 days to travel around the Sun.

U2 has won 22 Grammy Awards to date, the most of any band.

States of the Union

According to statistics, New Jersey has the lowest suicide rate of any state.

The state of Florida has the most golf courses in America. The fewest: Alaska.

Wisconsin leads the nation in production of paper and paper products.

Pennsylvania was the first state to display its Web site address on its license plates.

Rhode Island is the most heavily industrialized state in proportion to its size.

Because of its shape on a map, Oklahoma has been called "the nation's largest meat cleaver."

Only 54.3 percent of Louisiana high school students graduate, the lowest rate of any state.

On average, Hawaiian residents live longer than people in other U.S. states.

Indiana ranks first among U.S. states in both mobile-home sales...and "danger from tornadoes."

North Dakota is the only state in the United States never to have had an earthquake.

Dreams

THE 12 MOST COMMON BAD DREAMS

Falling or drowning
Being lost or trapped
Being chased or attacked
Being injured, ill, or dying
Car or other vehicle trouble
House or property loss or damage
Poor test or other poor performance
Missing a boat or other transport
Machine or telephone malfunction
Natural or man-made disasters
Being menaced by a spirit
Being naked or inappropriately dressed in public

* * *

DREAM SYMBOLS FOR FOODIES

Corn: abundance
Watermelon: fiery passion
Bread: the basic needs of life
Grapes: wealth and decadence
Gravy: failing health or business
Oranges: health and prosperity
Sandwich: pressure and stress
Apples: knowledge and prosperity
Eggs: fertility and creative potential
Vinegar: worries about a negative matter
Strawberries: sensual desires and temptation

Causes of Death

First victim of the guillotine: a highwayman named Nicolas Pelletier, on April 25, 1792, in Paris, France.

In 1940, German spy Josef Jakobs became the last person to be executed at the Tower of London.

The first attempt on Martin Luther King Jr.'s life came in 1958, when a woman stabbed him in the chest with a letter opener.

Indira Gandhi and her son Rajiv were both assassinated during their consecutive terms as prime minister of India.

In 1800, England's King George III survived two assassination attempts... in one day.

King Charles I of England wore two shirts to his execution because it was a cold day and he didn't want his shivering to be mistaken for fear.

Catherine the Great of Russia died from a stroke she suffered while sitting on the toilet.

At the Jonestown massacre, Jim Jones's followers drank Flavor Aid, not Kool-Aid.

King Alexander of Greece, who reigned from 1917 to 1920, died at age 27 from the bites of two pet monkeys.

Chinese premiers Mao Zedong and Deng Xiaoping both died of complications from Parkinson's disease.

French novelist Émile Zola died of carbon monoxide poisoning from a defective chimney flue.

England's King George II fell to his death...from a toilet seat.

The 1918 flu pandemic killed 25 million people in four months...more than were killed in all of World War I.

American Politics

In 1972, CREEP—the Committee to Re-elect the President—supported Richard Nixon.

When the NAACP was founded in 1909, its only African American officer was a newspaper editor.

The semiunderground Know Nothing political party formed in the 1840s. Its goal: to stop the influx of Irish immigrants to the United States. The name comes from the fact that, when asked about the party's activities, members were instructed to say, "I know nothing."

Founded by Union army officers, the National Rifle Association was originally established to improve marksmanship.

The ACLU began as an antimilitarism movement during World War I, headed by people who didn't support America's mandatory draft.

Congress once denounced Frank Sinatra and the Lone Ranger for turning American youths into delinquents.

In 1969, author Norman Mailer ran for Mayor of New York City. He wanted it to be the 51st state.

In 1676, an American colonist named Nathaniel Bacon led a tax rebellion against the governor of Virginia. The rebellion fell apart three months later when Bacon died of dysentery.

What did George Washington and Colonel Sanders have in common? They were both Freemasons.

In 2003, there were 135 people on the ballot to be governor of California.

President Harry S. Truman's mother refused to sleep in the White House's Lincoln Bedroom—she was a Confederate sympathizer.

Food Stuff

Americans now eat nine times more broccoli than they did 20 years ago.

In the Middle Ages, people added carrot juice to butter to make the color more appetizing.

If you shake a can of mixed nuts, the larger nuts will rise to the top.

Because fruits ferment, virtually all fruit juices contain minute amounts of alcohol.

More people on the West Coast prefer chunky peanut butter. East Coasters like theirs creamy.

Nondairy creamer is flammable.

The first fruit eaten on the Moon was a peach.

The average American child eats 15 pounds of cereal in a year.

It takes twelve ears of corn to make a tablespoon of corn oil.

Casu marzu, a cheese from Sardinia, is ready to eat when it's riddled with live maggots.

Young & Old

Paul McCartney wrote "When I'm Sixty-four" when he was 15.

Gladys Knight won first prize on *Ted Mack's Original Amateur Hour* TV show when she was seven years old.

Youngest golfer ever to compete in the Ryder Cup: Sergio Garcia, at age 19.

Elton John won a scholarship to the Royal Academy of Music at the age of 11.

Maggie Kuhn founded the senior citizens' activist group the Gray Panthers in 1971, at the age of 65.

The piano piece "Chopsticks" was written by 16-year-old Euphemia Allen.

Drummer Julian Pavone played at a Chicago Cubs game and made a CD called *Go, Baby!* He was three.

Conductor Leopold Stokowski founded the American Symphony Orchestra when he was 80...and signed a six-year recording contract at age 94. (He died a year later.)

Mark Twain didn't learn to ride a bicycle until he was nearly 50 years old.

Jack Kerouac wrote his first novel at the age of 11.

Youngest player ever to qualify for the PGA Tour: Ty Tryon, at age 17.

Bill Gates started programming computers at the age of 13.

Trumpeter Wynton Marsalis first played with the New Orleans Philharmonic when he was 14.

The value of Herbert Hoover's estate at his death at age 90 in 1964: more than $8 million.

On the Job

Five most dangerous jobs in the United States: logger, pilot, asbestos worker, metalworker, electrician.

Statistically, the most productive day of the workweek is Tuesday.

Professions most likely to require work at night: police, security guard. Least likely: construction worker.

Gum magnate William Wrigley Jr. was the first employer to give workers a two-day weekend.

Before the Civil War, the average person worked 11 hours a day, six days a week.

Day of the week most Americans call in sick: Friday (18 percent). The day fewest do: Tuesday (11 percent).

In 2000, France became the first country to adopt the 35-hour workweek.

Estimated number of plumbers in the United States: 500,000.

On average, Americans miss more than three million days of work each year due to allergies.

The average American salary during the 1960s was $4,743. Today: about $40,000.

The higher his income, the more likely an American man will cheat on his wife.

Among American men, those with the highest income are the most likely to be overweight—but among American women, those with the lowest income are.

U.S. men who drink moderately earn 7 percent higher pay than nondrinkers.

About 25 percent of male employees say they take naps on the job. Only half as many women do.

The Oregon Trail

TRANSPORTATION. The most common vehicle used on the Oregon Trail—the route many 19th-century pioneers took from the East to the West Coast—was the prairie schooner, a light, covered wagon. But they also used everything from wheelbarrows to handcarts to wind-powered wagons to make the trip. One inventor even tried to come up with a way to fly settlers to Oregon. In 1849, a man named Rufus Porter advertised that he could use balloons to carry people over the mountains. About 200 people signed up for the trip, but Porter ran out of money before he could make even one flight.

DANGER, DANGER! More than 10,000 people died traveling the Oregon Trail. The most common cause of death: disease. People caught smallpox and cholera in huge numbers, and their companions were so anxious to get moving that some of the sick were buried alive.

CHILD'S PLAY. Many kids traveling the Oregon Trail took up an unusual game: cow dung frisbee.

VALUABLE CARGO. In 1847, Iowan Henderson Luelling set out for Oregon with his wife, eight children, and three wagons. One was for the family and their belongings, but the other two carried about 700 young fruit trees (apple, pear, cherry, and others). People he passed on the trail thought Luelling was crazy, but when he arrived in the Willamette Valley in northwest Oregon, he planted the trees and established several orchards. Luelling was the first to introduce these fruits to Oregon, and later to California. Today, both are among the most profitable fruit-growing regions of the United States.

Facts of War

Shortest war in American history: the Spanish-American War, in 1898. It lasted less than four months.

More battles of the American Revolution were fought in South Carolina than in any other colony.

In the War of 1812, the British burned most of Washington, D.C., including the White House.

The only war ever fought by NATO was against Yugoslavia.

New Englanders so opposed the War of 1812 that many wanted to secede.

Buckingham Palace was bombed nine times during World War II, with one fatality.

The last battle of World War I was fought in what is now Zambia, Africa.

President James K. Polk was so involved with managing the details of the Mexican War that he even oversaw the purchase of mules.

During World War I, Germany offered Arizona, New Mexico, and Texas to Mexico if the country would change sides. (It didn't.)

And Now...Percents

Thirty-one percent of American workers skip lunch every day.

Eighty percent of the world's population regularly eats insects.

Twenty-five percent of Americans will catch more than four colds this year.

Fifty percent of the pizzas sold in the United States have pepperoni on them.

Fifty percent of all Oreo eaters say they pull the cookies apart before eating them.

How often do NFL teams try for a first down on fourth down? Less than 1 percent of the time.

Fifty-five percent of Americans say they'll let someone else into the bathroom with them.

Thirty percent of NBA players have tattoos.

World's biggest consumers of music: the British, who account for 7.2 percent of global sales.

Seventy percent of Fortune 500 CEOs regularly do business on the golf course.

Seventeen percent of sales reps who golf with clients say they intentionally let the clients win.

Odds that a cosmetic surgery patient is a woman: 89 percent.

Twenty percent more antacids are sold the day after the Super Bowl than on an average day.

Heinz sells more than 50 percent of all the ketchup in the world.

A British study found that people with facial piercings are 23 percent more likely to order vegetarian pizza.

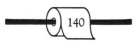

Laws Against Nature

Melbourne, Australia, has an 8:00 p.m. curfew...for cats.

A Memphis, Tennessee, ordinance bans frogs from croaking after 11:00 p.m.

In Wilbur, Washington, you can be fined for riding an ugly horse.

It's a crime to punch a bull in the nose in Washington, D.C.

In Zion, Illinois, it's illegal to give a lit cigar to a dog, cat, or other domesticated pet.

In Fairbanks, Alaska, moose are banned from mating within city limits.

In Florida, it's against the law to hunt deer while they're swimming.

It's against the law in Utah to fish from horseback.

It's illegal to put graffiti on someone else's cow in Texas.

Technically, you must have a hunting license to catch mice in California.

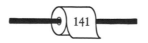

Historical Surprises

Joseph Stalin was studying to become a Russian Orthodox priest when he learned about communism.

While he was escaping, political prisoner Lev Bronstein stole his jailer's passport...and was thereafter known as Leon Trotsky.

Before he reunited Italy in the 1870s and became a national hero, Giuseppe Garibaldi lived briefly on Staten Island, New York, and worked as a candle maker.

Ho Chi Minh, whose name means "one who enlightens," once worked as a photo retoucher in Paris.

Later in life, Russian revolutionary Vladimir Lenin attacked the despotism of Communist leaders.

St. Patrick wasn't Irish. He was British but was kidnapped by Irish pirates.

Explorer John Cabot, who sailed to fame under the English flag, was really an Italian named Giovanni Caboto.

Although King John of England signed the Magna Carta, he promptly had Pope Innocent III annul it.

Cleopatra wasn't Egyptian. She was Greek.

During the French Revolution, King Louis XVI tried to escape, but he was easily recognized—because his portrait was on French currency.

Edward VIII abdicated the English throne in 1936, but he did rule again...as governor of the Bahamas.

Josephine Bonaparte's divorce from Napoléon was the first under the Napoleonic code of law, which allowed women to file for divorce.

142

Snakes & So On

Snakes don't blink because they don't have movable eyelids.

The "warts" on a toad are actually toxin-filled glands.

The American alligator derives its name from the Spanish *lagarto*, or "lizard."

During one summer, a single toad will eat about 10,000 insects.

The South American basilisk lizard is nicknamed the "Jesus Christ lizard" because it can run across the surface of water to escape predators.

During their lifetimes, alligators grow—and lose—about 3,000 teeth.

The poisonous copperhead snake gives off a scent like that of fresh-cut cucumbers.

More than 80 percent of the reptiles in Australia are native to the continent.

Horned toads are not toads—they're lizards.

The Sonoran coral snake and the western hook-nosed snake both fart to scare off predators. (The noise scares them, not the smell.)

Life in the Military

The U.S. Navy won't accept any recruit with an "obscene" tattoo.

In 1995, Rebecca Marier became the first woman to graduate at the top of the class at West Point.

When they're at sea, the crews of U.S. nuclear-powered submarines wear blue coveralls called "poopie-suits."

Granola bars, instant noodle soup, and freeze-dried coffee were all invented by the military.

The only woman to receive the congressional Medal of Honor was Dr. Mary Walker, a surgeon in the Civil War.

Item most requested by American soldiers serving in Iraq: toilet paper.

Fliers with the Blue Angels have to be active-duty Navy or Marine Corps tactical jet pilots with a minimum of 1,350 flight hours.

In January 2006, the U.S. Army raised its maximum enlistment age to 39.

The U.S. Navy aircraft carrier USS *Abraham Lincoln* has five gymnasiums and a basketball league with 22 teams.

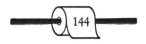

By George!

England's King George I (1660–1727) was German and could barely speak English.

At the 1912 Olympics, General George S. Patton placed fifth in the pentathlon.

If the 2004 U.S. presidential election had been held in Canada, John Kerry would have beaten George Bush 64 percent to 19 percent.

George magazine (a political publication named for George Washington) was founded by John Kennedy Jr. in 1995. Its first cover featured Cindy Crawford.

George Washington played a version of baseball with his men at Valley Forge.

King George VI changed the date of his birthday from December 14 to June 9, so it wouldn't interfere with Christmas.

Alabama governor George Wallace put himself through college by working as a professional boxer.

Author George Orwell was probably the first person to use the phrase "cold war," in 1945.

The speeches of England's King George VI (1895–1952) were written specifically to minimize his stammer.

On July 4, 1776, King George III wrote in his diary, "Nothing of importance happened today."

Writers George Sand and George Eliot were women.

George Washington Carver made more than 300 products out of peanuts during the early 1900s.

Priciest painting by a female artist: *Calla Lilies with Red Anemone* (Georgia O'Keeffe, sold for $6.1 million in 2001).

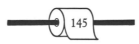

Ancient History

The Roman Empire was knit together by more than 50,000 miles of roads.

Early Egyptians buried their dead in the desert. The heat and dryness of the sand dehydrated the bodies quickly, creating natural mummies.

Horse racing originated around 4500 BC among nomadic tribesmen in central Asia.

Ancient Egyptians slept on headrests made of stone.

At its height in AD 117, the Roman Empire covered 2.5 million square miles.

According to paleontologists, Neanderthals probably had high-pitched voices.

Sit-in strikes were conducted by Egyptian graveyard workers in the 12th century BC.

In ancient Rome, being born with a crooked nose was a sign of a good leader.

In ancient Egypt, doctors sometimes prescribed warm donkey droppings to relieve sore eyes.

During the Three Kingdoms period (AD 220–280), China's name for Japan was Wa.

The earliest known pottery in the world comes from Japan's Jomon culture, which emerged around 14,000 BC.

Ancient Roman wrestling matches had only one rule: no eye gouging.

The ruins of Carthage are located in Tunisia.

The word gymnasium comes from the Greek *gymnos* (naked) because athletes in ancient Greece often competed in the nude.

Confection-ately Yours

America's oldest candy brand is the Necco wafer, sold since 1847. The eight original flavors: lemon, orange, lime, clove, cinnamon, wintergreen, licorice, and chocolate.

About 65 percent of American candy brands have been around for more than 50 years.

The marshmallows in Lucky Charms cereal are technically called "marbits."

In 1915, William Wrigley Jr. sent free chewing gum to every person listed in the Chicago phone book.

Pez dispensers got their first character heads in 1955.

Three out of every four Snickers bars in the world are made at the M&M/Mars plant in Waco, Texas.

Streetlamps in Hershey, Pennsylvania, are shaped like chocolate kisses.

Every year, Americans eat about 95 million pounds of marshmallows...and more than 2.5 billion pounds of chocolate.

Chocolatier Clarence Crane invented Life Savers in 1912; the original flavor was called Pep-O-Mint.

How many M&Ms are there in a pound? About 192 peanut or 512 plain.

In the late 1960s, Pez tried to market flower-flavored candies.

U.S. candy makers manufacture more than 16 million jelly beans every Easter.

The first chewing gum to be widely advertised in the United States was Tutti-Frutti.

Time needed to produce a marshmallow Peep: six seconds.

Ocean & Coast

The Sargasso Sea has no coastline. (It's in the middle of the North Atlantic Ocean.)

Florida's beaches lose 20 million cubic yards of sand every year.

The United States has 12,383 miles of coastline; 6,640 miles of it are in Alaska.

First national seashore: Cape Hatteras National Seashore, in North Carolina, established in 1953.

Seventy percent of San Francisco Bay is less than 12 feet deep.

New York City has 570 miles of shoreline.

Alaska's Glacier Bay has some of the largest tidal fluctuations in the world; high tide can be as much as 25 feet higher than low tide.

Tsunami waves can move from one shore of the Pacific to the other in less than a day.

The ocean off the Outer Banks of North Carolina has been called "the Graveyard of the Atlantic." The total number of vessels lost near Cape Hatteras is estimated at more than 2,000.

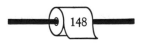

Scientific Streets

Many of the streets in Paris are named for famous scientists. Here are five you might recognize:

1. Rue Ampère. Named for French physicist André-Marie Ampère, who discovered electromagnetism. He initiated a standard system of measurement for electric currents, and the ampere unit of electric current was named for him.

2. Rue Copernic. Named for Polish astronomer Nicolaus Copernicus, who produced a workable model of the solar system with the Sun in the center in the 16th century.

3. Rue Pierre et Marie Curie. Named for the Nobel Prize–winning couple who pioneered the study of magnetism and radioactivity, and discovered the elements radium and polonium in 1898. (Polonium was named for Marie's homeland of Poland.)

4. Rue Galilée. Named for Italian physicist, mathematician, astronomer, and philosopher Galileo Galilei, who has been called the "father of modern science."

5. Rue Foucault. Named for Jean Bernard Léon Foucault, a French mathematician and astronomer who invented the gyroscope and a pendulum that demonstrated that earth rotates on its axis.

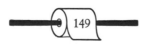

149

Biblical Facts

Worldwide, about 50 Bibles are sold every minute.

The Old Testament mentions almonds 73 times.

According to the Bible, King David played the harp.

The Bible is stolen more often than any other book in the world.

The word "and" is used 46,277 times in the King James Bible.

The five animals most often mentioned in the Bible are sheep, lambs, lions, oxen, and rams.

The word *bible* comes from the Greek *biblos*, meaning "book."

The bagpipe is mentioned in the Bible (Daniel 3:5).

Saint John was the only one of the 12 apostles to die of natural causes.

The first man to translate the entire Bible into English was Englishman Myles Coverdale, in 1535.

The seven deadly sins: lust, pride, anger, envy, sloth, avarice, and gluttony.

According to the Bible, Noah invented wine and was the first person to eat meat.

Number of words in the King James Bible: 783,137.

Nowhere in the Bible does it say that there were three wise men.

Salt is mentioned more than 30 times in the Bible.

There are two talking animals in the Bible: the serpent and Balaam's ass.

The final word in the Bible: "amen."

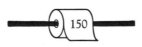

Women in Politics

In 1922, 87-year-old Rebecca Felton from Georgia became the first female senator. Time in office: two days. (It was a temporary appointment.)

Abigail Adams, the second First Lady, often expressed her political views openly, for which she was widely criticized as being "unladylike."

Franklin D. Roosevelt appointed the first female member of a presidential cabinet: Frances Perkins of New York was Secretary of Labor from 1933 to 1945.

Susan B. Anthony founded America's first female political party: the National Woman's Suffrage Society.

In 1980, Vigdís Finnbogadóttir became Iceland's first (and only) female head of state.

First woman to head an Islamic government: Benazir Bhutto, former prime minister of Pakistan.

Miriam "Ma" Ferguson became the first female governor of Texas on January 20, 1925.

Wyoming boasts the nation's first elected female public official: Estelle Reel, in 1895. She was Superintendent of Public Instruction.

One of the 19th century's leaders of women's suffrage, Victoria Woodhull, ran for U.S. president in 1872...even though she couldn't vote.

Lady Nancy Astor, the first woman elected to the British House of Commons, was born in Virginia.

In 1916, Montana's Jeannette Pickering Rankin became the first woman to serve in the U.S. Congress.

In August 2000, women filled the top five political and judicial posts in New Zealand.

Hillary Clinton was once a Republican.

England & France

The average life expectancy for Londoners in the 16th and 17th centuries was 39.7 years.

In 52 BC, Paris was attacked by the Romans, who called the city Lutetia, meaning "marshy place."

In 1014, Viking ships pulled down and destroyed the London Bridge.

In 1789, when a Paris mob stormed the Bastille to start the French Revolution, it missed rescuing the Marquis de Sade by just days. (He'd been transferred to an insane asylum outside Paris, accused of egging on the rioters from his cell's window.)

The 1666 Great Fire of London destroyed 13,200 homes but resulted in only six recorded fatalities.

The Great Plague of London (1865–66) was a bubonic plague that killed 20 percent of the city's residents.

A French executioner was once fired because he pawned his guillotine.

In the 1840s, French criminals couldn't be arrested from sundown to sunrise.

London was founded by the Romans in AD 47.

The first English historian was a monk known as the Venerable Bede (672–735).

During France's Reign of Terror (1793–4), 17,000 people were beheaded.

The Marquis de Lafayette (who fought in the American Revolution) was labeled a traitor during the French Revolution because he sided with the middle class.

After England conquered Quebec in 1760, it offered to trade the region back to France for the Caribbean islands of Guadeloupe. France declined.

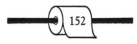

Ancient Designs

Estimated weight of Egypt's Great Pyramid of Giza: 6 million tons.

A Babylonian pyramid called Etemenanki may have inspired the Tower of Babel story.

Darius I of Persia connected the Nile to the Red Sea with a canal.

Stonehenge wasn't the work of Celtic druids—it was built about 2,000 years before they arrived in Great Britain. Today, most historians think the Britons (ancestors of the modern British) built the monument.

The Great Pyramid of Giza is made of 2.3 million limestone blocks; each weighs 2 ½ tons.

Byzantine architects built the largest domes in the ancient world. The most famous example: St. Sophia, constructed in Constantinople, modern-day Istanbul, Turkey.

The Parthenon in Athens was nearly destroyed in 1687 when Turkish soldiers used it to store gunpowder.

Looking for Cutthroat Castle? You'll find it in Colorado's Hovenweep National Monument. No pirates there, though—Hovenweep consists of pre-Columbian Indian ruins.

The Great Wall of China was actually made of four different walls that were rebuilt and linked over 2,000 years.

The Villa Romana del Casale in Sicily includes a famous mosaic of bikini-clad Roman women exercising.

The step pyramid at Saqqara, Egypt, is considered the oldest man-made building still standing.

Rome's ancient stadium, the Circus Maximus (for horse and chariot racing), could hold up to 250,000 people.

Sister Acts

MARY AND ANNE BOLEYN

Mary (a.k.a. the other Boleyn girl) became the mistress of England's King Henry VIII before her more famous sister ended up marrying him. Most historians think Mary was the older of the two, and some believe she had two children by Henry. In 1519, at the age of 20, Mary joined the English court as "maid of honor" to Catherine of Aragon, Henry's first wife, who was then the queen of England. Mary's sister Anne joined the court soon after.

Anne rejected Henry's amorous advances for at least a few years before he decided to divorce Catherine to marry her. Meanwhile, Mary married and was widowed. Her second husband was a commoner, which prompted the family to disown her. Mary, her husband, and their children moved to the countryside, where Mary lived out the rest of her days. (Things didn't go as well for Anne. She was beheaded in 1526 to make room for Henry's third wife, Jane Seymour.)

CHARLOTTE, EMILY, AND ANNE BRONTË

All three grew up in Yorkshire, England, during the 19th century, the daughters of an Anglican clergyman. They all published their first novels in the same year: 1847. Charlotte's *Jane Eyre* was an overnight success. Emily's *Wuthering Heights* wasn't an immediate hit with readers, but it caught on a few years later and today is considered one of the finest English novels ever written. Younger sister Anne's *Agnes Grey* was considered good but not great.

Emily never finished her next novel; she died at age 30 of tuberculosis. Anne died at 29, also of tuberculosis. Charlotte, the only one to marry, outlived them both and made it to age 38 before succumbing to an illness probably related to her pregnancy.

LILLIAN AND DOROTHY GISH

Lillian was in her late teens and Dorothy was about 13 years old when they started making silent movies for director D. W. Griffith

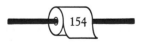

in 1912. Lillian starred in Griffith's classic *Birth of a Nation* (1915), and both had roles in his *Orphans of the Storm* (1921).

Later, Lillian took on Broadway roles in *Uncle Vanya* and *Camille* and made her last movie in 1987: *The Whales of August*, starring Bette Davis. She never married. The less-famous Dorothy specialized in comedies, but did drama, too. Dorothy's last movie was *The Cardinal* in 1963. She died of pneumonia at a clinic in Italy in 1970, with her sister by her side. Lillian died in her sleep in 1993 at the age of 99.

BARBIE AND SKIPPER ROBERTS

Barbie's younger, shorter (9.25 inches to Barbie's 11.5 inches) was introduced in 1964 in three varieties (blonde, brunette, and red-head) and had a demure sideways glance, as opposed to her big sister's forward gaze. Skipper's first accessories included a wire stand, comb and brush, red flats, headband, and swimsuit. Her older sister had been launched—as a blonde and a brunette—in 1959 with gold hoop earrings, sunglasses, and black open-toe heels.

Over time, Skipper's image changed, a marketing effort to make her more "appealing." By the time she was removed from the market in 2003, she was almost as long-legged and shapely as Barbie, who remains one of the most popular toys in the world.

VENUS AND SERENA WILLIAMS

Superstar tennis players Venus and Serena Williams have both been ranked number one in the world by the Women's Tennis Association. Born in 1980 and 1981, respectively, they're the youngest of five sisters. Their father Richard wanted all his daughters to play tennis—he'd admired the game since he was a young man—but only Venus and Serena showed a natural aptitude for the sport. Both started their training at the age of four.

The sisters have played each other more than 20 times professionally, and the results are fairly even. As a doubles team, they're near unbeatable—taking home two Olympic gold medals, in 2000 and 2008. Both women are also fashionistas and have their own designer clothing lines.

Firsts

First telephone call from Earth to the Moon: President Richard Nixon called the crew of *Apollo 11* on July 21, 1969.

Steve Jobs introduced the first iPod on October 23, 2001; it cost $400. Since then, more than 173 millions units have been sold, with the iPod Shuffle going for just $79.

On June 4, 1927, millionaire Charles A. Levine was the first passenger on a transatlantic flight leaving the United States.

First album released on compact disc: Billy Joel's *52nd Street*, on October 1, 1982.

First electronic computer: the ENIAC—Electronic Numerical Integrator And Computer. It was unveiled on February 14, 1946, and cost $500,000 to build.

Johnson & Johnson introduced the first decorative Band-Aid in 1951.

Year the first home video game console went on sale: 1972.

First popular transistor radio: the Regency TR-1. It was released in 1954 and cost $49.95, about $395 today.

The first interactive video game: a missile simulator created in 1947.

Inventor Martin Cooper, who worked for Motorola, made the first cell phone call on April 3, 1973. (He called his rivals at AT&T). His inspiration for the phone? The communicators on *Star Trek*.

The first *Uncle John's Bathroom Reader* was published in 1988.

The first direct-dial transcontinental call was made on November 10, 1951; it took 18 seconds to connect. This was an improvement on the first transcontinental call made in 1915, which took 23 minutes and needed five operators to connect.

Age Doesn't Matter

Youngest student ever admitted to the Baltimore Peabody Conservatory of Music: Tori Amos. She was five.

Sydney Greenstreet was 62 when he made his film debut in *The Maltese Falcon*.

By the age of four, Mozart could learn a new piece of music in half an hour.

John Cleese reached the height of six feet by the age of 12.

Jazz singer Mel Tormé's first gig: singing with the Coon Sanders Nighthawks Orchestra. He was four.

Julie Andrews had mastered a four-octave singing range by age eight. Average person's range: three octaves.

Fourteen-year-old Bobby Fischer became the youngest chess grand master in history when he won the title in 1958.

Laura Ingalls Wilder didn't publish her first book until she was 65.

William James Sidis, a child prodigy, entered Harvard University at the age of 11 in 1909. (The school had refused to let his father enroll him at age nine.)

Robert Redford turned down the lead in *The Graduate* because he felt he was too old for it. Dustin Hoffman, who took the part, was 30—the same age as Redford.

Katharine Hepburn, an avid golfer, started playing at the age of five.

Golfer Bobby Jones won the Georgia State Amateur Championship at age 14.

Sergei Prokofiev composed an opera at the age of nine.

Colonel Harlan Sanders started his finger-lickin'-good chicken business in his 60s.

Calls of the Wild

Studying the musical features of animal sounds—like cricket chirps and whale songs—is called zoomusicology.

According to scientists, frogs croak, bark, cluck, click, grunt, snore, squawk, chirp, whistle, trill, and yap.

Some male songbirds sing more than 2,000 times a day.

Mockingbirds can imitate almost any sound, from a car alarm to a cat's meow.

Giant pandas emit a bleat like sheep.

A lion's roar is about as loud as a chainsaw.

Apes gibber, deer bell, and hippos bray.

Cats can make more than 100 different vocal sounds; dogs can make about 10.

Dolphins communicate in several frequencies, many of which are higher than the human ear's limit. So we can only hear some of their vocalizations.

A lion's roar can be heard five miles away.

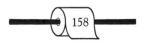

Burial Grounds

The Paris Catacombs were built in abandoned quarries in 1788 to house bones moved from overcrowded graveyards around the city.

A "graveyard" is usually associated with a church and located on church property. A "cemetery" is an independent burial ground.

Fairview Cemetery in Halifax, Nova Scotia, is the burial site for more *Titanic* casualties than any other cemetery in the world. Of the more than 1,500 victims of the disaster, 121 are buried there.

Jim Morrison, Isadora Duncan, Sarah Bernhardt, Moliere, and Marcel Marceau are all buried in the famous Père Lachaise Cemetery in Paris.

Composer Frederic Chopin's heart is encased in a pillar at the Holy Cross Church in Warsaw, Poland. (The rest of him is buried in Paris.)

A crematorium can cremate a 180-pound body in 1 ½ hours.

Largest cemetery in Europe: Zentralfriedhof in Austria. It opened in 1874 and holds more than 3 million bodies.

World's largest cemetery: Wadi-us-Salaam in Iraq, with more than 5 million graves.

World's oldest pet cemetery: the Cemetery of Dogs in Paris opened in 1899 in response to a new law stating that pet owners could no longer leave their animals' bodies in the city's streets or rivers.

Lenin's embalmed body has been on display in Moscow's Red Square since 1924.

People started building tombs aboveground in New Orleans in the 1700s because cemeteries often flooded during heavy rainstorms, and buried coffins would be pushed out of the ground.

Books

More than 100 romance novels are published every month in the United States.

Indiana University's main library sinks an inch per year...because of the weight of the books.

First published in 1985, the *Klingon Dictionary* has sold more than 250,000 copies.

One of ancient Persia's high-ranking government officials took his 117,000-volume library with him everywhere. The books were carried on the backs of camels trained to walk in alphabetical order.

Iceland publishes four times as many books per capita as the United States.

Later in his life, the famous lover Giovanni Casanova worked as a librarian.

By the year 1500, there were 10 million books in print.

Clergyman John Harvard didn't found the college; he donated a library to the school, which was named for him later.

The Oxford English Dictionary lists 39 euphemisms for "bathroom" and 49 words that can be used to describe buttocks.

In 2007, Harlequin introduced a series of romance novels about NASCAR.

More than 450,000 of Bob Hope's jokes are housed at the Library of Congress.

The pages of this book will eventually turn brown, due to oxidation.

In the 1700s, the best-selling book in the world was the multivolume *Diderot's Encyclopedia*, compiled by Frenchman Denis Diderot.

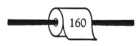

Cash Crops

Leading producer of cranberries in the United States: Wisconsin.

MSG is found naturally in wheat.

A single acre of wheat can produce more than 3,000 loaves of bread.

There are about 1,300 kernels in a pound of corn.

Bugs Bunny's favorite type of carrot is called Danvers.

There are more than 7,000 varieties of tomatoes.

Oranges and strawberries do not ripen after being picked. Avocados and bananas do.

The celtuce plant is a hybrid, part celery, part lettuce.

The indentation on the bottom of an apple is called the calyx basin.

Tomato juice is the state beverage of Ohio.

Avocados are often called a "perfect" food because they contain nearly all the vitamins, minerals, and other nutrients (including protein) that the human body needs.

Cranberries are sorted for ripeness by bouncing them. A ripe berry can be dribbled like a tiny basketball.

There are 7,500 varieties of apples—2,500 of them grow in the United States.

On average, there are seven peas in a pod.

Potatoes and sweet potatoes are distantly related. But yams and sweet potatoes aren't related at all.

Ninety-nine percent of the pumpkins sold in the United States end up as jack-o-lanterns.

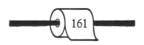

Crime and...

Number of shopping carts stolen from Los Angeles stores in 2005: 6.2 million.

People most often killed during bank robberies: the robbers.

In 1981, a Los Angeles man was arrested for hiding under tables and painting women's toenails.

About 509 million songs were legally downloaded in 2006—in the same year, 5 billion were downloaded illegally.

Your risk of being murdered is greater on January 1 than on any other day of the year.

Four most common arrests in the United States: drunk driving, theft, drug possession, and public drunkenness.

First rock star ever arrested onstage: Jim Morrison. (It happened twice—in 1967 and 1968.)

*   *   *

BIG OOPS
In 1965, Johnny Cash accidentally started a fire in California's Los Padres National Forest. He destroyed 508 acres.

...Punishment

In 2008, one out of every 100 Americans spent time in jail.

When the FBI was founded in 1908, it had 34 investigators. Today there are more than 15,000.

Only seven women have ever made the FBI's 10 Most Wanted list.

In convict lingo, "Getting a Valentine" means to receive a one-year jail sentence.

Last state to abolish flogging as a legal punishment: Delaware...in 1972.

In Charleston, South Carolina, people who are arrested can be charged $1 for the ride to jail.

The only formal qualification needed to be appointed a Florida executioner: You must be at least 18 years old.

*　　*　　*

BORED?

A Virginia man made an eight-mile-long chain of chewing-gum wrappers. (It took him 38 years.)

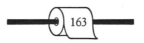

Average Humans

On average, people can hold their breath for one minute. (World record: nine minutes, eight seconds.)

According to polls, more people sing in the car than in the shower.

It's estimated that a third of all adults have difficulty distinguishing right from left. But...

Ninety-five percent of people put on their left sock first.

Eighty-five percent of people can curl their tongue into a tube.

Approximately 50 million Americans snore.

About 27 people die each year of suffocation from a dry-cleaning bag.

People with schizophrenia rarely yawn.

Fifteen percent of Americans bite their toenails.

You're four times more likely to choke to death on a nonedible object than on food.

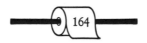

Dim Bulbs

"It's time for the human race to enter the solar system."
—Dan Quayle

"The skin is an important interface between man and the environment."
—OSHA pamphlet

"We've got to ask ourselves: How much clean air do we need?"
—Lee Iacocca

"I don't really think, I just walk."
—Paris Hilton

"I am for the death penalty. Who commits terrible acts must get a fitting punishment. That way, he learns the lesson for the next time."
—Britney Spears

"For your convenience, we will be closed Christmas Day."
—Sign at a Boston supermarket

"I don't want to make the wrong mistake."
—Yogi Berra

"Solutions are not the answer."
—Richard Nixon

Bodies at Work

When you see something you like, your pupils dilate.

The average person swallows 295 times while eating a meal.

Right-handed people tend to chew their food on the right side of their mouths.

Between death and the onset of rigor mortis, muscle contractions sometimes cause the body to turn onto its side.

Talking on the phone, laughing, or taking notes burns about 1.3 calories per minute.

More than 90 percent of the actions performed by the nervous system are reflexes.

Fastest-healing part of the human body: the tongue.

With each breath, humans exchange about 17 percent of the air in their lungs.

Chewing gum can help improve your memory (but you have to remember to buy the gum).

It's physically impossible to tickle yourself because your brain anticipates the tickle.

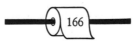

World War II

Exclusive supplier of rice to the U.S. military during World War II: Uncle Ben's.

James Bond creator Ian Fleming worked with the United Kingdom's Naval Intelligence during World War II.

Boy Scouts founder Robert Baden Powell once wrote a book on how to recognize German spies by their walk.

After the end of World War II, Albert Einstein was offered the presidency of Israel. He declined.

Missionary John Birch was killed by the Chinese 10 days after World War II ended; some consider him the first victim of the Cold War.

Iva Toguri D'Aquino, an American citizen who lived in Japan during World War II and was convicted of being a "Tokyo Rose," served six years in prison for treason. Much later, in 1977, she was pardoned by President Gerald Ford.

Nazi doctor Josef Mengele escaped from Germany at the end of the war and moved to South America. He drowned in Brazil in 1979, where he had been living under the name Wolfgang Gerhard.

Founded in 1923 in Vienna, Austria, Interpol was absorbed into the Gestapo during the Nazi era.

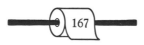

8 Ways to Crack a Safe

Your Aunt Selma died recently, and among her possessions is an old safe. The only problem is that she didn't tell you the combination. Here are some ways to get inside:

1. Many people either write the combination down somewhere or don't change the one set by the company that made the safe. First, try to find that.

2. Listening with a stethoscope might do the trick. Each number is connected to a wheel right behind the dial. When the combination's numbers are chosen correctly, the wheels click into place. A safecracker listens for the sound of each wheel's clicking, and when the corresponding numbers line up, the safe can be opened.

3. Drill through the back of the safe and unscrew the lock from the inside with a long screwdriver.

4. Drill all the way around the lock in the front, right through to the wheels, then insert a metal rod to push out the bolt that locks them.

5. Burn out the lock with a blowtorch if it's an old-fashioned safe. Newer safes will need a "metal-cutting torch," a device that heats and cuts through metal.

6. If noise isn't a problem—and if you can take a chance on damaging or destroying the safe's contents—you can always blow it up. Pour a liquid explosive like nitroglycerin into the safe's door frame and attach a fuse.

7. Electronic safes (the kind with a number pad) can often be opened easily by spraying the keypad with ultraviolet ink. Then shine a UV flashlight to reveal finger marks.

8. Another way of opening an electronic safe is to connect it to a computer with safecracking software installed and let the machine do the work.

168

Beatlemania

The Beatles' last concert was at Candlestick Park in San Francisco on August 29, 1966. Last song they played: "Long Tall Sally."

In 1964, the BBC reported that Ringo Starr had his toenails removed. (It was actually his tonsils.)

George Harrison owned a musical toilet that played "Lucy in the Sky with Diamonds."

Second-highest album sales in the United States after the Beatles (106 million): Garth Brooks (92 million).

John Lennon and Paul McCartney met at a church picnic.

John Lennon recorded and produced under 15 different aliases.

The Beatles' *White Album* is officially titled *The Beatles*.

Beatles song that has been recorded more than any other in history: "Yesterday."

The Beatles were the first living celebrities to be featured in an animated TV show. They had their own Saturday morning cartoon (1965–69).

Linda McCartney and Wings released one single under the name Suzy and the Red Stripes.

Former Rolling Stone Brian Jones played sax on the Beatles song "You Know My Name."

The Beatles were once known as Johnny and the Moondogs.

The Beatles recorded their first album, *Please Please Me*, in 10 hours. It cost about $1,000 to make.

First person on the cover of *Rolling Stone*: John Lennon (1967).

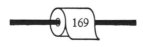

First, Last & Once

Carole King's first single as a performer was called "Baby Sittin'" (1959).

Ted Williams's final major-league hit was a home run.

First culture to serve meals in courses: the Russians. It was called *dining a la russe*, and Russian prince Alexander Kurakin introduced the technique to the French around 1800.

Golfer Arnold Palmer once hit balls off the second tier of the Eiffel Tower. His longest: 403 yards.

French tailor Barthelemy Thimonnier developed the first sewing machine in 1829.

In the rough: Nils Lied drove a golf ball 2,640 yards…on a sheet of ice in Antarctica.

Bob Dylan's first professional performance: opening for John Lee Hooker in New York City in 1961.

The first (and only) unassisted triple play in the World Series: Bill Wambsganss of the Cleveland Indians, in 1920.

The last legal spitball in the minor leagues was thrown by Burleigh Grimes on September 10, 1934.

Pamela Anderson was named Canada's "Centennial Baby" in 1967 for being the first person born on the centennial of Canada's independence.

John L. Sullivan (1858–1918), the "Boston Strong Boy," was the last bare-knuckle fighting champion.

Mark Twain published his first short story when he was 30.

Honus Wagner was the first baseball player to have his signature branded into a Louisville Slugger bat (1905).

Mozart's last composition: *Requiem Mass in D Minor* (1791).

It's an Honor

Charles Lindbergh was *Time* magazine's first Man of the Year, in 1927.

Baseball player with the most World Series rings: Yogi Berra (10).

Only 17 Negro League players are members of the National Baseball Hall of Fame.

Pope John Paul I once wrote a fan letter to Pinocchio, and Pope John Paul II was an honorary Harlem Globetrotter.

Tom Brokaw and KISS's Gene Simmons have both been honored by bobblehead nights at baseball parks.

Two British prime ministers are named in the Beatles' song "Taxman": Harold Wilson and Edward Heath.

Manager Tommy Lasorda has been inducted into both the Canadian and American baseball halls of fame.

Steve Miller was given—and taught to play—his first guitar by Les Paul.

Colette, author of *Gigi*, was one of the few Frenchwomen to become a grand officer of the French Legion of Honor.

Easter in Sweden

THE EASTER WITCH. Since the 1800s, children in Sweden have dressed up as witches to celebrate Easter. According to Scandinavian legend, in the week before Easter, witches (disguised as townspeople most of the year) flew into the mountains to dance and celebrate spring with the devil. Traditionally, the Swedes lit fires to drive the witches away. Today, people light bonfires and set off fireworks, and children paint their faces, wear long skirts, and go from house to house, handing out small pictures they've drawn in the hopes of getting a piece of candy.

DINNER. Instead of ham, the traditional meal consists of pickled herring, salmon, deviled eggs topped with caviar, meatballs, Swedish sausage, and a type of cola called *Paskmust*.

BY ANOTHER NAME. Easter is called *Paskafton*, and most celebrations take place on Holy Saturday, the day before Easter, because that's when the witches supposedly left the mountains and turned back into regular people...just in time to go to church on Easter Sunday.

SOLEMN DAYS. Over the years, as people drifted away from the church, religious traditions became less strict, but Easter used to be one of the most revered holidays in Sweden. It was so important that other religious events (like weddings and christenings) were forbidden from taking place during Holy Week—from Palm Sunday (the Sunday before Easter) to Holy Saturday.

TWIGS. The Swedes decorate birch or willow twigs with feathers and beads and display them around their houses. The twigs represent the palms spread before Jesus on Palm Sunday.

Nicknames

James Earl Carter Jr. was the first president sworn in using his nickname—"Jimmy."

ESPN's pick for best nickname in baseball history: Ted "the Splendid Splinter" Williams.

Real name of 50 Cent: Curtis James Jackson III.

As a girl, Sophia Loren was called "Stechetto" (Italian for "stick") because she was so skinny. Cameron Diaz was called "Skeletor."

Where did Harry Lillis Crosby get the nickname "Bing"? From the comic strip *The Bingsville Bugle*.

At Choate prep school, John F. Kennedy was nicknamed "Rat Face" for his scrawny appearance.

Dolly Parton's CB handle was "Booby Trap."

Prince William's nickname is "Wombat."

Cy Young's real name was Denton True Young. His nickname, "Cy," was short for "cyclone."

Samuel L. Jackson was called "Machine Gun" as a child because of his stutter.

Francisco Franco adopted the nickname "El Caudillo" (the Leader).

Whitey Ford nicknamed Pete Rose "Charlie Hustle" in 1963 after Rose ran to first base on a walk.

George Herman "Babe" Ruth got his nickname as a young player on the Baltimore Orioles. The team's manager, Jack Dunn, adopted him, and he was known as Dunn's "baby."

Houston Oilers running back Charlie Tolar was known as "the Human Bowling Ball."

Jesse James's nickname: "Dingus."

Myth-conceptions

Until about 100 years ago, jump rope was considered a boy's game.

The 1969 Woodstock concert was not held in the town of Woodstock, but at a farm in Bethel, New York.

Charles Lindbergh was actually the 61st person to fly across the Atlantic. His was the first solo flight.

Morse code is named for Samuel Morse, but it was invented by Alfred Vail, one of Morse's colleagues.

Although it is widely attributed to him, William Shakespeare never used the word "gadzooks."

Napoléon Bonaparte was not that short—he was slightly taller than the average Frenchman.

In the 19th century, "Shirley" was a popular name for boys.

Anthony "Zorba the Greek" Quinn was born in Chihuahua, Mexico.

Aristotle believed that the most important purpose of the human brain was to cool the blood.

Benito Mussolini never did make the trains run on time in Italy.

Real Headlines

Dead Man Remains Dead

Purgatory Tickets to Remain at $27

High-Crime Areas Said to Be Safer

Drunk Gets Nine Months in Violin Case

Slow Driver Arrested After 4-County Chase

Woman Born Feb. 29 Has Baby Same Day

Helicopter Powered by Human Flies

Clinton Wins on Budget, but
More Lies Ahead

Outside Consultants Sought for
Test of Gas Chamber

Man Is Fatally Slain

Mortuary Adds Drive-Through

Man Stuck on Toilet; Stool Suspected

Man Thought Hurt, but Slightly Dead

One-Legged Man Competent to Stand Trial

For What Ails You

Sixty percent of all chicken soup sold in the United States is bought during cold and flu season.

A fever can cause brain damage if it goes above 107.6°F.

What do your tailbone and appendix have in common? Nobody knows what they're for.

Penicillin causes about 300 deaths per year in the United States.

Most frequently broken bone: the clavicle (collarbone).

Streptomycin, an antibiotic, was discovered in fungus found in a chicken's throat.

Fifty-five percent of Americans are registered organ donors.

Country with the most kidney donors per capita: Iran. (The United States is second.)

About one in five humans has no reaction to the toxic oil in poison oak or poison ivy.

Best-selling medicines worldwide: cholesterol reducers, antidepressants, and ulcer drugs.

Chance of getting a cold within a week after taking a two-hour flight: 20 percent.

Among amateur golfers, lowerback injuries are the most common ailment.

Old English word for "sneeze": *fneosan.*

Sales of Rolaids, Alka-Seltzer, and Tums jump 20 percent in December.

According to medical texts from 1552 BC, the ancient Egyptian cure for indigestion was to crush a hog's tooth, put it inside four sugar cakes, and eat one a day for four days.

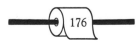

Range of Facts

Mount Everest's name in Nepali (the main language of Nepal) is Sagarmatha, which means "Goddess of the Sky."

Officially, the definition of a mountain is "a land-mass that projects conspicuously above its surroundings and is higher than a hill."

Utah is home to the United States' only major east-west mountain range, the Uintas.

Until the 1830s, most Americans thought the Rocky Mountains were impassable.

Washington State's North Cascades are often called "the American Alps."

Most mountainous state in the United States: Nevada, with more than 300 ranges.

The Himalayas cover one-tenth of the land on earth.

The dinosaurs were already extinct by the time the Alps were formed.

World's longest mountain range: the Andes, which stretch more than 4,000 miles through seven nations.

Number of corpses abandoned and still remaining on Mount Everest: about 120.

Animal Tales

In Old English, snakes were called "nadders" until a misspelling turned them into "adders."

Fifteen people have died during the annual "Running of the Bulls" in Pamplona, Spain.

During the Great Depression, armadillos were a popular food in the American Southwest. Many people nicknamed them "Hoover hogs."

More than 40 horse "actors" appeared in *Seabiscuit* (2003), with 10 sharing the title role.

Vermont's Panache restaurant offers musk ox, lion, and giraffe dishes on its menu.

The small intestine of an average ostrich is 46 feet long. (A human's is between 19 and 26 feet.)

Goat meat contains about 40 percent less saturated fat than chicken.

Odds that a can of fish sold in the United States will be eaten by a cat, not a human: one in three.

What do you call a saddle on an elephant? A howdah.

Comparisons

Iowa is bigger than Portugal.

The entire area of Japan (population: 127 million) is slightly smaller than California (population: 34 million).

Iguassu Falls in Brazil and Argentina has about nine times the water volume of Niagara Falls.

Golf courses cover about as much of the United States as Delaware and Rhode Island combined.

Israel is about the size of Massachusetts, and has about the same population.

Minnesota has 90,000 miles of shoreline, more than California, Florida, and Hawaii combined.

Idaho's Craters of the Moon National Monument and Preserve covers more than 1,100 square miles, about the size of Rhode Island.

The combined area of the entire United Kingdom is smaller than the state of Oregon.

The 21 smallest U.S. states combined are still smaller than Alaska.

Dallas/Fort Worth International Airport is larger than Manhattan Island.

The Amazon River basin could hold the country of France 13 times over.

San Francisco's Golden Gate Park is 174 acres larger than New York's Central Park.

Genghis Khan conquered more land than Alexander the Great, Napoléon Bonaparte, and Adolf Hitler.

There are more people of Irish descent in Boston and surrounding New England than there are in Ireland.

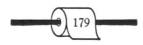

The Nation's Locations

California's Disneyland and Florida's Disney World are both are located in Orange County.

Easternmost capital city in the United States: Augusta, Maine.

Chicago has America's tallest building and the world's only drive-through post office.

Smallest post office in the United States: Ochopee, Florida, a town in the western Everglades. The 8'4" by 7'3" building was originally a farmer's shed.

Fastest-growing city since 1990: Gilbert, Arizona. Fastest-shrinking city since 1990: Detroit, Michigan.

The oldest capital city in the United States is Santa Fe, New Mexico, founded in 1608.

The official state fish of Nevada is the cutthroat trout.

Montpelier, Vermont, is the smallest state capital in the United States. Population: 8,035.

Only 2 percent of the immigrants who were processed through Ellis Island were not allowed to enter the United States.

Maine is the largest U.S. producer of blueberries, with 25 percent of the country's production. And...

Nearly 90 percent of the nation's lobster supply is caught off the coast of Maine.

The government owns 85 percent of all the land in Nevada.

High life: 74 percent of New York City residents live at least one flight of stairs aboveground.

October 4, 2004, was the first day since 1999 on which no one was shot in Chicago.

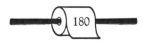
180

In the Olden Days

Before 1920, it was technically legal to send children through the mail.

Who looked after a knight's estate while he was away fighting the Crusades? Usually his lawyer.

In ancient China, criminals who were caught robbing travelers had their noses cut off.

Between 800 and 1500, English law decreed that every male had to practice archery daily.

The notorious pirate Blackbeard took hostages, but there's no proof that he ever killed one.

In 1908, New York City passed a law forbidding women from smoking in public.

In 19th-century Britain, you could be hanged for associating with Gypsies…or for stealing bread.

The Colt revolver—a six-shooter patented in 1836—is still used today by the Texas Rangers.

During Prohibition, there were more than 100,000 illegal drinking establishments in New York City.

Since the 1950s, it has been against the law for a flying saucer to touch down in any of France's vineyards.

Historical Transportation

The USS *Phoenix* survived the 1941 attack on Pearl Harbor, was sold to Argentina, and sank in the 1980s during the Falklands War.

The primary presidential helicopter is a Sikorsky VH-3D called the Sea King.

Gordon Lightfoot's song "The Wreck of the Edmund Fitzgerald" chronicles the sinking of the SS *Edmund Fitzgerald*, a freighter that went down in Lake Superior in 1975 without sending a single distress call.

Seaworthy replicas of the *Niña*, *Pinta*, and *Santa Maria* have been docked at Corpus Christi, Texas, since 1992.

William Howard Taft was the second president to own a car, but he was too fat to drive it.

First acting president to ride a train: Andrew Jackson (1833).

The tidewater coastline of Texas contains more than 600 historic shipwrecks.

Lyndon Johnson was the only U.S. president to be sworn in on an airplane.

President James Madison's reasons for declaring the War of 1812: He wanted to stop the British navy from harassing U.S. ships and prevent the British government from forming alliances with American Indians.

In Galveston, Texas, you can see a yacht that once belonged to Benito Mussolini.

While president, Ulysses S. Grant was fined $20 for driving his carriage too fast.

Only fully intact British warship ever found in the Great Lakes: the HMS *Ontario*, which sank in Lake Ontario in 1780 during the American Revolution.

Money, Money, Money

The average take from a bank robbery is less than $5,000.

Peter the Great of Russia taxed Russian men who wore beards.

The first insurance policy in the American colonies was written in 1721.

The NASDAQ was totally disabled in December 1987 when a squirrel chewed through a phone line.

During the Depression, 44 percent of all U.S. banks failed.

NASDAQ is short for the National Association of Securities Dealers Automated Quotations.

The first income tax was levied in China in AD 10, at a rate of 10 percent of the profits of skilled professionals.

When Al Capone was finally convicted, it was not for murder but for income-tax evasion.

In 1864, the top U.S. income tax rate was 3 percent.

The Jesse James gang's final bank robbery netted them just $26.70.

In England in the 1700s, you could buy insurance against going to hell.

Some insurance companies offer hole-in-one insurance for golf tournaments that award a prize to any player who makes a hole in one.

The IRS processes more than 2 billion pieces of paper each year.

The most likely time for a bank robbery is on a Friday between 9:00 and 11:00 a.m. The least likely time is on a Wednesday between 3:00 and 6:00 p.m.

According to the FBI, 74 percent of the threats against federal workers are directed at IRS employees.

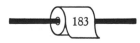

The White House

Theodore Roosevelt officially gave the White House its current name in 1901. Before that, it was called the President's Palace, the President's House, or the Executive Mansion.

In 1915, to celebrate the completion of the first transcontinental phone line (from New York to San Francisco), President Woodrow Wilson made a call from the Oval Office.

Bulletproof glass wasn't installed at the White House until 1941. It went into three windows of the Oval Office.

The White House has 412 doors, 147 windows, 132 rooms, 35 bathrooms, 28 fireplaces, 8 stair-cases, 6 levels, and 3 elevators.

The White House is the only private residence of a head of state that the public can visit free of charge.

The six floors of the White House have a total area of about 55,000 square feet.

Every day, about 6,000 people visit the White House.

The first solar panels were installed at the White House in 2002. Where? Atop the pool house.

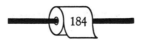

Body Numbers

Weigh yourself; multiply it by 0.0028. That's how many grams of salt are in your body.

Every day, your eyes are closed for a total of 30 minutes...blinking.

The adult human body requires about 88 pounds of oxygen daily.

When people see someone they like, their eyebrows raise for about two-tenths of a second.

By age 60, you will have lost 50 percent of your taste buds and 40 percent of your sense of smell.

If unwound, your DNA would reach from Earth to the Sun and back...more than 400 times.

Women are 70 percent more likely than men to live past the age of 100.

When you walk down a steep hill, the pressure on your knees is equal to three times your body weight.

Take your height and divide by eight. That's how "tall" your head is.

A human body includes about 50 trillion cells.

A single gram of human feces contains 100,000,000,000 microbes.

Human capillaries are about 0.0003 inch in diameter...thinner than a hair.

Your eyeballs are 3.5 percent salt.

Each person sheds about 100 billion flakes of skin every day.

The average speaker sprays 2.5 microscopic droplets of saliva for every word spoken.

Love & Marriage

A gamomaniac is someone obsessed with proposing marriage.

In South Korea, a can of Spam is considered a great wedding gift.

By law, Princess Diana had to call Prince Charles "sir" until they were formally engaged.

Catherine Parr was married twice before she wed Henry VIII. She wed a fourth time after he died.

Inspiration for the Rolling Stones song "Angie": David Bowie's first wife, Angela.

To choose a wife, Ivan the Terrible had 1,500 women sent to Moscow for him to choose from.

Queen Victoria's wedding cake had a circumference of more than nine feet.

Diana was the first British subject to marry an heir to the throne since 1659.

Most remarried couple: Richard and Carol Roble from New York, with 56 ceremonies. (The first was in 1969.)

Berengaria of Navarre (Spain) became the British queen when she married Richard I in 1191, but she never actually set foot in England.

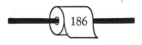

It's Elemental

Most abundant element in the universe: hydrogen. (Helium is second.)

There's no mercury on Mercury—most of the planet is solid iron.

Mineral seepage creates the colors at Michigan's Pictured Rocks National Lakeshore. Red and orange are copper, green and blue are iron, black is manganese, and white is lime.

Most tin cans are actually made of steel, with a thin layer of tin to prevent corrosion.

Iron weighs more after it rusts. Why? Iron oxide (what iron becomes when it rusts) is heavier than iron alone.

The name of the radioactive element in smoke detectors is americium.

Among the ingredients in stannous fluoride, the cavity fighter found in toothpaste: tin.

Most-used metals in the world (in order): iron, aluminum, copper.

The element astatine gets its name from the Greek word *astatos*, meaning "unstable."

Ewww!

Salvador Dalí wore a home-made perfume composed of artist's glue and cow dung.

In 16th-century England, people who cleaned out cesspits were known as "gong farmers."

The contents of King Louis XIV's chamber pot were noted daily and entered in a logbook.

Cloacina was the Roman goddess of sewers.

The word "vomit" has the most entries in *The American Dictionary of Slang*.

A healthy human bladder can hold two cups of urine for up to five hours.

In the fourth century, Rome levied a tax on the sale of urine and excrement.

Geoffrey Chaucer, François Rabelais, Benjamin Franklin, and Mark Twain all wrote about flatulence.

If you're average, you'll swallow three spiders this year.

Tommy Bolt is the only pro golfer to have been fined for passing gas. (He did it in 1959 while an opponent was putting.)

You can't burp in outer space.

There is a British beer called Old Fart.

Astronauts get "spacesick" so often that the space shuttle toilet has a special setting for vomit.

In French folklore, dreaming about poop is an omen that good fortune is on the way.

The bagpipe was originally made from the skin of a dead sheep.

The man who invented Jell-O was originally looking for a way to make a palatable laxative.

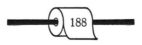

Canadian City Names

TORONTO. North of the city is Lake Toronto. The Iroquois who once lived there called it Toronto, meaning "place where trees stand in water." Who put trees in the lake? Another native group, the Hurons, planted saplings there to help trap fish.

CALGARY. In the 1870s, when the area was a post for the Mounties (Mounted Police), it was named Fort Brisebois after officer Ephrem Brisebois. But in 1876, after Brisebois declared a woman from the nearby Metis tribe his common-law wife, his superior, Colonel James Macleod, angrily renamed the town. Macleod had just returned from a trip to Calgary—a popular white sand beach on the Isle of Mull off Scotland—so Fort Brisebois became Fort Calgary. The word "calgary" comes from the Gaelic *cala ghearraidh*, which means "beach of the meadow."

QUÉBEC. Before the French colonists arrived in the 1500s, the area was inhabited by the Algonquin people. The Algonquins called it Kebek, meaning "straight" or "narrow," referring to the way the river (now the St. Lawrence) narrows at the Algonquins' settlement (now Québec City). Explorer Samuel de Champlain made the word French in 1613, spelling it "Québec."

OTTAWA. In 1832, the British government hired a group of engineers, headed by Colonel John By, to build a canal in the colony of Upper Canada. The large camp that housed workers—called Bytown in the colonel's honor—eventually grew into a town. In 1855, it became officially incorporated as a city, and took a new name from the Adàwe, the native people with whom Europeans traded during early colonization of the area. French settlers had corrupted the name Adàwe to Outaouak, and British settlers corrupted it to Ottawa.

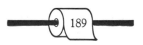

Learning the Language

Longest one-syllable word in the English language: "screeched."

Hoping to improve the world's communication, Ludwig Zamenhof created a language he called Esperanto ("one who hopes") in 1887. It didn't catch on.

The average American knows only about 10 percent of the words in the English language.

Five oldest English words still in use: town, priest, earl, this, ward.

According to language experts, virtually every language on earth has a word for "yes-man."

More than 1,000 different languages are spoken on the African continent.

Most-studied foreign languages in the United States: Spanish, French, German, Italian, and Japanese.

An ancient Chinese written language called Nushu was created and used exclusively by women.

The world's most widely spoken language is Mandarin Chinese.

Dante's *Divine Comedy* established the Tuscan dialect as the basis of modern Italian.

Most common languages on the Internet: English, Japanese, and Spanish.

The Quechua language of Peru has 1,000 words for "potato."

Until 1399, the first language of English kings was French.

The 1980s group Bananarama's first single, "Aie A Mwana," was sung in Swahili.

Studies show: most English speakers say "uh" before a short pause and "um" before a long pause.

Everyday Americans

The average American 12-year-old gets about $15 in weekly allowance.

About 10 percent of American households pay their bills with cash.

Eighty percent of U.S. Super Bowl viewers watch just for the commercials.

Eighteen percent of all the money spent on sporting goods is used to buy golf equipment.

Most Americans spend 45 minutes a day listening to recorded music.

Americans consume about 11.7 pounds of chocolate per person every year.

Americans have the highest average caloric intake in the world: 3,790 calories a day.

According to polls, the most popular sport in America is football.

Americans consume 450 hot dogs per second.

The average American ate 120 restaurant meals in 2008.

Number-one store-bought cookie in the United States: Oreos.

The average American credit card holder owes almost $2,200.

Americans spend over $630 million a year on golf balls.

Americans purchase about 40 percent of the indigestion remedies sold in the world.

More than 75 percent of all American homes have at least one can of WD-40.

Americans spend $2 billion per year on candles.

At any one time, there are 100 million phone conversations going on in the United States.

Menagerie

Rats can find their way through a maze faster when Mozart's music is playing.

The Loch Ness Monster is protected by Scotland's 1912 Protection of Animals Acts.

In the 1964 TV series, Flipper was played mainly by a dolphin named Suzy.

Jumbo the Elephant, a premier attraction at P. T. Barnum's circus in the 1880s, brought the word "jumbo" into common usage.

Emperor Caligula issued invitations to banquets in his horse's name and considered making the animal a consul.

Nabisco's Barnum's Animal Crackers celebrated its hundredth anniversary by adding koalas.

In 1948, four men took a cow up Switzerland's 14,000-foot Matterhorn. They all froze to death.

Queen Henrietta of Belgium trained a llama to spit at people.

Russian czar Ivan the Terrible once had an elephant killed because it did not bow to him.

There are more tigers (in zoos and as pets) in the United States than there are tigers in the wild.

Costs in 1910

A loaf of bread...5¢

A postage stamp...2¢

The average house...$4,000

The average car...$500

A Coca-Cola...5¢

A movie ticket...7¢

A dozen eggs...34¢

A pound of flour...3¢

A camera...$6.95

A bathing suit...$1.75

A teddy bear...75¢

An apron...17¢

A lace parasol...$1.29

A pair of suspenders...18¢

The average yearly wage was $963.

A steak at the butcher shop went for 18¢ a pound.

Relatively Speaking

Alexander Graham Bell's father-in-law was the first president of the National Geographic Society.

Actor Kiefer Sutherland's grandfather was the premier of Saskatchewan, Canada, for 17 years.

George Dern, actress Laura Dern's grandfather, was Secretary of War under Franklin D. Roosevelt.

Actress Helena Bonham Carter's great-grandfather was former British prime minister Herbert Asquith.

James K. Polk was a great-grandnephew of John Knox, founder of Scottish Presbyterianism.

Whitney Houston and Dionne Warwick are cousins. So were James Madison and Zachary Taylor.

Tom Hanks is a descendant of Abraham Lincoln's uncle.

Moe Howard of *Three Stooges* fame married Harry Houdini's cousin.

Kaiser Wilhelm II, Czar Nicholas II, and King George V were all grandchildren of Queen Victoria.

Charles Bonaparte, who was the grandnephew of Napoléon, founded the FBI.

George W. Bush is related to Benedict Arnold, Marilyn Monroe, Winston Churchill, Princess Diana, Franklin Pierce, Abraham Lincoln, Theodore and Franklin D. Roosevelt, and Gerald Ford.

President John Tyler was a granduncle of Harry S. Truman.

American Idol 2002 runner-up Justin Guarini is a cousin of actor Samuel L. Jackson.

Hugh Hefner and Bing Crosby both had ancestors on the *Mayflower*.

American Institutions

The U.S. Pledge of Allegiance was written in 1892 by Francis Bellamy...a socialist.

The Liberty Bell was nearly sold for scrap metal in 1828.

The American flag flies 24 hours a day at the White House (if the president is at home), at Valley Forge...and on the moon.

From 1790 to 1800, Philadelphia was the capital of the United States.

The United States actually declared its independence from Britain on July 2, 1776. But the Declaration of Independence wasn't approved until July 4, 1776.

The green ink used for U.S currency was invented by chemist Thomas Sterry Hunt, who worked in Canada.

Drafts of the Declaration of Independence were written on hemp paper.

Under the U.S. Constitution, there is no way to remove a Supreme Court justice for incompetence.

Jacob Shallus, the calligrapher of the U.S. Constitution, was paid $30 for his work.

Connecticut, Georgia, and Massachusetts waited until 1939 to ratify the Bill of Rights.

Average cost to run for U.S. Congress in 2006: $1 million.

The original Bill of Rights prevented congressmen from raising their own salaries. (Today, they vote on their raises.)

During his administration, John Adams made it a crime to publish anything scandalous about the U.S. government.

Members of Congress don't need postage stamps for official mail—their signature counts as a stamp.

Go Fish

Fish have been swimming on our planet for more than 400 million years.

Mackerel and tuna will die if they stop swimming.

Deep-sea fish can explode when brought to the ocean's surface because of the rapid decrease in outside pressure.

Sea horses don't have scales.

The bioluminescent lantern fish produces enough light to read by (if you could read underwater).

A bluefin tuna can weigh over 1,000 pounds.

Electric eels can produce discharges of up to 650 volts.

Flying fish can swim—and glide through the air—as fast as 40 mph.

Only animal that can see both infrared and ultraviolet light: the goldfish.

What fish can leave the water and walk on land? The spotted climbing perch, which uses its pectoral fins like legs.

Forty percent of the world's fish species live in freshwater.

Catfish have 100,000 taste buds.

A shoal is a group of fish that swims loosely grouped together. A school is a tight-knit, organized group that swims at the same speed.

Fish yawn.

Scientists estimate that up to 15,000 fish species have yet to be identified.

World's most venomous fish? The stonefish, which lives in the Pacific near Australia. It has 13 venomous spines on its back, and one sting can kill a human.

A giant squid's eye is the size of a dinner plate.

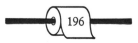

The Information Age

More than 10 million LP (long-playing) records are still sold every year.

There are 250 million TVs in the United States—and 400 million in China.

From 1897 until the 1950s, most records were made of a mix of shellac, slate, cotton, and wax.

In 2007, the number of recorded CDs sold was about equal to the number of blank CDs sold.

In the Soviet Union, people often made homemade records called "bones"—they were etched onto discarded medical X-rays.

A standard DVD includes 7.5 miles of information.

The 1889 Nickel-in-the-Slot, a coin-operated phonograph that was a precursor to the jukebox, made $1,000 in six months.

Guglielmo Marconi, the inventor of radio, opened the first radio station in England in 1897.

These days, most records are pressed onto recycled vinyl.

Betamax VCRs were available from 1975 until 2002.

The fax machine has been around since 1843...longer than the telephone.

Radio waves from broadcasts of the 1930s have already traveled past 100,000 stars.

Western Union invented singing telegrams to improve its "bad news" reputation.

World's fastest computer: IBM's Roadrunner can perform 1,000 trillion calculations per second.

Last movie released on laser disc: *Star Wars Episode 1: The Phantom Menace.*

Grave Matters

The title of Phil Spector's "To Know Him Is to Love Him" was taken from his father's tombstone.

The earliest known will was written in 2550 BC.

About 50 people a week visit the grave of Harry Potter, a British man who died in 1939 and is buried in Israel.

King Tut's third and inner coffin was made from 243 pounds of solid gold.

The three wise men are said to be interred in a cathedral in Cologne, Germany.

Hitler's jawbone is reportedly kept "in a safe place" in Russia.

For decades after Emperor Nero's death, people in Rome claimed to have seen him.

English poet Dante Rossetti put many of his unpublished poems in his wife's coffin when she died in 1862. Seven years later, he retrieved them.

American outlaw Clay Allison's tombstone reads, "He never killed a man that did not need killing."

Marilyn Monroe, Natalie Wood, Walter Matthau, and Roy Orbison are all buried in the small Westwood Memorial Park in Los Angeles.

In 1813, a British doctor turned the vertebrae of King Charles I into a saltshaker.

* * *

LAWYERS

- Every 30 seconds, someone files a lawsuit in the United States.
- More than 60 percent of the world's lawyers live in the United States.

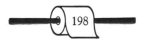

Uncommon in Common

Stephen Colbert, Vin Diesel, and Mike Myers all like to play Dungeons and Dragons.

Little Richard and MC Hammer are both ordained ministers.

Keanu Reeves, Johnny Depp, and Russell Crowe play in bands.

Walter Matthau, Goldie Hawn, and Sylvester Stallone all released albums...that bombed.

Bob Dylan and Prince are both from Minnesota.

Real people on Pez dispensers: Betsy Ross, Daniel Boone, and Paul Revere.

The Sex Pistols covered songs by Frank Sinatra, Bill Haley, and the Monkees.

As a session musician, Jimmy Page played with the Kinks, Joe Cocker, and Engelbert Humperdinck.

B. B. King, Bill Haley, James Brown, and Ike Turner were former DJs.

What do Elvis Presley and Liberace have in common? Both had a twin who died at birth.

Frank Capra, Irving Berlin, Max Factor, and Bob Hope were immigrants processed through Ellis Island.

Winston Churchill, Benito Mussolini, and Pope John Paul II all wrote movie scripts.

Famous people from Arkansas: Maya Angelou, Johnny Cash, and Douglas MacArthur.

Nick Cave, David Lee Roth, Henry Rollins, and Sting are all published authors.

Laura Bush, J. Edgar Hoover, and Pope Pius XI were all librarians.

Google, Apple, and Amazon started in home garages.

Basic Feng Shui

WHAT IS IT?
Pronounced "fung shway," it's the ancient Chinese art of how things are placed in a home, business, or office in order to attract and circulate positive energy, or "chi." Some unfavorable architectural details are impossible to change, so feng shui experts have come up with ways to "cure" them. Here are a few:

THE ENTRY. The approach to your home should be unblocked and as clutter-free as possible. A curved path is okay, as long as it isn't "too" curvy. A straight path can allow the chi to rush in. You're looking for a nice, calm flow, outside and inside.

THE FRONT DOOR. It should be easy to find. If it isn't, make it obvious by adding an arbor, lining up plants along the walkway, or installing a sign that says "Welcome."

INSIDE THE FRONT DOOR. The space as you step inside the front door should be unblocked, and a blank wall facing the front door can stop the chi from entering. The cure: experts suggest putting up a mirror on that wall, even a small one.

THE LIVING ROOM. Furniture should open toward you as you enter the room. The biggest piece, the sofa, is most important. Don't let it block the entry into the room and try not to place it with its back facing the entry.

THE BATHROOM. This is where the most dangerous fixture in feng shui resides: the toilet. Chi can go down the toilet, so keep the lid down and keep the door closed whether you're in there or not.

THE BEDROOM. Position the bed so that you have a full view of the room and the door. If windows and such make that impossible, put a mirror across from the bed and try to angle it so that you can

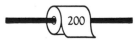

see the reflection of the door. Whatever you do, don't put a bed directly in line with the door. That's what feng shui experts call the "coffin" position—if you were dead, your pallbearers could pick you up and take you (feet first) straight out the door. Nightstands on both sides of the bed will encourage balance in relationships.

THE KITCHEN. The stove, a symbol of prosperity, is the most important fixture in the kitchen. Very few stoves face the doorway to the kitchen, so cures abound. Experts suggest putting a mirror (or something shiny) on the wall behind the stove. You can also just put a shiny kettle or pot on one of the burners. Not only will this enable the cook to be aware of anyone entering the room, the reflection will increase the number of the burners—from four to seven or eight—thereby increasing prospects for wealth.

THE OFFICE. In the office—at home or at work—position the desk so that you're facing the entrance when you sit, closer to the wall behind you than the doorway. It puts you "in command" and takes away any prospect of your being startled by someone entering the room without your knowledge.

THE RELATIONSHIP AREA. The far right corner of your home is the relationship corner. If you want to have a harmonious relationship, put something pink there and decorate with things like hearts that symbolize love.

FENG SHUI DON'TS
- Dried flowers are a no-no because they're dead. Plastic, silk, or real flowers are better. And when real flowers start to die, throw them out.

- Knives on display in the kitchen can create conflict. Stow them in a drawer or in a wooden block.

- Overhead beams—especially in a bedroom—are considered bad for chi flow and can upset a couple's relationship. The higher the beams, the better. But either way, try to paint them a light color, cover them up, or have them removed.

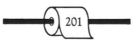

For the Birds

The first bird mentioned in the Bible is a raven (Genesis 8:7). Second is a dove, in verse 8:8.

The queen is the only person in Britain who is legally allowed to eat swan.

Time needed to hard-boil an ostrich egg: two hours.

The Baltimore Ravens have three mascots: Edgar, Allan, and Poe.

The Pacific island of Nauru's economy is based almost entirely on harvested bird droppings.

Florence Nightingale had a pet owl named Athena.

The shortest word ending in "ology" (meaning "the study of") is oology—the study of eggs.

The left drumstick of a chicken is more tender than the right one.

During one insanity attack, King George III of England ended every sentence with "peacock."

At the 1900 Olympics, the archery competition used live pigeons as targets.

If you actually ate "like a bird," you'd eat about 28 pounds of food per day.

The rock band the Eagles once sued the American Eagle Foundation for name infringement. (The band later dropped the suit.)

There's no such thing as a Cornish game hen—they're just young chickens of two pounds or less.

Rule at Yellowknife Golf Club in Canada: "No penalty assessed when ball carried off by raven."

In the 12th century, many Europeans believed that trees gave birth to birds.

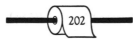

Behave in Public

It's against the law to run out of gas in Youngstown, Ohio.

In Los Angeles, it's against the law for infants to dance in public halls.

If you've just eaten garlic in Gary, Indiana, you must wait at least four hours before you can attend a theater or ride on a public streetcar.

In Rochester, Michigan, anyone swimming in public must have their suit inspected by a police officer.

In Massachusetts, it is illegal for a mourner at a funeral to eat more than three sandwiches.

In Elkhart, Indiana, it's against the law for a barber to threaten to cut off a child's ears.

In Xenia, Ohio, it's a crime to spit on a salad bar.

It's illegal to drive without a steering wheel in Decatur, Illinois.

By law, all Washington, D.C., taxis must carry a broom and a shovel.

In Louisiana, it is illegal to gargle in public.

It's against the law in Jefferson City, Missouri, to tie a boat to the railroad tracks.

In Winchester, Massachusetts, it is illegal for a woman to dance on a tight-rope...unless she's in a church.

In Florida, you may not pass gas in a public place after 6:00 p.m.

* * *

"Speak softly and wear a loud shirt." —**Hawaiian proverb**

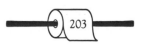

203

Mr. President

8 Presidents from Virginia
1. George Washington
2. Thomas Jefferson
3. James Madison
4. James Monroe
5. William Henry Harrison
6. John Tyler
7. Zachary Taylor
8. Woodrow Wilson

6 Presidents Who Owned Slaves
1. George Washington
2. Thomas Jefferson
3. James Madison
4. Andrew Jackson
5. James Polk
6. Zachary Taylor

5 Presidents Who Were Never Elected
1. John Tyler
2. Millard Fillmore
3. Andrew Johnson
4. Chester Arthur
5. Gerald Ford

3 Presidents Who Lost the Popular Vote But Won Anyway
1. Rutherford B. Hayes
2. Benjamin Harrison
3. George W. Bush

2 Musical Pieces Played When the President Enters a Room
1. "Ruffles and Flourishes"
2. "Hail to the Chief"

3 Requirements to Be Elected
1. Must be at least 35 years old.
2. Must be a natural-born citizen.
3. Must have lived in the United States as a permanent resident for at least 14 years.

6 Jobs Before They Were President
1. Sheriff: Grover Cleveland
2. Elevator operator: Lyndon B. Johnson
3. Janitor: James Garfield
4. Lifeguard: Ronald Reagan
5. Male model: Gerald Ford
6. Tavern worker: Martin Van Buren

Military Miscellany

When Saigon fell during the Vietnam War, the radio alert for Americans to evacuate was the song "White Christmas."

Pope John XXIII was a sergeant in the Italian army during World War I.

The range of a medieval longbow was about 220 yards—more than two football fields.

First people to wear T-shirts: sailors in the U.S. Navy.

Annie Oakley taught soldiers marksmanship during World War I.

Humphrey Bogart's lisp was the result of a navy injury—a prisoner punched him in the mouth.

Early guns took so long to load and fire that a bow and arrow was often more efficient.

Jimmy Stewart was awarded the Distinguished Flying Cross and the Croix de Guerre in World War II.

The groove around the rim of a bullet is called the cannelure.

There's a G.I. Joe action figure modeled after General Colin Powell.

Hollywood Prop-erty

Fifty gallons of fake blood were used during the filming of *Scream*. But combined, the *Kill Bill* movies used more than 450 gallons.

The famous "horse's head" in *The Godfather* was real—the producers got it from a dog-food company.

The battered hat worn by Henry Fonda in *On Golden Pond* once belonged to Spencer Tracy.

The original Godzilla weighed 220 pounds. It was made of urethane and bamboo.

Groucho Marx's mustache was often painted on.

The stage crew added milk to the rain in *Singin' in the Rain* so it would show up better on film.

An actual barn was built during the barn-raising scene in *Witness* (1985), but it was torn down shortly afterward.

The fit-all jeans in *The Sisterhood of the Traveling Pants* (2005) were Levi's.

In the brain scene in *Hannibal* (2001), the brain is dark chicken meat.

Dustin Hoffman's four-pound silicone breasts in *Tootsie* (1982) cost $175 each.

For the 2002 film *Spider-Man*, the props department created Spider-Man several costumes at about $100,000 each. Four were stolen from the set and eventually recovered—a security guard and his accomplice had taken them.

John Wayne's silver-and-leather hatband in *True Grit* was originally Gary Cooper's.

In *Seabiscuit* (2003), most of the "spectators" at the Pimlico racetrack were inflatable mannequins.

Cost to make the alien puppet in *E.T.*: $1 million.

Mailbag

The junk mail Americans receive in one day could provide enough fuel to heat 250,000 homes.

In 1893, Queen Isabella of Spain was the first woman to appear on a U.S. postage stamp.

There was a post office on the Russian space station *Mir*.

In most cases, if a chain letter were never broken, within 15 cycles the entire world would have read it.

World's oldest working post office: Sanquer, Scotland, in continuous operation since 1712.

Booker T. Washington was the first African American to appear on a U.S. stamp, in 1956.

London's post office still gets letters sent to 221B Baker Street, asking for Sherlock Holmes's help.

Jack Nicholson once had a job answering the fan mail for cartoon characters Tom and Jerry.

A "timbromaniac" is someone obsessed with postage stamps.

Eddie Lowery, who caddied for golfer Francis Ouimet, is the only caddie to have appeared on a U.S. postage stamp.

The first postage stamps were issued in Great Britain in 1840.

A photo of Queen Elizabeth taken by singer Bryan Adams was made into a Canadian postage stamp.

The United States Post Office handles about 46 percent of the world's mail.

The first nonroyal to be portrayed on a British stamp: William Shakespeare, in 1964.

Actor Ryan O'Neal once mailed a live tarantula to gossip columnist Rona Barrett.

What to Wear?

Americans buy more than 73,000 miles of neckties each year.

John "Johnny Appleseed" Chapman (1774–1845) wore a tin pot for a hat.

Alexander the Great often led parades dressed as the goddess Artemis.

In the 19th century, "sideburns" were named after Civil War general Ambrose Burnside because of his own thick sideburns that connected to his mustache.

Twenty percent of tuxedo rentals take place in May.

The winged hat worn by the Greek god Hermes is called a petasos.

One of Bonnie Prince Charlie's supporters, Flora MacDonald, smuggled him to safety by dressing him as her maid.

Chuck Berry came up with his famous duck walk while trying to distract audiences from his wrinkled suit.

Director Tim Burton wears mostly black because he "doesn't like having to match colors."

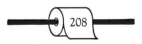

In the Name of Love

Most sought-after Cracker Jack prizes: toy rings. They're often used as engagement rings.

Rod Stewart has told some reporters that he wrote "You're in My Heart" for his ex-wife. (He's also claimed that it's about Liverpool's soccer team.)

Tibetan dating ritual: A man steals a woman's hat. If she likes him, she asks for it back.

Over the course of his life, Mormon leader Brigham Young had 55 wives.

One in 20 married Americans will begin an affair this year.

Twenty-three percent of American couples sleep in separate beds.

Worldwide, 60 percent of marriages are arranged.

Divorce statistics are lowest among people who say they're atheists.

Men did not start wearing wedding rings until the early 1900s.

Less than 5 percent of U.S. weddings take place in January.

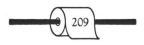

To the Teeth

The hardest substance in the human body: tooth enamel.

Half of all Americans say that a smile is the first thing they notice about a person.

The world's most valuable tooth: one of Sir Isaac Newton's. After Newton's death in 1727, a nobleman bought the tooth for $4,650 and used it as the setting for a ring.

In ancient Rome, some people whitened their teeth with urine.

George Washington had dentures made out of gold, lead, ivory, and hippopotamus teeth, not wood.

Early toothbrushes were twigs with frayed ends.

First toothpaste in a tube: Dr. Sheffield's Creme Dentifrice, created in 1892.

Sixty percent of people older than 65 still have all of their own teeth.

On average, Americans buy about 14 million gallons of toothpaste every year.

In Mexico, the tooth fairy is called the tooth mouse.

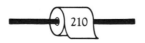

Merry Christmas!

In the late 1600s, it was illegal to celebrate Christmas in Massachusetts because the Puritains believed December 25 had been arbitrarily assigned as Christ's birthday.

Say "Merry Christmas" in Japanese: *Merii Kurisumasu.*

Approximately 10 percent of Jewish households have Christmas trees.

In 1841, Prince Albert brought the first royal family Christmas tree to Windsor Castle.

In 1836, Alabama was the first state to declare Christmas a legal holiday.

In 1932, King George V became the first British monarch to broadcast a Christmas message.

President Franklin Pierce decorated the first official White House Christmas tree in 1856.

During the Middle Ages, Christmas trees were hung upside down.

In Russia, Santa Claus wears a blue suit.

In Ukraine, it's considered good luck if you find a spiderweb on Christmas morning.

The first Santa Claus School opened in September 1937 in Albion, New York.

Jazz great Louis Armstrong was 40 before he got his first Christmas tree. He liked it so much that he took it on tour with him.

The First Lady has trimmed the White House Christmas tree since 1929.

At Christmas, Greeks burn all their old shoes to ward off bad luck in the coming year.

Kanakaloka is the Hawaiian word for Santa Claus.

Duck, Duck, Goose

Only female ducks quack.

Ducks' bones are hollow; that makes their bodies lighter, enabling them to fly.

Geese fly in a V to reduce wind resistance and to keep track of their group.

Ducks can dive as deep as 20 feet underwater to find food.

Ducks waddle because their legs are short and spaced farther apart than those of many other animals. To take steps, they have to swing their bodies from side to side.

There are 11 different kinds of Canadian geese...and they live all over North America.

Male ducks are called drakes. Females are ducks or hens.

Duck feathers are coated with oil and are waterproof. Ducks use their beaks to spread the oil from a special gland at the base of their tail feathers.

Many Canadian geese mate for life.

With one exception (Muscovy), all domesticated ducks are descended from mallards.

It's a Shoe-In

Most common woman's shoe size: 7 ½.

Dr. William Scholl was a podiatrist who became a shoemaker.

A woman wearing stiletto heels exerts 552 pounds of pressure per square inch at the heel.

According to some scholars, Jesus wore a size-10 ½ sandal.

An athletic shoe can stay afloat in the ocean for 10 years.

Sam Snead practiced golfing barefoot.

Shaquille O'Neal wears size-22 shoes.

If your feet just smell bad, it's foot odor. If they smell really bad, it's called "bromidrosis."

Music legend Fats Domino owned over 300 pairs of shoes.

France's King Charles VIII had six toes. This led to the invention of a square-toed men's shoe.

The Battle of Gettysburg began when Confederate soldiers marched into the small town of Gettysburg, Pennsylvania, because they needed new shoes.

First record to make the pop, country, and R&B charts at the same time: Carl Perkins's "Blue Suede Shoes."

Right shoes typically wear out faster than left shoes.

Paris Hilton's feet are so big (size 11) that designers have to custom-make her shoes.

Among the ancient Incas, a couple was considered married when they exchanged sandals.

The "boots" eaten by Charlie Chaplin in *The Gold Rush* (1925) were made of licorice.

U.S. Firsts

First chairman of the Joint Chiefs of Staff:
General Omar Bradley.

Pennsylvania had the United States' first circulating library and the first medical college (at what's now the University of Pennsylvania).

Sanford Dole was the first and only president of the Republic of Hawaii (1894–98).

The first commercial oil well in the United States was dug in Titusville, Pennsylvania, in 1859.

First sorority in the United States: Alpha Delta Pi at Wesleyan College in Macon, Georgia, in 1851.

First state to outlaw slavery: Vermont, in 1777.

Lyndon B. Johnson was the first (and so far the only) U.S. president to be sworn in by a woman...federal judge Sarah T. Hughes, after John F. Kennedy's assassination.

First city to have mechanized street cleaners: Philadelphia.

Stanford graduate Lou Hoover, wife of Herbert Hoover, was the first woman in the United States to receive a geology degree.

Golf Hazards

At many Australian courses, a ball that hits a kangaroo must be played where it lies.

Hubert Green had to play the 1977 U.S. Open with an armed escort due to a death threat.

In golf lingo, a "Captain Kirk" is a shot that goes "where no man has gone before." "Divorce court" is slang for a couple who play together. And caddying for a player who has an awful round is called a "safari."

Among the hazards at the Stanley Golf Course in the Falkland Islands: minefields.

Richard Boxall broke his leg teeing off at the 1991 British Open.

Iowa's Laurens Golf Course is also an airport. (Planes have the right of way.)

At the April Foolish Open in Florida, players have to contend with hazards like clotheslines of laundry.

Pro golfer Andy Bean once had to grab a six-foot alligator by the tail and move it to play his shot.

The Body

Most of your body's motor neurons aren't replaced when they die, so the older you are, the fewer you have.

The mineral content and structure of human bone is nearly identical to some species of South Pacific coral.

When frozen, red blood cells can last up to 10 years.

The aorta, the largest artery in the human body, is about the diameter of a garden hose.

Five largest internal organs of the body: liver, brain, lungs, heart, and kidneys.

Fifteen percent of people have a second toe that's longer than the others.

Blond hair is the finest; black hair is the coarsest.

A human head can remain conscious for about 15 to 20 seconds after it has been decapitated.

Length of a single human DNA molecule, when extended: about 5'5". But all the DNA in a human body could fit inside one ice cube.

It takes 20 different muscles to kiss someone. But beware: kissing can cause wrinkles.

Wrinkles have three main causes: the sun, gravity, and facial expression.

An adult human head weighs 11 pounds—about as much as an average bowling ball.

Human babies are born with 300 bones; adults have 206. The smaller bones fuse together over time to form stronger ones.

Eyelashes are typically the darkest hairs on the body.

Tears are 0.9 percent salt.

Human sweat contains chemicals similar to what skunks spray.

Happy Birthday to You

On March 8, 1969, the *Apollo IX* astronauts sang "Happy Birthday" in outer space.

Stephen Hawking was born on January 8, 1942...the 300th anniversary of the death of Galileo.

First singing telegram: July 28, 1933, delivered to entertainer Rudy Vallee. The song: "Happy Birthday."

On an average day, 7,918 Americans turn 60 years old.

First major leaguer to choose his birthday as his uniform number: Carlos May (#17), born on May 17, 1948.

Instead of birthday cake, Russian children get birthday pie.

CBS anchor Dan Rather was born on Halloween: October 31, 1931.

Most people share their birthdays with at least 9 million other people.

* * *

MNEMONIC DEVICES

- **Every good boy does fine:** The notes on the five lines of the treble clef musical scale, from bottom to top—E, G, B, D, F.

- **Roy G. Biv:** Colors of the rainbow—red, orange, yellow, green, blue, indigo, violet.

- **Some men hate each other:** The Great Lakes—Superior, Michigan, Huron, Erie, and Ontario.

- **Please excuse my dear Aunt Sally:** The order in which mathematical operations should be performed—parentheses, exponents, multiplication, division, addition, subtraction.

An Average Page

If you're older than 65, there's an above-average chance you put relish on your hot dog.

The average player's height in the NBA: 6' 7.4".

Average age of a PGA Tour pro: 35.

Average participant in fantasy football: white male, married, age 37, with a household income of $78,000.

Swing speed of the average male golfer: 93.75 mph. Of Tiger Woods: 125 mph.

If you're average, your lifetime will last about 2,475,576,000 seconds.

If you're average, you'll visit the bathroom 2,500 times this year. (Happy reading!)

The average British adult drinks 228 pints of beer per year.

In a lifetime, most people eat around 60,000 pounds of food.

Altogether, American kids make about $8.6 million per year in allowance.

More World Records

The world's shortest escalator is at a shopping mall in Japan. It rises two feet, eight inches.

Bertha Van der Merwe from South Africa holds the record for staying awake: 282 hours, 55 minutes.

Record name: a Florida baby was named Truewilllaughinglifebuckyboomermanifestdestiny. (Middle name: George.)

World's tallest identical twins: Michael and James Lanier—they're both 7'4" tall.

World's shortest stage play: Samuel Beckett's *Breath*— 35 seconds of screams and heavy breathing.

World record for the cat with the most toes: Jake, who has 28 (seven on each paw).

In New Mexico, don't miss the "World's Largest Roadrunner." He stands 20 feet tall and is made of garbage.

In 2003, Andy Martell of Canada created the world's largest ball of plastic wrap: 54 inches across.

World's longest national highway: the Trans-Canada Highway, at 10,781 kilometers (6,699 miles).

Largest age difference for a married couple: 83 years— 22-year-old bride Ely Maryulianti Rahmat from Malaysia married 105-year-old Sudar Marto.

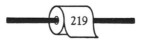

Random Origins

TELETHONS. After writer Damon Runyon died of cancer in 1946, his friends in the entertainment industry established the Damon Runyon Cancer Research Foundation. The charity held its first big fund-raiser in April 1949—an unprecedented 16-hour television broadcast to solicit donations. This "telethon" ("television" plus "marathon") was the idea of NBC executive Sylvester Weaver, who thought big TV events would entice people to buy television sets. That first telethon wasn't much different from today's telethons: a big star (Milton Berle) hosted; an on-screen bank of phone operators accepted call-in donations; and stars of movies, TV, and Broadway performed and pleaded for money. The broadcast raised $100,000 for cancer research.

TREE-SHAPED AIR FRESHENERS. In 1951, in his garage laboratory, a New York chemist named Julius Sämann created the world's first air freshener made just for the car. Made of a material similar to a disposable beer coaster, Sämann's prototype was pine-scented...so he cut the freshener into the shape of a tree. Sämann got a patent and opened the Car-Freshener Corporation. Today, Little Trees are the top selling air fresheners in the world. And all of them are tree-shaped, even the top-selling "New Car Scent."

READER'S DIGEST. In 1914, DeWitt Wallace suffered injuries fighting in World War I and was sent to a French hospital to recover. He was incredibly bored and wanted something to read. That gave Wallace an idea: a pocket-size anthology of short articles on many topics, written in basic, easy-to-understand English. When he got back to the United States after the war, he approached several publishers with his idea. They all rejected it. So in 1922, he printed 5,000 copies of his magazine himself. All of them sold, and the popularity of *Reader's Digest* grew quickly. By 1926, the magazine had a circulation of 40,000. Today its readership is 38 million.

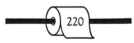

Exceptional Talents

Helen Keller could identify her friends by their odors.

An Australian man named Simon Robinson holds the record for the loudest scream: 128 decibels—almost as loud as a jet engine.

On his debut album, *For You*, Prince played 27 different instruments.

Franz Schubert had a great memory. He wrote versions of his song "Die Forelle" from memory for his friends.

Born in 1795, Miranda Stuart from England posed as a man to attend medical school and become a doctor. She was one of the most successful of her era, and her gender wasn't discovered until she died in 1865.

England's King James I was thinking ahead; he wrote about the health hazards of smoking in his 1604 treatise "Counterblaste to Tobacco."

Muhammad Ali had a hit single on his 1963 album *I Am the Greatest*—a cover of "Stand by Me."

The father of the early 20th-century Supreme Court justice Oliver Wendell Holmes Jr. discovered the adrenal gland.

Trick-shot golfer Wedgy Winchester could chip a coin into a golf hole from 20 yards.

Most successful song by a solo female artist: Whitney Houston's "I Will Always Love You."

Marie Tussad, who was suspected of royalist sympathies and arrested during the French Revolution, was sentenced to die on the guillotine, but was spared because of her wax-sculpting talents.

At 16, Rick James went AWOL from the U.S. Navy, fled to Canada, and joined a band with Neil Young.

Ah, Britannia

First recorded appearance of a garden gnome in England: 1840. (They were first made in Germany.)

In Lancashire, in 1617, King James I knighted a piece of steak Sir Loin, thus coining the term. Why? He thought it was especially tasty.

According to studies, married people in England spend about 25 minutes per week kissing.

Nine percent of the people in England drink neither tea nor coffee.

A 2006 study found that the average white middle-aged Briton was healthier than the average white middle-aged American.

Fifty-eight percent of the London Underground, the city's transit system, is actually above-ground.

There are 66 cities in the United Kingdom: 50 in England, five in Wales, six in Scotland, and five in Northern Ireland.

In the United Kingdom, about 50 instant lottery tickets are sold every second.

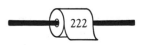

Leaders of the World

Nine U.S. presidents never attended college: George Washington, Abraham Lincoln, Harry S. Truman, Andrew Jackson, Martin Van Buren, Zachary Taylor, Millard Fillmore, Andrew Johnson, and Grover Cleveland.

Former British prime ministers John Major and Tony Blair once worked for London's power company.

Shortest time in office for a Canadian prime minister: John Turner, 79 days in 1984.

Said Musa—prime minister of Belize from 1998 to 2008—wore jeans and a T-shirt to his inauguration.

U.S. president Woodrow Wilson couldn't read until he was 10 years old.

Mexico's president Felipe Calderon (who took office in 2006) once told MTV that he "regretted not having more fun as a child."

Former U.S. president Jimmy Carter's English teacher introduced him to *War and Peace* when he was 12. He was disappointed to learn that it wasn't about cowboys and Indians.

In 2007, the magazine *Vanity Fair* listed French president Nicolas Sarkozy as number 68 on its 100 best-dressed list.

Vaclav Havel, former president of the Czech Republic, is a huge fan of both Frank Zappa and Lou Reed.

U.S. president James A. Garfield could write Latin with one hand and Greek with the other—at the same time.

British journalist Carol Thatcher, the daughter of former prime minister Margaret Thatcher, won the 2005 season of the UK reality show *I'm a Celebrity... Get Me Out of Here!*

223

Under the Weather

You can use pinecones to forecast the weather: when rain is on the way, the scales close.

Technically, a drizzle is 14 drops of rain per square foot per second; a light rain is 26 drops.

The first type of umbrella was invented by the ancient Egyptians as a sun shield.

According to weather forecasters, "scattered showers" means a 10 percent chance of rain.

In 1823, Charles Macintosh patented the waterproof cloth later used to make raincoats.

A whistle sounds louder just before it rains.

Average life span of an umbrella: 1 ½ years.

According to the U.S. Weather Service, one-day forecasts are right 75 percent of the time.

The Chinese invented the first waterproof umbrella using wax and lacquer.

A lightning bolt can travel at a speed of 60,000 miles per second.

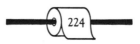

Celebrity Gossip

James Earl Jones, who was the voice of Darth Vader in the *Star Wars* series, used to stutter. When he was in high school, the stuttering was so severe that he rarely spoke to anyone.

Before he became famous, Sylvester Stallone cleaned lion cages.

On his business cards, Verne Troyer, who played Mini Me in the *Austin Powers* movies, calls himself "the biggest little guy in the business."

Oscar-winning movie stars live longer than those who don't win.

French artist Henri Rousseau—famous for painting exotic jungle scenes—never left the city of Paris.

Track and field star Jackie Joyner-Kersee suffers from asthma.

After only three months in school, seven-year-old Thomas Edison was sent home for constantly asking "Why?" His frustrated teacher sent a note home to Edison's parents claiming that the boy was slow.

They Write the Songs

Sting wrote the Police song "Every Breath You Take" on Noel Coward's piano.

Neil Sedaka composed "Oh! Carol" for Carole King in 1959. She later recorded "Oh! Neil."

Cole Porter's original lyrics to "I Get a Kick Out of You" referenced the Lindberghs: he changed them after the couple's baby was kidnapped.

Carl Perkins wrote the song "Blue Suede Shoes" on an old potato sack.

Willie Nelson wrote "Crazy" for country singer Billy Walker—and Walker turned it down. (Patsy Cline didn't.)

Songwriter Jim Weatherly wrote "Midnight Train to Georgia" in the 1970s after a conversation with actress Farrah Fawcett, in which she said she had to run to catch a "midnight plane to Houston."

The melody for Nat King Cole's 1954 hit "Smile" was composed by Charlie Chaplin.

Henry Wadsworth Longfellow never actually saw the 53-foot waterfall Minnehaha that he wrote about in his 1853 poem "The Song of Hiawatha."

Barry Manilow didn't write "I Write the Songs"—Bruce Johnston did...and it was about Beach Boy Brian Wilson.

Kris Kristofferson, Janis Joplin's former boyfriend, penned her hit single "Me and Bobby McGee."

The John Fogerty song "Centerfield" plays continuously at the National Baseball Hall of Fame in Cooperstown, New York.

John Lennon's inspiration for the 1967 song "Good Morning, Good Morning" was a cereal commercial.

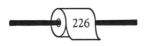

Men & Women

During a conversation, women make eye contact 15 percent more often than men do.

In 2008, there were 140,000 stay-at-home dads in the United States, up 64 percent from a decade before.

According to the *Boston Globe*, the estimated salary for a stay-at-home parent is $138,000.

Women look at other women more often than they look at men.

At age 21, women are more likely than men to be enrolled in college.

Almost twice as many women as men buy gifts for Mother's Day.

Thirty-five percent of teenage girls who use the Internet write blogs; only 20 percent of teen boys do.

Men who have a heart attack in a public place often walk outside when they start to feel ill, but women are more likely to go into the bathroom.

Men can read smaller print than women can, but women can hear better.

Men are more likely than women to be left-handed.

Studies reveal that men prefer classical music while on hold; women prefer light jazz.

More women than men talk to their cars.

*   *   *

"Have you noticed that all the people in favor of birth control are already born?"

—Benny Hill

Money Matters

The U.S. Treasury began printing paper money in 1862 because there was a coin shortage.

There are $171 million worth of pennies and $2.6 billion worth of dimes in circulation.

The paper for U.S. currency is made exclusively by the Massachusetts-based Crane & Company.

There are 26 states named on the back of a $5 bill.

In 1792, the United States established the dollar as its official currency.

It costs about 1.2 cents to mint a penny.

At the end of the Civil War, 33 percent of U.S. paper currency was counterfeit.

Eighteen percent of U.S. coins are contaminated with the *E. coli* bacteria.

The three people shown on today's U.S. currency who weren't presidents: Alexander Hamilton, Benjamin Franklin, and Sacagawea.

Who's on the $500 bill? William McKinley. The $1,000 bill? Grover Cleveland.

U.S. paper currency is fluorescent under UV light.

The only First Lady to have her image used on U.S. currency: Martha Washington, on a silver certificate in 1886.

Original gold coins included $10, $5, and $2.50 values.

About half of the U.S. currency printed are $1 bills.

The U.S. Mint once considered producing doughnut-shaped coins.

Alabama's state quarter spells Helen Keller's name in Braille.

Everyday Dangers

According to statistics, about 7,000 people a year are injured by falling off of chairs.

Most dangerous cheerleading moves: the "pyramid" and the "basket toss."

What recreational activity causes more bone fractures than any other? Aerobic dancing.

Hot drinks cause more injuries than lawn mowers do.

About 2,000 people are injured every year from trying to pry frozen foods apart.

More people die while playing golf than any other sport. Leading causes: heart attacks and strokes.

Deadliest weather phenomenon in the United States: lightning.

Cotton swabs cause more injuries than razor blades.

More than 6,000 Americans are injured every year by toilet seats.

Odds of being killed by fireworks: one in 615,488.

Survivor Realities

The inaugural 2000 season of *Survivor* is often credited as the beginning of the "reality television revolution."

The fourth season of *Survivor* was supposed to take place in Jordan, but because of the 9/11 terrorist attacks, the producers relocated to the Marquesas Islands in French Polynesia.

The show's host, Jeff Probst, is also an ordained minister.

All of the show's contestants receive a stipend (between $2,500 to $100,000) for participating. The amount increases the longer they're in the game.

Michael Skupin, who took part in the Australian season, fell into a campfire during filming and was evacuated from the set. Then, after he got home, members of the animal rights group PETA attacked him with pepper spray for killing a pig on the show.

British television producer Charlie Parsons came up with the idea and format for *Survivor* in 1992.

Tina Wesson, winner of the 2001 season, wasn't originally selected to be on the show. The producers called her when someone else dropped out.

Oldest *Survivor* contestant: Rudy Boesch was 72 when he competed on the first season. Youngest: 19-year-old Spencer Duhm (season 18).

The first season's winner, Richard Hatch, spent three years in jail for tax evasion. Why? He didn't properly report his $1 million prize to the IRS.

The Australian season didn't actually take place in the Outback. The camps were in a semiremote area about three hours from Cairns, a coastal city in the northeastern part of the country.

Presidential Pastimes

When John Tyler was told that he'd been elected president, he was on his knees playing marbles.

Calvin Coolidge liked to have his head rubbed while he ate breakfast in bed.

Abraham Lincoln enjoyed Edgar Allan Poe's poem "The Raven."

James A. Garfield was a fan of Jane Austen.

Benjamin Harrison liked to play billiards and go duck hunting.

For fun, Calvin Coolidge rode a mechanical horse that he kept in the White House.

An avid collector, Franklin D. Roosevelt had a stamp collection that grew to 25,000 stamps by the 1930s and was worth millions.

Calvin Coolidge played the harmonica.

Speed-reader Jimmy Carter was once clocked reading 2,000 words a minute.

James A. Garfield juggled Indian clubs, which look like bowling pins, to build his muscles.

Thomas Jefferson, James A. Garfield, and Rutherford B. Hayes all liked to play chess.

Thomas Jefferson collected maps, minerals, fossils, bones, and Native American artifacts.

John F. Kennedy collected scrimshaw—carved or engraved ivory.

Harry S. Truman walked two miles every morning at a brisk clip of 128 steps per minute.

Jimmy Carter is an avid fan of Putt-Putt golf.

Franklin D. Roosevelt watched only short films with happy endings.

Can't Win 'Em All

In 1966, British fans booed Bob Dylan when he used an electric guitar for the first time onstage.

Winston Churchill called Mahatma Gandhi "a seditious lawyer...posing as a half-dressed fakir."

Japanese pro golfer Masashi Ozaki was uninvited from the 1988 Masters when rumors of his mob connections surfaced.

Tchaikovsky called Brahms's piano concertos "dried stuff."

In 1967, Jimi Hendrix opened for the Monkees...and was booed.

After pitcher Buck O'Brien gave up five runs in the first inning of a 1912 World Series game, his Red Sox teammates beat him up.

German psychologist Karen Horney challenged Sigmund Freud's theories and suggested that men suffered from "womb envy."

The term "fan" was first used to insult baseball "fanatics" in the late 1800s.

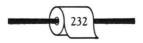

It's Called a...

Siffleuse...a female wrestler

Cheek...the side of a hammer

Flink...a group of 12 or more cows

Pintle...the pin that holds a hinge
together

Archetier...a person who makes bows for
violins and other instruments

Yeevil...a fork used for pitching manure

Zugzwang...making a bad move in chess

Plectrum...a tool used to pluck or strum a
stringed instrument, like a guitar pick

Skirl...a group of pipers (A group of
harpists is called a melody.)

Peloton...the main cluster of riders
in a bicycle race

Digitabulists...a person who collects
thimbles

Alipile...a person who removes armpit
hair professionally

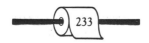

Anthems

Hawaii's unofficial anthem, "Aloha 'Oe" ("Farewell to Thee") was written in 1877 by Lili'uokalani, the islands' last queen.

Spain's national anthem has no official lyrics.

The 1862 Civil War song "Battle Cry of Freedom" was so popular in the northern United States that 14 printing presses couldn't meet the demand for sheet music.

The theme song for *Monty Python's Flying Circus*: "The Liberty Bell" by John Philip Sousa.

"Taps," written by Union general Daniel Butterfield, was also used by the Confederate army.

Michael Jackson's estate owns the rights to South Carolina's state anthem, "South Carolina on My Mind."

Teacher Katharine Bates wrote "America the Beautiful" in 1893 after viewing Colorado's Pike's Peak.

The Beatles' "All You Need Is Love" opens with a few bars of the French national anthem.

The Dutch national anthem, "Het Wilhelmus," is the world's oldest. It was first performed in 1574.

Woody Guthrie wrote the folk anthem "This Land Is Your Land" as a protest of Irving Berlin's "God Bless America."

World's newest national anthem: Nepal's "Sayaun Thunga Phool Ka" ("Hundreds of Flowers"), adopted in 2007.

The music for California's state anthem ("I Love You, California") was composed by a man named Abraham F. Frankenstein.

Hard Workers

With 8,833 wins, Bill Shoemaker is the most successful jockey of all time.

King Frederick II of Prussia (1712–86) wrote 120 flute concertos, more than any other composer.

Author Isaac Asimov (1920–92) wrote or edited more than 500 books in his lifetime.

Total number of concerts played by the Grateful Dead: 2,317.

Susan Butcher won the world's longest dogsled race, the Iditarod, four times.

Russian songwriter Irving Berlin wrote more than 1,000 tunes.

Vin Scully has been the "Voice of the Dodgers" since 1950—the longest tenure of any sportscaster with one team.

It took Leo Tolstoy nearly 10 years to write *War and Peace*, and it was originally published in six volumes.

Antonio Vivaldi composed 488 concertos, more than any other composer.

Movie Price Tags

Marlon Brando was paid $3.7 million for two weeks of work for his cameo role in *Superman.*

First movie to earn $100 million: *Jaws* (1975). First movie to earn $200 million: *Jaws.*

Highest-grossing golf movies: *Tin Cup* ($53.9 million) and *Caddyshack* ($39.8 million).

Biggest Hollywood bomb ever: *The Adventures of Pluto Nash* (2002). It lost more than $95 million.

Clint Eastwood's salary for the 1964 spaghetti Western *A Fistful of Dollars*: $15,000.

Julia Roberts earned $50,000 for *Mystic Pizza* in 1988, $300,000 for *Pretty Woman* in 1990, and $20 million for *Erin Brockovich* in 2000.

Dustin Hoffman's salary for *The Graduate* (1967): $17,000.

Kevin Smith's comedy *Clerks* (1994) was made on a budget of $26,800.

Highest-grossing Western: *Dances with Wolves*, which made $394.2 million worldwide.

At $3.9 million, *Ben-Hur* (1925) was the most expensive silent film ever made.

Pulp Fiction cost $8 million to make, of which $5 million was for actors' salaries.

The Miami Police Department's annual budget equals 83 percent of what it cost to make the movie *Miami Vice* in 2006.

For her role in *Cleopatra*, Elizabeth Taylor was the first female actor to get a $1 million film contract.

It cost $3 million to build the *Titanic*...and $100 million to make the movie.

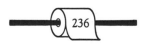

236

X-treme Weather

The temperature has never reached 100°F in either Alaska or Hawaii.

Cherrapunji, India, is the wettest inhabited place on earth, with 428 inches of rain per year.

Highest temperature ever recorded at the South Pole: 8°F.

Chicago's average winter temperature is colder than that of Reykjavik, Iceland.

Tornadoes strike most often between 4:00 and 6:00 p.m., March through July.

In 1921, a hurricane deposited 23 inches of rain on Texas in one day.

A lightning bolt strikes so fast that it could circle the globe eight times in a second.

The warmest city in the United States, on average, is Key West, Florida. Coldest: International Falls, Minnesota.

Dust from the Sahara desert has been carried by the wind as far as Chicago.

Wettest city in the United States: Hilo, Hawaii. Driest: Yuma, Arizona.

Driest inhabited place on earth: Aswan, Egypt, receives only 0.02 inch of rain per year.

Snowiest city in the United States: Blue Canyon, California, with 204 inches (17 feet) per year.

Winds that blow toward the equator curve west.

Florida has more tornadoes per square mile than any other state.

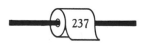

All About Words

There are no words in the English language that rhyme with "orange," "silver," "month," and "purple."

The letter combination "ough" can be pronounced eight different ways.

The Swedish group ABBA learned to sing their English songs phonetically.

ABBA also had the highest-charting single in which both the song and band's name were palindromes: "SOS."

The only three English words that end in "ceed": succeed, proceed, and exceed.

Stevie Wonder released a 1968 album under the name Eivets Rednow.

What does KGB stand for? *Komitet Gosudarstvennoy Bezopasnosti* (or Committee for State Security, in English.)

The Japanese word *koroski* means "death induced by overwork."

In Canada, a left-hander is known as a "silly-sider."

*Saippuakivikauppias…*Finnish for "lye merchant."

Only word in the English language that begins and ends with "und": underground.

What is *Nessiteras rhombopteryx*? The scientific name for the Loch Ness Monster...and an anagram for "monster hoax by Sir Peters."

The "Ye" in "Ye Olde Taverne" is pronounced "the," not "yee."

The Simpsons cartoonist Matt Groening's name rhymes with "raining."

In *The Matrix*, Neo is often referred to as "the One." (One is an anagram of Neo.)

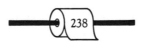

Higher Education

Most college grads live in urban areas—about twice as many as elsewhere.

Harvard University started out as New College in 1636 with nine students and one instructor.

Over a lifetime, a college graduate earns an average of $1 million more than a high school grad.

In 2008, about 18 million students were enrolled in U.S. colleges and universities.

Oldest continuously operating high school in America: Boston Latin, established in 1635.

In 1963, Rice University in Houston became the first U.S. university to establish a department of space science.

Yale University granted the first medical diploma in the United States in 1729.

Oberlin College in Ohio was one of the first U.S. colleges to admit African Americans and women.

Usually, a "college" provides only undergraduate programs, whereas a "university" offers both undergraduate and graduate courses of study.

During the 1960s, Stephen King wrote a column called "King's Garbage Truck" for a University of Maine magazine.

Mary Lyon founded the first women's college in America, Mount Holyoke Seminary in Massachusetts, in 1837.

Yale University is home to the oldest college newspaper in the United States, the Yale Daily News.

Adjusted for inflation, it now costs twice as much to attend a four-year college than it did 25 years ago.

Doctor! Doctor!

Every year, U.S. doctors leave surgical tools inside about 1,500 patients.

What do revolutionary Che Guevara and clairvoyant Nostradamus have in common? Both had careers as doctors.

Jane Delano, a relative of Franklin Delano Roosevelt, founded the American Red Cross Nursing Service.

Elizabeth Blackwell was the first woman to graduate from a U.S. medical school and the first female doctor in the United States.

Busiest time of year for plastic surgeons: Christmas.

Only 11 percent of American doctors play golf.

Walt Whitman served for three years in the Civil War...as a nurse.

In 1988, Beach Boy Brian Wilson and his psychiatrist, Dr. Eugene Landy, recorded a rap song called "Smart Girls."

The number-one reason Americans give for visiting the doctor is "upper respiratory tract infection."

Swiss psychiatrist Carl Jung introduced the concepts of extroverted and introverted personalities.

There are more psychiatrists than mail carriers in the United States.

Child-care guru Dr. Benjamin Spock won the 1924 Olympic gold medal in rowing.

Hippocrates, the "father of medicine," prescribed pigeon poop as a cure for baldness.

Sigmund Freud pioneered the use of cocaine as an anesthetic.

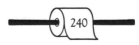

A Pirate's Life

THE GILDED AGE. The "Golden Age of Piracy" was an outbreak of piracy in nearly all the world's oceans that lasted from about 1650 until 1725. Most modern ideas of pirates come from this period, and history's most notorious pirate leaders—like Blackbeard, Henry Morgan, and William Kidd—all sailed during this time.

NOT A BAD JOB. During the 17th and 18th centuries, pirates made more money and had better working conditions than men onboard merchant and navy ships. Pirates voted before mounting an attack, and all booty was distributed among the crew, with the captain getting a larger portion and the rest shared evenly.

UNCONVENTIONAL PIRATES. Youngest known pirate: John King was nine years old when he was killed on the *Whydah*, which sank in a 1717 storm off the coast of Massachusetts. And Grace O'Malley, a 16th-century Irish female pirate, commanded three ships and employed about 200 men.

PIRATE JUSTICE. A pirate who broke his oath to his crew (by hoarding more than his share of the loot, for example) would be marooned on an island with a container of water and a loaded gun.

DON'T MESS WITH CAESAR. Around 75 BC, before he became emperor of Rome, Julius Caesar was a popular soldier and speaker who was captured by pirates. Initially, they wanted to ransom him for 20 gold pieces, but Caesar said he was worth more and convinced them to ask for 50 instead. After the Roman government paid the ransom, Caesar put together a search party, found the pirates, and had them all killed.

Hot & Cold

Iceland is home to 120 glaciers...and more than 100 volcanoes.

Only two U.S. towns have an extinct volcano within their city limits: Portland and Bend, Oregon.

During most of earth's geologic history, the North and South poles had no ice.

You can't make snowballs at the South Pole...the snow is too dry.

The only still-growing glacier in the world is Argentina's Perito Moreno.

On the scenic Icefields Parkway in Alberta, Canada, you can drive past three massive glaciers.

Antarctica's only active volcano: Mount Erebus. Its only river: the Onyx.

Largest desert in the world: Antarctica. Technically, the definition of a desert is a place with little or no rainfall, so Antarctica, which receives almost no rain, is the world's largest.

More Real Headlines

Man Eating Piranha Mistakenly
Sold as Pet Fish

Smithsonian May Cancel Bombing
of Japan Exhibits

A Reason for Odor Found at Sewer Plant

Man Accused of Shooting Neighbor,
Dog Held for Trial

Something Went Wrong in Jet Crash,
Experts Say

Utah Girl Does Well in Dog Shows

Arafat Swears in Cabinet

Lansing Residents Can Drop Off Trees

Poll Says 53 Percent Believe that
Media Often Makes Mistakes

Blind Woman Gets New Kidney from Dad
She Hasn't Seen in Years

Some Pieces of Rock Hudson Sold at Auction

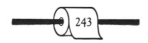

Assorted Animals

Ninety percent of all animal species in history are now extinct.

The ancient Egyptians bought jewelry for their pet crocodiles.

Cats were first domesticated around 8000 BC.

Menoceras, a prehistoric rhinoceros that was the size of a pony, roamed America's Midwest about 20 million years ago.

The last cow to be kept at the White House: Pauline, who belonged to William Howard Taft (1909–13).

Most dinosaurs walked on their toes.

In ancient Egypt, killing a cat was a capital offense.

Giraffes have seven vertebrae in their necks...the same as humans. Theirs are just much larger.

Some ferrets sleep so soundly that they won't wake up even if you jostle them.

Napoléon's favorite horse was a gray Arabian named Marengo.

Before lawn mowers, grazing sheep often kept golf courses trim. One course in Florida tried using goats, but it didn't work—alligators ate them.

Giant pandas have evolved to eat mostly bamboo, but technically they're carnivores.

Benjamin Franklin wanted to make the turkey, not the eagle, America's national bird. He believed the bald eagle didn't live its life "honestly" and considered the turkey a more "respectable" bird.

World's largest frog: the goliath from Africa. It can grow to be 12 ½ inches long and weigh about seven pounds.

Land o' Lakes

The Great Salt Lake is about eight times saltier than seawater.

Lake Mashu, Japan, has the world's clearest water. It's transparent to a depth of 136 feet.

Biggest source of pollution in Lake Ontario: Lake Erie.

Deepest lake in the United States: Crater Lake in Oregon, at 1,943 feet.

Lake Huron's Manitoulin Island is the largest island in a freshwater lake.

Minnesota has 201 lakes named Mud, 154 named Long, and 123 named Rice.

Texas has just one natural lake—Caddo Lake—and 190 man-made lakes and reservoirs.

The largest underground lake in the United States: the Lost Sea in (or under) Sweetwater, Tennessee.

Largest aquifer in the United States: the Ogallala Aquifer in the Great Plains, which covers more than 170,000 square miles in eight states.

There are about 3 million lakes in Canada.

Quirky Folks

Frank Sinatra showered four times a day.

King George III once referred to Benjamin Franklin as an "evil genius."

Napoléon Bonaparte was afraid of cats.

Lou Gehrig's only film role was as himself—a former baseball player turned rancher in the movie *Rawhide*.

Kevin Spacey initially wanted to be a stand-up comic.

Artist Paul Gauguin worked on the Panama Canal in 1887.

Robin Williams grew up in a 30-room mansion in Bloomfield Hills, Michigan.

Early job for French actor Gerard Depardieu: door-to-door soap salesman.

Shirley Temple failed a screen test for the *Our Gang* movie comedies.

Bob Hope was jailed as a youth for stealing tennis balls.

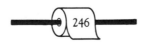

Wheel of Fortune

Since it first went on the air in 1975,*Wheel of Fortune* has given away more than $180 million in cash and prizes.

On average, Vanna White claps her hands 720 times per episode.

First letter White turned on the show's puzzle board: T.

Wheel of Fortune's wheel weighs about 4,000 pounds.

Of the more than 3,000 people who try out, fewer than 500 make it onto the show.

Biggest winner: in 2008, New Jersey's Michelle Loewenstein won $1,026,080.

Inspiration for the show's puzzle board: the children's game Hangman.

Host Pat Sajak served in the army during Vietnam, where he worked on a military radio show in Saigon. He began each day with the phrase "Good morning, Vietnam!"

Wheel of Fortune is the longest-running syndicated show in television history.

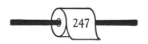

What Could've Been

W. C. Fields was the first choice for the Wizard in *The Wizard of Oz*.

Kate Hudson was originally cast as William's sister in *Almost Famous* (2000). She took over the Penny Lane role when Sarah Polley dropped out of the film.

Meryl Streep's role in *Out of Africa* (1985) was first offered to Audrey Hepburn.

Harrison Ford turned down the lead role in *Jurassic Park*.

Uma Thurman originally turned down the role of Mia in *Pulp Fiction* (1994). Director Quentin Tarantino persuaded her by reading the script to her over the phone.

The roles played by Tom Cruise and Renee Zellweger in *Jerry Maguire* were originally written for Tom Hanks and Winona Ryder.

One actor considered for the Don Corleone role in *The Godfather*: Laurence Olivier.

Chris O'Donnell was offered Will Smith's role in *Men in Black*, but turned it down.

The first choices for leads in *The African Queen* were John Mills and Bette Davis.

Director David Lean wanted Albert Finney for the lead in *Lawrence of Arabia*, but Katharine Hepburn urged the producer to cast Peter O'Toole instead.

Eddie Murphy's role in *Beverly Hills Cop* (1984) was originally written for Sylvester Stallone.

Marie Osmond turned down the female lead (Sandy) in *Grease*.

Mel Gibson and Tim Curry both auditioned for the role of Mozart in *Amadeus* (1984).

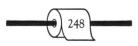

Human Relations

According to studies, the primary cause of depression in married people is being married. In unmarried people, it's being single.

Forty million Americans use online dating services.

Forty percent of American women say they have asked a man out on a date. (And 93 percent of them got a "yes.")

A third of all pet owners admit to having more photos of their pet than of their spouse.

The U.S. divorce rate has dropped almost every year since 1979.

About 80 percent of the talking you do each day is to yourself.

Thirty-five percent of parents play video games with their kids. Of those parents, 47 percent are women.

On average, people stand 14 inches apart when having a conversation.

The three most common fears among American adults: spiders, social situations, and flying.

Tasty Titles

The St. Louis grocer who created Log Cabin syrup named it in honor of Abe Lincoln's first home.

In Italian, *muscatel* means "wine with flies in it."

The French name for potato: *pomme de terre,* or "apple of the earth."

James H. Salisbury, an American doctor who advocated eating red meat, gave his name to the Salisbury steak.

The Big Dipper constellation is known as "the Casserole" in France.

Pretzels that have no salt on them are called "baldies."

Mrs. Smith of pie fame was actually a Pennsylvania woman named Amanda Smith who supported her family by cooking pies.

The lollipop was named in 1908 by George Smith after a popular racehorse, Lolly Pop.

Burrito is Spanish for "little donkey."

Amazing Animals

In 2007, British marine biologists discovered the oldest living animal, a clam more than 400 years old.

The longest recorded flight of a chicken: 13 seconds.

Of the world's 10 deadliest snakes, seven live in Australia. But only about four people die of snakebites there each year.

According to scientists: the five smartest primates after humans are orangutans, chimpanzees, spider monkeys, gorillas, and surilis.

Rats can go without water longer than camels can.

The most endangered mammal in the United States: the black-footed ferret. It's also the only ferret species native to the region.

Longest flying-squirrel flight on record: 2.5 miles.

By the age of 15, most tuna have swum more than a million miles.

As a species, the platypus is 150 million years old. (Humans are about 200,000 years old.)

Gray whales make the longest annual migration of any mammal...12,000 miles round-trip.

Domestic cats thrive in more places on earth than any other mammal species besides humans.

North America has the greatest diversity of freshwater mussels in the world—297 species.

Alpaca wool comes in 22 natural colors—the most color variety of any wool-bearing animal.

In 2004, an English mastiff named Tia gave birth to a world-record 24 puppies in one litter.

Real Names

Sandra Dee...Alexandra Cymbliak Zuck

Roy Rogers...Leonard Franklin Slye

Boris Karloff...William Henry Pratt

Demi Moore...Demetria Guynes

Sade...Helen Folassade Adu

Johnny Cash...J. R. Cash

Jane Seymour...Joyce Frankenberg

Minnesota Fats...Rudolf Wanderone

Audrey Hepburn...Edda Kathleen van
Heemstra Hepburn-Ruston

Albert Brooks...Albert Lawrence Einstein

Whoopi Goldberg...Caryn Elaine Johnson

Michael Caine...Maurice Joseph Mickelwhite

* * *

"My wife and I were happy for 20 years.
Then we met." —Henny Youngman

Opera Notes

Jacopo Peri's *Dafne*, composed in 1594, was the first Italian opera.

"Here Comes the Bride," from Richard Wagner's 1850 opera *Lohengrin*, was first used as a wedding march during the Civil War.

The 1957 Bugs Bunny cartoon *What's Opera, Doc?* adapted music from Wagner's operas.

The female lead in an opera is the *prima donna*. The male lead is the *primo uomo*.

Giuseppe Verdi's opera *Aida* premiered in Cairo, Egypt, in 1871 to celebrate the opening of the Suez Canal two years earlier.

In 1955, Marian Anderson became the first African American to perform at the Metropolitan Opera in New York.

In *Pretty Woman* (1990), the opera Richard Gere takes Julia Roberts to is *La Traviata*... which is about a prostitute who falls for a wealthy man.

Record number of curtain calls after an opera performance: Luciano Pavarotti, with 165.

Hawaii's Spooky Spots

THE NU'UANU PALI LOOKOUT

Today, this is a tourist attraction overlooking the northeastern coast of Oahu, but in 1795, it was the site of one of the deadliest battles in Hawaii's history. That year, King Kamehameha I, who became one of the islands' most powerful rulers, had nearly completed his quest to unite the islands' various tribes under one king. He'd already conquered several other islands, and only Oahu stood in his way. So he gathered 10,000 soldiers and attacked the island's chief. As the battle raged, the fighting spread into the mountains and Kamehameha's army gained ground. Finally, his soldiers trapped their enemies on a cliff atop the Nu'uanu Pali, a pass through the mountains. Kamehameha pressed on, eventually driving hundreds of enemy soldiers over the cliff—a 1,000-foot plunge to their deaths. Eventually, the leader of Oahu surrendered, and soon after, Kamehameha seized power and became the first official monarch of the Kingdom of Hawaii.

In the years that followed, rumors about the pass being haunted began circulating. The Hawaiians already observed many superstitions: They didn't carry pork over the pass, because they believed the fire goddess Pele, who lived on the eastern side of the mountains, didn't approve. (She was in an ongoing battle with a half-man, half-pig god.) In another story, a lizardlike creature that could take the form of a beautiful woman would lure men into the mountains and kill them. Finally, during the 1800s, men building a road through the pass found several hundred skulls, believed to be the remains of Kamehameha's enemies. That just fueled the legends, and today, locals aren't surprised when tourists report hearing whispers and cries in the fierce winds atop the Pali lookout.

THE PU-U O MAHUKA HEIAU

This particular site on Oahu's North Shore was one of Hawaii's largest and most sacred heiaus, or religious temples. It was a place

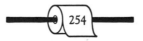

where tribal chiefs held important meetings, their wives gave birth, and their subjects sacrificed humans to the gods.

Supposedly, the heiau is also in the path of a group of mythical apparitions called the Night Marchers. They look like ancient warriors, carry shields and weapons, and pound on battle drums. No one's sure where they're headed or what they're looking for, but locals and tourists who visit the heiau's ruins after dark have reported seeing footprints in the sand and hearing drumbeats and chants in the distance. Fortunately, according to legend, as long as human interlopers don't interrupt a night march or make eye contact with one of the ghosts, they won't be harmed.

THE KONA BEACH HOTEL

Located on the Big Island of Hawaii, this hotel was completely renovated in 2008, but couldn't erase its eerie past: the hotel sits on a plot of land where King Kamehameha I lived until his death in 1819, and his body is buried somewhere beneath the structure. (In accordance with ancient Hawaiian custom, his exact burial site was never disclosed.)

Strange occurrences at the hotel include whispered battle cries, the sound of marchers, and footsteps. But most unsettling is the portrait of Lilioukalani, Hawaii's last queen, on the hotel's first floor. Guests report that the portrait—which hangs at the end of a series honoring the islands' monarchs—glares at people who stop to look at it...and appears to breathe.

* * *

REAL TOMBSTONE INSCRIPTIONS

- "Here lies the body of Jonathan Blake; stepped on the gas instead of the brake."
- "I told you that I was sick!"
- "Looked up the elevator shaft to see if the car was on its way down. It was."

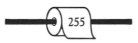

Celebrity Hodgepodge

Princess Diana was ¹⁄₆₄ Armenian.

First left-handed pitcher to win a Cy Young Award: Warren Spahn, in 1957.

Tommy Tune won his third Tony Award for directing the Broadway musical *Nine* in 1982.

When Nicole Richie was nabbed for DUI in 2006, the arrest report listed her weight as 85 pounds.

What position did George W. Bush play for the Midland, Texas, Central Little League? Catcher.

Teddy Roosevelt invited Booker T. Washington to dine at the White House.

American rock band with the most Top-40 hits: the Beach Boys, with 36.

Actor William Bendix, who played Babe Ruth in *The Babe Ruth Story*, was a batboy for the New York Yankees.

Donald Sutherland starred in the 1975 film *Day of the Locust* as a character named Homer Simpson.

The F in F. Murray Abraham's name stands for Fahrid. He's of Italian and Syrian descent.

In the 1951 film *The Tall Target*, Dick Powell played a reporter who tried to stop the assassination of Abraham Lincoln. His name? John Kennedy.

Ronald Reagan asked to use "Born in the U.S.A." for his 1984 campaign song. Bruce Springsteen said no.

In two episodes of TV's *Batman*, Liberace played both the villain Chandell…and his twin brother Harry.

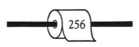

Presidential Numbers

After the Library of Congress burned down in 1814, Thomas Jefferson replenished it with his own 6,000-book collection.

Ronald Reagan saved the lives of 77 people when he worked as a lifeguard.

Oldest presidential candidate: Peter Cooper was 85 when nominated in 1876.

James A. Garfield's monthly wage as a 17-year-old boatman on the Ohio Canal: $14.

Alben W. Barkley, Harry S. Truman's vice president, married his 38-year-old girlfriend while in office. Barkley was 71.

Of all the presidents, Warren G. Harding had the biggest feet. He wore size-14 shoes.

Heaviest U.S. president: William Howard Taft (332 pounds). Lightest: James Madison (100 pounds).

Harry S. Truman's first day as president was on Friday the 13th, 1945.

Tallest U.S. president: Abraham Lincoln (6' 4"). Shortest: James Madison (5' 4").

After William McKinley's assassination, Teddy Roosevelt became the youngest U.S. president at age 42.

President Lyndon B. Johnson flew to his Texas ranch 74 times during his time in office.

William Henry Harrison's inaugural address lasted nearly two hours.

The person most often featured on the cover of Time magazine: Richard Nixon, with 55 appearances.

John Tyler was so poor after leaving office that he was unable to pay his bills until he sold his corn crop.

257

From Our Sponsors

Coca-Cola slogan from 1906: "The Great National Temperance Beverage."

In 1955, Quaker Oats gave away deeds to one square inch of Yukon land with boxes of its cereal.

1940s Wurlitzer Jukebox slogan: "The magic that changes moods."

Ad that enticed Paul "Ace" Frehley to audition for KISS: "Lead guitarist wanted with flash and ability. Album out shortly. No time wasters please."

Ernest Hemingway appeared in magazine ads for Parker Pens and Ballantine Ale.

In 1984, a Canadian farmer rented out ad space on his cows.

First spokesman for Mr. Coffee: Joe DiMaggio.

In the 1890s, Nancy Green became the first living person whose image was trademarked...as Aunt Jemima.

Grape-Nuts cereal was once advertised as an aid to maintaining sobriety.

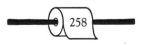

International Landmarks

The Eiffel Tower is repainted by hand every seven years.

World's tallest cathedral spire: the Ulm Cathedral in Germany, at 528 feet.

Largest bell on earth: the Tsar Kolokol in Moscow. It weighs about 200 tons...and has never been rung.

Amsterdam's Homomonument—a pink, triangle-shaped granite platform on one of the city's canals—is a memorial to persecuted gays and lesbians.

World's tallest "pyramid": the Transamerica Pyramid in San Francisco, at 853 feet. World's tallest Egyptian pyramid: the Great Pyramid of Giza, at 481 feet.

The Itaipú Dam on the border of Paraguay and Brasil is the largest hydroelectric complex in the world.

Construction of Milan's great cathedral, the Duomo di Milano, lasted more than 450 years. The first bricks were laid in 1386, and the structure was finished in the 1880s.

It took 20,000 people 22 years to build the Taj Mahal.

More Communications

In 1996, approximately 45 million people worldwide were using the Internet. By 2002, there were 544 million people online.

The average person makes 1,140 phone calls a year.

How much would a year's worth of *New York Times* newspapers weigh? About 520 pounds.

Every day, 7 million new documents are added to the World Wide Web.

One million phone calls are made from the Pentagon every day.

The word "Internet" was coined in 1982.

The first world leader to send an e-mail: Queen Elizabeth II, in 1976.

Martin Cooper created the first cell phone in 1973. It weighed two pounds and looked like a brick.

The first spam e-mail went out on May 3, 1978, and advertised a computer system.

More Americans read supermarket tabloids than newspapers.

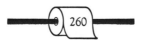

Religion

The three largest religions in the world: Christianity, Islam, and Hinduism.

Worldwide, 16 percent of people say they're non-religious.

Sedlec Ossuary, a Catholic church in the Czech Republic, has a chandelier made out of human bones.

Members of the Old Order Amish speak German during worship services.

Followers of Wicca, a nature-based religion, use pentagrams as symbols of their faith.

About 70,000 people in Australia follow the Jedi religion (inspired by the *Star Wars* films).

In Arabic, the word *Islam* means "submission."

The Bible has been translated into pig latin and Klingon.

In a poll, 12 percent of adults believed Joan of Arc was "Noah's wife."

Shinto originated in Japan around AD 700.

Membership in the Church of Scientology doesn't rule out membership in another religion—some Scientologists cite another religion as their primary one.

According to studies, only three in ten Anglican ministers know how to recite the Ten Commandments correctly.

The seven archangels: Uriel, Raphael, Raguel, Michael, Sariel, Gabriel, and Remiel.

When the world's first automatic telephone answering machine was invented in 1935, it was a big hit with Orthodox Jews—their religion forbids them from answering the phone on the Sabbath.

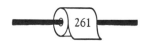

Don't Mess with Texas

Texas was an independent nation from 1836 to 1845.

Sam Houston (the first president of Texas) was adopted into the Cherokee Nation at age 16 and married a Cherokee woman.

In 1860s Fort Worth, a buffalo hide was worth about $1.

In 1844, Dallas consisted of "two small log cabins, and two families of ten to twelve souls." The next year, the United States annexed Texas, and by 1850, Dallas had nearly 1,000 people.

The earliest known Texas pottery dates back to around 500 BC.

The Louisiana Purchase established the northeastern boundary of Texas in 1803.

Despite popular mythology, there were 20 survivors of the 1836 Battle of the Alamo.

The first black man in Texas: a slave named Esteban who traveled with Spanish explorer Cabeza de Vaca during the 1500s.

The first Texas ranches were the 18th-century Spanish mission ranches along the San Antonio River.

Between 1867 and 1887, about 5 million cattle traveled along the Chisholm Trail, a cattle-drive trail from Texas to Kansas, to be shipped and sold to buyers in the East.

First European exploration of the Texas coastline: Spaniard Alonso Alvarez de Pineda in 1519.

Theodore Roosevelt owned the Texas ranch El Capote, which provided horses for him and his Rough Riders at the Battle of San Juan Hill.

The state sport of Texas: rodeo.

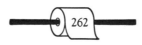

Found in the Ground

Worldwide, about 152,000 metric tons of gold have been mined to date...enough to fill 60 tractor-trailers.

What's fulgerite? "Fossilized lightning," which occurs when a bolt melts sand or soil into a glass tube.

If you hit a diamond hard with a hammer, it will shatter.

Chemical most used by humans: salt. It has more than 14,000 known uses.

New Mexico's White Sands National Monument is in the world's largest field of gypsum sand, a fine white rock that dissolves in water.

More than 10 percent of the world's annual salt supply is used to de-ice American roads.

Obsidian—volcanic glass—is so sharp it's used in cardiac and eye surgery.

Petrified wood was once so abundant that the Pueblo Indians in New Mexico and Arizona used it for building material.

About 130 million carats of diamonds are mined every year.

Why you're not supposed to touch stalactites or stalagmites in a cave: the oil and sweat on human hands can stop the growth of these natural calcite formations forever.

The Dead Sea contains about 11.6 billion tons of dissolved salt.

Fossilized termite farts have been found preserved in amber.

Salt has been found in meteors in outer space.

All marble starts out as limestone.

Go International

At the Wangfujing Snack Street in Beijing, you can nibble on deep-fried centipedes, insect pupae, scorpions, sea horses, and snakes.

Almost 20 percent of South Korean residents are named Kim.

n 2009, politicians in Volkach, Germany, proposed setting up a DNA database for all the dogs in town. That way, they could run tests on any dog poop left behind on streets or lawns, match it to the database, and find—and fine—the dogs' owners. The idea never took off.

The Emirates Palace—one of only three seven-star hotels in the world—is in the United Arab Emirates. (The others are in Dubai and Italy.) Room rates include a $15,000 bottle of cognac and a 24-hour butler.

As early as the fifth century BC, vendors in Greece's outdoor markets sold snow cones made with ice, honey, and fruit.

World's tallest people: residents of the Netherlands. Men average 6'; women average 5'7".

The world's only remaining grand duchy (a country whose head of state is a grand duke or duchess.): Luxembourg.

Baby Animals

A baby oyster is called a spat, beluga whales are piddlins, infant beavers are called kittens, and baby eels are elvers.

On average, an elephant's gestation takes 660 days.

Seventy-five percent of wild birds die before they're six months old.

Why do puppies lick your face? They're instinctively searching for food.

Odds that a baby sea turtle will survive to adulthood: one in 10,000.

Dusty, a tabby cat from Texas, gave birth to a record 420 kittens in her lifetime.

Baby sea lions have to be taught how to swim.

Whales are born tail first.

Porcupine babies (called porcupettes) can climb trees within an hour of birth.

Buffalo milk has more protein than cow's milk.

Puppies from the same litter can have different fathers.

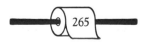

George Washington

George Washington's salary as president: $25,000 a year.

He was the only president to be elected unanimously, and the only one for whom a state was named.

Washington designed a stercorary, a special building to compost horse manure.

Some of Washington's pets: Polly the parrot and 36 hounds.

Washington is the only president who didn't live in Washington, D.C., while he was in office.

Washington lost his first tooth at age 22. Over the next 35 years, he lost all but one.

Washington is credited with introducing the mule to America.

Washington divided his estate, covering more than 3,000 acres, into five farms named Union Farm, Dogue Run, Muddy Hole, Mansion House, and River Farm.

At 16, Washington was an enthusiastic spelunker—he loved exploring caves.

Sybil's Personalities

Sybil **was a 1973 best-selling book** based on the work of psychiatrist Cornelia B. Wilbur and a patient with multiple personality disorder (now called "dissociative identity disorder"). The patient's name in the book (Sybil) was a pseudonym; her real name (Shirley Ardell Mason) wasn't revealed until after her death in 1998. During their sessions, Wilbur discovered that her patient had 16 separate personalities:

- Sybil Isabel Dorsett: the original self.
- Vicky Scharleau: a sophisticated blonde.
- Peggy Lou Baldwin: an often angry pixie type.
- Peggy Ann Baldwin: similar to Peggy Lou but more fearful than angry.
- Mary Dorsett: a plump, little old lady type.
- Marcia Dorsett/Baldwin: a writer and painter.
- Nancy Lou Ann Baldwin: similar to the Peggys, hence the middle names Lou and Ann.
- Mike Dorsett: a boy/carpenter with olive skin, dark hair, and brown eyes.
- Vanessa Dorsett: an intensely dramatic redhead.
- Ruthie Dorsett: a toddler.
- Sid Dorsett: a boy/carpenter with fair skin, dark hair, and blue eyes.
- Sybil Ann Dorsett: a pale and timid type.
- Clara Dorsett: an intensely religious type, highly critical of the original Sybil.
- Helen Dorsett: a fearful but determined woman with light brown hair.
- Marjorie Dorsett: a vivacious brunette.
- The Blonde: the girl Sybil would like to be.

Living Colors

Three top-selling towel colors: navy, burgundy, and hunter green.

Most of the villains in the Bible have red hair.

In 1976, the Rolling Stones took down their billboard for the album *Black and Blue* after feminists complained it promoted violence.

In one year, Crayola produces 2 billion crayons—enough to make a giant crayon 35 feet wide and 100 feet taller than the Statue of Liberty.

Golf illusion: red golf balls appear bigger and closer; blue golf balls appear smaller and farther away.

In 1996, TV's Mr. Rogers named Crayola's 100 billionth crayon color: "Blue Ribbon."

The colors magenta, sienna, and Venetian red are all named after Italian cities.

Excited neon atoms release red light.

The green bleachers in Boston's Fenway Park have one red seat—the spot where Ted Williams's stadium-record 502-foot home run (allegedly) landed in 1946.

People tend to eat less when food is served on a blue plate.

Most-used crayon color: black.

According to astronomers at Johns Hopkins University, the color of the universe is beige.

Most common school colors in America: blue and white.

All the song titles on Bobby Vinton's 1963 album *Blue Velvet* include the word "blue."

Color most associated with weddings in ancient Rome: yellow.

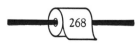

The Boozery

In East Africa, people brew beer from bananas.

The year on a bottle of wine refers to when the grapes were picked, not when the wine was bottled.

A bottle of champagne has three times as much air pressure as a car tire.

When Guinness beer is poured into a glass, the bubbles rise to the top and then are pushed to the bottom.

In the 1906 San Francisco earthquake, 15 million gallons of wine were destroyed.

Enough beer is poured every Saturday across America to fill a football stadium.

Clint Eastwood has his own beer, Pale Rider Ale, named for his 1985 film *Pale Rider*.

White wine gets darker as it ages. Red wine gets lighter.

The earliest beer recipe was found on a Sumerian tablet dating from about 4000 BC.

Popular drink in Greece: white wine mixed with Coca-Cola.

The scum found on top of aged wine is called "beeswing."

The alcohol content of a can of beer and a shot of whiskey are about the same.

Egyptian pyramid builders got three beer breaks a day.

Beer doesn't come up once in the Bible.

According to the experts, the smaller the bubbles, the better the champagne.

Ancient Egypt had at least six known types of beer.

Worldwide, about 20 million acres are devoted to growing wine grapes.

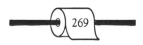

At the Movies

The world's longest movie: *Cure for Insomnia* (1987) runs for 87 hours.

First Western: *The Great Train Robbery* (1903).

First Western movie star: Bronco Billy Anderson. His career lasted from 1903 to 1916.

First movie made in Hollywood: *In Old California* 1910.

Number 1 on the AFI's "Greatest American Movies" list: *Citizen Kane* (1941).

First African American actor to win an Academy Award: Sidney Poitier for *Lilies of the Field* (1963).

First feature-length film documentary: the Eskimo saga *Nanook of the North* (1922).

Best-selling DVD of 2008: *Wall-E*.

Armageddon (1998) was the first film in which actual NASA space suits were used.

The first copyrighted motion picture (made in 1894) is of a man sneezing.

Most-watched film in history: *The Wizard of Oz*. More than a billion people have seen it.

Most successful year at U.S. movie theaters: 1947, with 4.7 billion tickets sold. (Only 1.42 billion were sold in 2007.)

*   *   *

First television sitcom: *The Goldbergs* (1949). CBS canceled the show in 1951 when one of its stars was blacklisted during the McCarthy era.

Indigenous People

The Cherokees' name for themselves is Aniyunwiya, which means "Principal People."

Giant noses are a mark of beauty to the San Blas Indians of Panama. Women paint black lines down the center of their noses to make them appear longer.

The 1954 film *Sitting Bull* was shot near Mexico City, and most of the American Indians were played by Mexican actors.

Before Europeans arrived in the New World, no American Indians had type B blood.

The oldest sandals known were made of sagebrush bark fibers about 9,500 years ago and were found in Catlow Cave in central Oregon.

The Mentawai tribe of Indonesia file their teeth into sharp points.

The ancient Indus civilization—centered mostly in Pakistan, India, and Afghanistan—had a written language of more than 400 pictograph scripts. But to this day, scientists have been unable to decode the language.

Woodrow Wilson's second wife, Edith, was a descendant of Pocahontas.

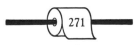

Random Facts

Pants with elastic waists were first introduced during World War II, when metal zippers were in short supply.

Richard Nixon gave away autographed golf balls as presidential gifts.

In the 15th century, the houses of York and Lancaster fought the War of the Roses to control the English monarchy. (The Lancasters won.)

The Kalashnikov AK-47 assault rifle and its variants have been used in more than 75 wars.

Smiley buttons were used as logos by presidential candidate George McGovern and Good Humor Ice Cream.

Playing cards were issued to some British pilots in World War II. If they were captured, the cards could be soaked in water and unfolded to reveal escape maps.

In a 1946 contest in Tokyo, an abacus added more quickly than an electric calculator.

President George H. W. Bush once accidentally beaned his vice president, Dan Quayle, with a golf ball.

State beverage of Nebraska: Kool-Aid.

Having trouble hitting the high notes? According to some experts, breathing in helium before playing the clarinet will raise its pitch.

*   *   *

Studies show: One in seven Americans say they or someone they know has had an experience involving a UFO.

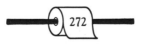

Elvis Lives!

Elvis Presley once volunteered to be an FBI drug informant. (His services were refused.)

Last song Elvis performed in public: "Bridge Over Troubled Water."

At a 2007 auction, a pill bottle once used by Elvis sold for $2,460.

According to sources, in *West Side Story*, producer Robert Wise wanted Elvis to play Tony.

Who's Al Dvorin? The American talent agent who first said, "Elvis has left the building."

The most flowers sold in one day in U.S. history was the day after Elvis Presley died in 1977.

The Jordanaires have sung backup on more than 30,000 recordings, including 361 Elvis songs.

Sixty-five percent of Elvis impersonators are of Asian descent.

Elvis nearly always closed his concerts with "Can't Help Falling in Love."

In 2007, Garth Brooks passed Elvis to become the best-selling solo artist in U.S. history.

Elvis owned a pet mynah bird that said, "Elvis! Go to hell!"

More than 100 Elvis Presley albums made the *Billboard* Top 40.

Elvis collected police badges from cities he performed in.

Elvis made only one commercial: a radio spot for Southern Maid Donuts in 1954.

In 1988, Director Quentin Tarantino played an Elvis impersonator on TV's *The Golden Girls*.

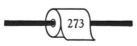

Page of Lists

3 WOODWORKING AXIOMS
1. Measure twice; cut once.
2. Always sand with the grain.
3. You can never have too many clamps.

7 STARS IN THE BIG DIPPER
1. Dubhe
2. Merak
3. Phecda
4. Megrez
5. Alioth
6. Mizar
7. Alkaid

4 MATRIARCHS OF JUDAISM
1. Sarah
2. Rebecca
3. Leah
4. Rachel

3 LAWS OF ROBOTICS IN ISAAC ASIMOV'S SCIENCE-FICTION NOVELS

1. A robot may not injure a human being or, through inaction, allow a human being to come to harm.

2. A robot must obey any orders given to it by human beings, except where such orders would conflict with the first law.

3. A robot must protect its own existence as long as such protection does not conflict with the first or second law.

9 HIGHEST-PAID SPORTS STARS IN 2008
1. Tiger Woods
2. Phil Mickelson
3. LeBron James
4. Floyd Mayweather
5. Kobe Bryant
6. Shaquille O'Neal
7. Alex Rodriguez
8. Kevin Garnett
9. Peyton Manning

5 FAMOUS MILITARY HORSES
1. Traveller (Robert E. Lee)
2. Black Jack (U.S. Army)
3. Bucephalus (Alexander the Great)
4. Comanche (George Custer)
5. Little Sorrel (Stonewall Jackson)

A Way with Words

The word "daisy" comes from the Old English *daegeseage*, meaning "the eye of the sun."

A "Motown" is a poker term for two jacks and two fives—jacks on fives. (Get it? Jackson Fives.)

In golf, a score of eight on a single hole is called "making a snowman."

A lynchobite is someone who works at night and sleeps during the day.

Despite the fact that Julius Caesar was bald, his surname "Caesar" means "hairy" in Latin. (Supposedly, his family was known for their thick hair.)

The words "loosen" and "unloosen" mean the same thing; so do "flammable" and "inflammable."

Forks originally had two tines and were called "split spoons."

Until the 19th century, an "accident" referred to anything that happened, good or bad.

The terms "Caribbean" and "cannibal" come from the same root, *Carib*, a group of indigenous people from South and Central America.

Technically, juice boxes are known as "aseptic packaging."

The all-night diner's term for the hour when a city's bars close: "drunk thirty."

The investing term "blue chip" comes from the color of the highest value of poker chip...blue.

What is a bladder pipe? A bagpipe made from a hedge-hog bladder.

The lead character in the 2001 movie *Shrek* got his name from the Yiddish word for "fear."

All Over the Map

Eight countries have land that lies within the Arctic Circle: Norway, Sweden, Finland, Canada, the United States, Russia, Denmark, and Iceland.

Hong Kong is made up of a peninsula and 236 islands.

American Samoa is the only U.S. territory south of the equator.

More than 90 percent of Egypt is desert.

The Tonga Islands in the South Pacific move about ¾ of an inch every year.

China borders 16 other countries.

The only South American countries with no coastline: Bolivia and Paraguay.

The Cape of Good Hope is not the southern-most point of South Africa. Cape Agulhas, 100 miles to the southeast, is farther south.

Of the 700 or so islands that make up the Bahamas, only 30 are inhabited.

Hawaii is moving toward Japan at a rate of four inches per year.

More Military Miscellany

Soldiers from every country in the world salute with their right hands.

Until 1864, men drafted into the U.S. military could hire someone to take their place. Grover Cleveland did this in 1863 and was ridiculed for it by his political opponent, James Blaine...who had done the same thing himself.

During World War II, Japanese officers killed in battle were promoted to a higher rank posthumously.

Rutherford B. Hayes was a major general in the Union army in the Civil War.

The doors that cover U.S. nuclear missile silos weigh 748 tons.

In 1943, at age 19, George H. W. Bush became the youngest pilot in the U.S. Navy.

For at least five years, the U.S. Army didn't acknowledge the fact that the Wright brothers had built a machine that could fly.

There are 92 known cases of nuclear bombs lost at sea.

The only time a soldier is not required to salute: when he is a prisoner.

The secret code for unlocking U.S. nuclear missiles during the Cold War was 00000000.

When the president is aboard any HMX-1 Marine helicopter, it goes by the name "Marine One."

The U.S. Air Force uses half of the fuel purchased by the government.

The U.S. Army includes Tabasco sauce in all of its ration kits.

6 Ways to Spot a Lie

1. Watch for sweating and squirming. The alleged liar may be sweating more than normal or making fidgety adjustments to his clothing. (Don't put too much stock in this one alone, especially when the stakes are high. The higher the stakes, the more nervous almost everyone is, so you'll want to look for multiple clues.)

2. Notice if "barriers" have been put up. Are the alleged liar's arms crossed across his chest, or is he protecting himself by sitting behind a table or standing behind some kind of barrier, like part of a doorway?

3. Watch the eyes. Liars often avoid eye contact and blink more often than normal. They also have difficulty transmitting emotions to their eyes: If a suspected liar is smiling, watch carefully to see if his eyes are "smiling," too. Dilated pupils can be a sign of a lie.

4. Ask for details. Often, a liar's story will fall apart if he's asked to explain it. A con artist, for instance, will have a story rehearsed— and look at ease while telling it—but you may be able to trip him up by interrupting and asking for details.

5. Listen for inconsistencies. Police interrogators ask suspects to repeat their stories in the hopes of uncovering contradictions.

6. Listen for giveaways. Experts have found that liars are generally less cooperative and less friendly than someone who's telling the truth. Liars often pepper their speech with negative statements and complaints. They also inject phrases like "to be honest" in an effort to make you think they're honest.

Creepy Crawlies

Live adult scorpions glow a greenish color when exposed to ultraviolet light.

If your bed is typical, about 6 million dust mites live in it.

Human tapeworms can grow to be 75 feet long.

Most spiders are cannibals.

Female Brazilian railroad worms have bioluminescent red and green spots.

Ribbon worms can turn themselves completely inside out.

Cockroaches have white blood.

Pill bugs are more closely related to shrimp than to insects.

There are about 650 different species of leeches in the world.

A spider sheds its skin as many as 15 times during its life.

If a cockroach touches a human, it runs to safety and cleans itself.

Foreign Words

In England, the game of checkers is called "draughts."

Modern bowling comes from the German game of *Heidenwerfen*, which translates to "strike down the heathens."

Karaoke means "empty orchestra" in Japanese.

The term "kangaroo court" was unknown in Australia until it was brought over from the United States.

In Arabic, *harem* means "forbidden."

Terra incognita is Latin for "unknown territory."

The word *anthology* is Greek for "a collection of flowers."

Mafia comes from the old Arabic word for "swagger."

In Chinese, saying "Yeeha" means you need to use the restroom.

Seersucker comes from a Persian word—*shir-o-shakar*—that means "milk and sugar."

The word *piccolo* means "small" in Italian.

The word *xylophone* is Greek for "wooden sound."

The word *divot* means, appropriately, "piece of turf" in Scottish.

The word *guitar* comes from the Greek *kithara*, a seven-stringed lyre.

Japanese slang for "nice shot": *Nice-su shot-o.* (Really.)

Glockenspiel means "play of bells" in German.

The word *alcohol* comes from the Arabic *al-kuhul*, meaning "the kohl," a powdered cosmetic used for darkening the eyelids.

Pencil is Latin for "little tail."

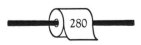

Happy Holidays

Coloring Easter eggs dates back to the ancient Egyptians and Persians, who practiced the custom during their spring festivals.

Juneteenth, a multiday celebration of the emancipation of slaves, originated in Galveston, Texas.

Traditional Christmas dish in medieval England: swan.

The average adult American male receives six Christmas presents.

Americans buy approximately 165 million Easter cards every year.

President Woodrow Wilson made Mother's Day a national holiday in 1914.

The Easter Egg Roll, held on Easter Monday, has been a White House tradition since 1878.

Americans generate an extra 5 million tons of trash between Thanksgiving and New Year's.

Best-selling Christmas record of all time: *Elvis' Christmas Album* (1957).

Cost to decorate a Christmas tree with electric lights in 1899: $300.

All Around Town

The only state capital with three words in its name: Salt Lake City (Utah).

Kansas City, Missouri, has more fountains than any city but Rome.

In Key Largo, Florida, there's an underwater statue of Jesus called *Christ of the Deep*.

Two state capitals include part of the states' names: Oklahoma City and Indianapolis.

The second-largest French-speaking city in the world: Montreal, Canada. (Paris is first.)

What do California, Idaho, Delaware, Florida, Oregon, Wyoming, Kansas, Nevada, and New Hampshire have in common? They're all cities in Ohio.

Waterford, Pennsylvania, has a statue depicting George Washington in a British uniform.

Churchill, Manitoba, calls itself the "Polar Bear Capital of the World."

Montpelier, Vermont, is the only state capital with no McDonald's within its city limits.

Cincinnati was named for Cincinnatus, a politician who ruled Rome for 16 days in 458 BC.

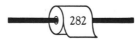

Cotton

First people to cultivate cotton: a prehistoric community that lived in the Indus River valley in modern-day Pakistan, China, and India around 4000 B.C.

During the Middle Ages in Europe, people knew that imported cotton came from a plant, but they didn't know what the plant looked like. Some believed the plants "grew" lamblike animals that produced the fiber.

The first recorded cotton crop in the United States was in Florida in 1556. Virginia followed in 1607.

The world uses more cotton today than any other type of fiber.

After the invention of the cotton gin in the 1790s, the U.S. cotton crop doubled. By 1850, the United States was growing 75 percent of the world's cotton.

The first machine-woven cotton cloth was made in England in 1730.

The United States produces nearly 21 million 500-pound bales of cotton each year, nearly twice the production of 1950.

Cotton's quality is based on three things: color, purity, and fiber strength.

During the American Revolution, the British and French were cut off from cheap American cotton, so they bought the fiber from Egypt instead. (After the war, they went back to buying American.)

Today, Egyptian cotton is softer, stronger, and more expensive than American cotton.

Cottonseed is crushed to produce three products: oil, meal, and hulls.

A River Runs Through It

Around the turn of the 20th century, engineers changed the direction of the Chicago River. It used to flow north into Lake Michigan, but they redirected it to flow south so that waste and debris would float away from the city's downtown area.

A "shut-in" is a rocky, narrow, and unnavigable river channel.

Ten of the tributaries flowing into the Amazon River are as big as the Mississippi River.

America's first national river: Buffalo National River in the Ozarks, part of the National Park Service.

Minnesota is the only state with the source of three main river systems: the Mississippi, St. Lawrence, and Red River of the North.

There are no rivers in Saudi Arabia.

The Amazon River is visible from outer space.

The Mississippi River is only about three feet deep at its headwaters in Minnesota.

The Everglades swamp is the widest river on earth.

The Buffalo National River in Arkansas is one of the nation's few remaining unpolluted rivers.

Texas's Colorado River is not the same river as the one in Colorado, Utah, and Arizona. The Colorado River in Texas starts and ends in the state.

The Rio Grande separates Texas from Mexico for 1,254 miles.

World's longest river: the Nile, at 4,132 miles.

The place where a stream disappears underground is called a "swallet."

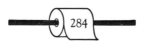

More Averages

Worldwide average life expectancy: 64.3 years.

Most people pass one to three pints of gas a day, in 14 different "episodes."

The average adult has about 46 miles of nerves and 10–20 billion miles of DNA.

A human who sits all day burns 104 calories per hour.

In humans, the left lung is smaller than the right.

Rope woven from human hair can support the weight of 400 people.

During his lifetime, the average man shaves off about 27 feet of hair.

The average dream lasts about 20 minutes.

During the first trimester, a human fetus is about the size of a sesame seed.

Most people suffer about 200 colds in their lifetime.

Most human scalps contain 120,000 and 150,000 hairs.

Alaska

With more than 663,000 square miles, Alaska contains about one-fifth of all the land in the United States.

Alaska's 33,000 miles of coastline touch three different bodies of water: the Arctic Ocean, the Atlantic Ocean, and the Bering Sea.

Alaska's state sport: dogsled racing.

Highest mountain in the United States: Denali (aka, Mount McKinley), at more than 20,000 feet tall.

About one-third of Alaska is inside the Arctic Circle.

The first European to visit Alaska was Danish fur trader Vitus Bering in 1741.

During World War II, the Japanese invaded three of the state's Aleutian Islands, the only time the Japanese occupied American soil during the conflict.

The Trans-Alaska Pipeline runs 800 miles from the Arctic Ocean in the north to the Gulf of Alaska in the south. Since it was completed in 1977, more than 15 billion barrels of oil have passed through the pipeline—about 88,000 barrels an hour.

About 22 indigenous languages are spoken in Alaska.

The United States bought Alaska from Russia in 1867 for two cents an acre...or a little over $7.2 million.

In 1927, Benny Benson, a 13-year-old from Seward, won a contest to design the state's flag. His design: a blue background (to symbolize the sky, lakes, and ocean) with eight gold stars representing the Big Dipper and the North Star.

Juneau is the only capital in the United States that's accessible only by boat or airplane.

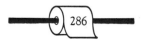

The Circle of Life

An octopus can lay more than 100,000 microscopic eggs at one time.

Male emperor penguins incubate their eggs on top of their feet. In the time it takes to hatch a single egg, the male loses a third of its body weight.

Pregnant bottlenose dolphins gestate for a year.

The only animals born with horns: giraffes.

Male sea catfish keep the eggs of their young in their mouths until the babies are ready to hatch.

Typical life span of a cow: 20–25 years. Typical life span of a dairy cow: 3–4 years.

Mother orangutans nurse their young for up to six years.

An arctic woolly bear caterpillar can live for 14 years before it turns into a moth.

The paradoxical frog, which lives in Trinidad, starts as a foot-long tadpole and "grows" into an inch-long frog.

Human birth-control pills are also effective on gorillas.

The 200 million wild rabbits living in Australia today come from 12 original breeding pairs.

In Liechtenstein, dairy farmers publish obituaries for their deceased cows.

Every year, approximately a billion seabirds and mammals die from ingesting plastic bags.

Dehydrated brine shrimp eggs can lie dormant for years, but once they're put in salt water, they rehydrate and will hatch within a few hours.

On average, a giraffe is about six feet tall at birth.

Worldy Matters

World's oldest country: Egypt, which was unified into a single nation in 3100 BC.

As of 2009, there are 193 countries in the world.

Since 1990, 27 new countries have formed. Fourteen of them came from the collapse of the Soviet Union and five came from the former Yugoslavia.

The country with the largest land area: Russia (6.5 million square miles). The country with the most people: China (1.3 billion).

Antarctica isn't a country—it's a scientific preserve. In 1961, 12 nations, including the United States, signed a treaty declaring it a "zone of peace" dedicated to science. No wars have ever been fought there.

After gaining independence from Serbia, Kosovo became the world's newest country in 2008.

Andorra, which sits between Spain and France, is one of the smallest countries in the world. Although it's a democracy, Andorra has two princes: one representing Spain and one representing France.

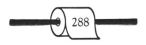

Get Lost

In 1959, Tommy Allsup, a member of Buddy Holly's band, lost his seat on the singer's ill-fated plane to Fargo in a coin toss. The "winner": Richie Valens.

Last reported sighting of Jimmy Hoffa: at the Machus Red Fox restaurant in Bloomfield Township, Michigan, in 1975.

When it was shown in China, *Oliver Twist* was called *Lost Child in Foggy City.*

In 1216, England's King John sent a ship containing some of the crown jewels on a voyage across the North Sea. The ship sank, and the jewels were lost.

In 1871, the *New York Herald* sent reporter Henry Stanley to find missing explorer David Livingstone in Africa. When he found him, Stanley posed the famous question, "Dr. Livingstone, I presume?"

The average bank teller loses about $250 every year.

The wreckage from Glenn Miller's plane crash in the English Channel has never been found.

No one has ever identified the man who stood in front of the tanks in Tiananmen Square in 1989.

Columnist and writer Ambrose Bierce vanished in 1913 while traveling with Pancho Villa's army.

Drew Barrymore wrote her autobiography, *Little Girl Lost,* when she was 14 years old.

Thirty-three percent of American fourth graders can't find their own state on an unmarked map.

Twenty-four hours from now, you'll have forgotten 80 percent of what you learned today.

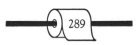

Who Coined the Term?

Genes...Danish biologist Wilhelm
Johannsen (1857–1927)

Jitterbug...Cab Calloway (1907–94)

Carport...Frank Lloyd Wright (1867–1959)

Refrigerator...Maryland engineer Thomas
Moore (1779–1852)

Disc jockey...Journalist Walter Winchell
(1897–1972)

Aromatherapy...French chemist René-
Maurice Gattefossé (1881–1950)

Cowabunga...Writers for the 1950s TV
program *The Howdy Doody Show.*

Third world...Economist Alfred
Sauvy (1898–1990)

Synchronicity...Psychologist Carl Jung
(1875–1961)

Software...Princeton University statistician
John W. Tukey (1915–2000)

Nerd...Dr. Seuss, in the book *If I Ran
the Zoo* (1950)

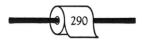

The First Family

John Quincy Adams named one of his sons George Washington.

Abraham Lincoln and Paul Revere were distant relatives.

George W. Bush is the only U.S. president to have fathered twins.

Martin Van Buren's autobiography does not mention his wife once.

Andrew Jackson's parents came from the village of Boneybefore in Carrickfergus, Northern Ireland.

James K. Polk's family name had originally been Pollock, a common Irish name.

As an infant, Franklin D. Roosevelt was name-less for seven weeks because his parents couldn't agree on what to call him. His father liked Isaac, and his mother preferred Warren.

At 18, Grover Cleveland worked on an uncle's cattle farm for room, board, and $10 a month.

Millard Fillmore's wife, Abigail, established the White House library.

A Bug's Life

There are 1.5 million insects for every human on earth.

An ant's smell sensors are located in its antennae and are about as sharp as a dog's.

There are more insects in 10 square feet of a rain forest than there are people in Manhattan.

In 2002, a species of ant from Central America was named after actor Harrison Ford. Why? To honor his work as a conservationist.

Cockroaches spend most of their time resting.

One of every three insects in the world is a beetle.

After bacteria and viruses, insects are the most dominant life-form on earth.

Termite mounds can grow up to 20 feet high.

Cockroaches have at least 18 knees, though scientists think they may have more.

Insects shiver when they're cold.

Among army ants, the "general" is always female.

There are about 140,000 ladybugs to the gallon.

Butterflies can get drunk on the juice of rotten fruit.

* * *

ALWAYS BE PREPARED
The Boy Scout handshake is done with the left hand.

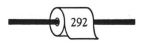

Bad Luck

Classical composers Antonio Vivaldi and Antonin Dvorak both died broke.

Cyrus McCormick's 1831 invention of a horse-drawn reaper took almost 30 years to catch on.

Agatha Christie's first book, *The Mysterious Affair at Styles,* was rejected by the first six publishers she submitted it to.

During Herman Melville's lifetime, *Moby-Dick* sold only 3,000 copies.

C. S. Lewis received more than 800 rejection letters before he sold his first book.

When he died in 1750, Johann Sebastian Bach was remembered mainly as an organist, not as a composer.

Dracula author Bram Stoker also wrote children's stories. Critics called them "morbid."

Guitarist Stephen Stills auditioned for the Monkees. (He didn't get the job.)

In 1862, abolitionist and poet Julia Ward Howe sold "The Battle Hymn of the Republic" to the *Atlantic Monthly* for $4.

Iron Butterfly was scheduled to play at Woodstock, but didn't. They got stuck at the airport.

Federico Fellini was nominated for 12 Oscars for writing or directing. Wins: 0.

Although Mahatma Gandhi was nominated for the Nobel Peace Prize five times, he never won it.

In his dozen appearances at the Masters golf tournament, Bobby Jones never broke par.

Mark Twain turned down a chance to invest in Alexander Graham Bell's telephone company.

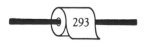

Oops!

Pro baseball player Richie Ashburn once hit the same fan twice with foul balls...in the same at bat.

The first time Norma Jean Mortensen signed an autograph as Marilyn Monroe, she had to ask someone how to spell her new name.

At the 2001 U.S. Open tennis match, Diana Ross lip-synched "God Bless America"...and forgot the words.

Al Capone once accidentally shot himself in the foot while golfing.

Jason Patric turned down the lead role in *The Firm*. The part went to Tom Cruise, and *The Firm* went on to become the third-highest-grossing film of 1993.

Raymond Floyd is the only pro golfer to have hit a drive that landed in his own golf bag.

Will Smith was offered the lead in *The Matrix*, but turned it down to make *Wild Wild West*, which tanked.

Dave Chappelle turned down the role of Bubba in *Forrest Gump* (1994). He thought the movie would be a failure.

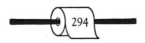

Moms & Dads

Winston Churchill's mother was the daughter of an American millionaire; his father was an English lord.

Will Ferrell's father played keyboard for the Righteous Brothers.

J. Edgar Hoover once gave his mother a canary raised by the "Birdman of Alcatraz."

Sean Connery has a tattoo that says "Mum and Dad."

Dwight D. Eisenhower's mother was a pacifist.

Actress Kathleen Turner's father was held as a POW by the Japanese during World War II.

In *Rain Man*, the "Boy at Pancake Counter" is Jake Hoffman, Dustin Hoffman's son.

The father of the United Kingdom's former prime minister John Major was a trapeze artist.

June Frances Nicholson, the woman Jack Nicholson always thought was his sister, turned out to be his mother. He was 37 before he learned the truth.

Charlemagne's parents were Pepin the Short and Bertha Broadfoot.

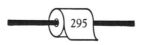

Twister!

In 1971, University of Chicago professor Dr. Tetsuya Fujita created the Fujita Tornado Scale to classify the destructive power of tornadoes into one of six categories based on wind speed:

- F0, 40–72 mph
- F1, 73–112 mph
- F2, 113–157 mph
- F3, 158–206 mph
- F4, 207–260 mph
- F5, 261–318 mph

An "inconceivable tornado" is an F6—it has wind speeds greater than 318 mph. There has never been a documented F6 tornado.

Generally, tornadoes last for just a few minutes and are on the ground for a few miles. But some tornadoes go on for hours and travel up to 100 miles.

Most tornadoes occur between 3:00 p.m. and 9:00 p.m.

Deadliest tornado on record: the Tri-State Tornado. In 1925, it killed 690 people in Missiouri, Illinois, and Indiana.

Tornadoes hit every continent except Antarctica, but the United States experiences between 700 and 800 per year, more than any other country.

Almost 40 percent of all tornadoes occur between 2:00 p.m and 6:00 p.m. That's when thunderstorms are also most frequent.

Contrary to popular belief, opening the doors and windows of a house will not protect it during a tornado.

On May 3, 1999, the most powerful F5 on record swept through Oklahoma. Top wind speed: 302 mph.

States in Tornado Alley: Texas, Colorado, Oklahoma, Kansas, Nebraska, Arkansas.

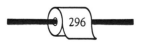

Animals Attack

Most dangerous animal in the zoo, according to zookeepers: the giant panda. The elephant is second.

Snakes can continue to bite after they're dead. It's a reflex action and often contains more venom than a live bite because the snake isn't controlling how much venom it releases.

There are more poisonous snakes per square foot on Komodo Island, Indonesia, than anywhere else on earth.

Of the world's more than 400 species of sharks, only four have a history of attacking humans: great whites, bull sharks, tiger sharks, and oceanic whitetips.

The tarantula hawk, a type of wasp, paralyzes tarantulas and lays an egg on the living spider. Then, when the egg hatches, the wasp larva has a fresh, living supply of food.

A single tiger can eat six tons of meat a year...the equivalent of about 50,000 Quarter Pounders.

The cougar, whose average weight is about 100 pounds, is such a skilled hunter that it can take down a 600-pound elk.

Body part most often bitten by insects: the foot.

More people die from bee stings every year than from skydiving or shark attacks.

Polar bears can eat 50 pounds of meat in one sitting. Their favorite meals? Ringed seals, young walruses, and beluga whales.

In an average year, 311 New York City residents report being bitten by a rat.

Aardvarks have been known to attack and kill lions.

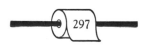

Translated Titles

The Sound of Music in Mexico:
The Rebel Novice Nun

Bad Santa in the Czech Republic:
Santa Is a Pervert

Grease in Venezuela: *Vaselina*

The Parent Trap in Germany:
A Twin Seldom Comes Alone

The Full Monty in China:
Six Naked Pigs

Knocked Up in Peru:
Slightly Pregnant
In China:
One Night, Big Belly

Dr. No in Japan:
We Don't Want a Doctor

Nixon in China: *The Big Liar*

The Matrix in France:
*The Young People Who Traverse
Dimensions While Wearing Sunglasses*

Boogie Nights in China:
His Great Device Makes Him Famous

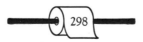

People & Places

Most common first name in the world: Muhammad.

Number 10 Downing Street in London has been the official home of British prime ministers since 1732.

When he was 17, Ehrich Weiss changed his name to Harry Houdini.

Dust devils are called "willy-willys" and "cock-eyed bobs" in Western Australia.

The speed limit along the crooked quarter-mile section of San Francisco's Lombard Street: 5 mph.

When Jim Henson needed a word to describe his creations, which combined marionettes and puppets, he came up with the term "Muppets."

U.S. Forest Service mascot Smokey Bear received so much fan mail in 1964 that he was got his own ZIP code: 20252.

Led Zeppelin took its name from the phrase "lead balloon," which means "an ill-conceived idea." Drummer Keith Moon embellished the term to "lead zeppelin" for emphasis. The band liked that so much that they took it on but modified the first word because they worried people would mispronounce "lead."

It took eight years to build the White House.

Of the more than 42,000 ZIP codes in the United States, the highest is 99950, for Ketchikan, Alaska. The lowest is 00501, for the IRS.

President Barack Obama's secret service code name is "Renegade."

Calling a butler "Jeeves" originated with the character Reginald Jeeves, a butler in many P. G. Wodehouse stories.

Most common last name in the United States: Smith.

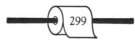

Dictator Dictations

"Ideas are more powerful than guns. We would not let our enemies have guns; why should we let them have ideas?"
—Joseph Stalin

"There must be a world revolution which puts an end to all materialistic conditions hindering woman from performing her natural role in life and driving her to carry out man's duties in order to be equal in rights."
—Muammar al-Gaddafi

"The universities are available only to those who share my revolutionary beliefs."
—Fidel Castro

"I'm quite modest. I don't want to tell people I'm a leader."
—Pol Pot

"If you tell a big enough lie and tell it frequently enough, it will be believed."
—Adolf Hitler

"Communists should be crushed like worms."
—Francisco Franco

"Politics is when you say you are going to do one thing while intending to do another. Then you do neither what you said nor what you intended."
—Saddam Hussein

"Sooner will a camel pass through a needle's eye than a great man be 'discovered' by an election."
—Adolf Hitler

"It may be necessary to use methods other than constitutional ones."
—Robert Mugabe

"Death is the solution to all problems. No man—no problem."
—Joseph Stalin

"It's good to trust others, but not to do so is much better."
—Benito Mussolini

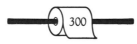

300

Alphabet Soup

The English alphabet is about 700 years old.

Irving Berlin could play the piano only in the key of F sharp.

Most common first letter for words in the English language: s.

What's the only letter in the alphabet with more than one syllable? Answer: *w*.

All Japanese words end in one of three letters: a, y, or n.

The dial tone of most telephones is in the key of F.

The Maltese alphabet has 29 letters but does not contain the Latin letter y.

According to linguists, the letter *p* in "ptarmigan" has no etymological justification whatsoever.

The most common American surname initial is S; the least common is X.

The D in "D-Day" stands for "Day," so June 6, 1944, was "Day-Day."

The first letters of the months July through November spell the name "Jason."

The only words in English with the letters *uu* are vacuum, residuum, and continuum.

Alice Cooper owns one of the original *o*'s from the "Hollywood" sign.

Houseflies hum in the key of F.

J is the only letter that doesn't appear anywhere on the periodic table of the elements.

The word "alphabet" comes from the Greek *alphabetos*.

Also Known As...

In the early part of his career, pianist Liberace performed under the name Walter Busterkeys.

The "real" name of the Comic Book Guy on *The Simpsons*: Jeff Albertson.

First Lady Barbara Bush was nicknamed "the Silver Fox."

President Reagan's Secret Service code name: Rawhide.

Musician Captain Beefheart's real name is Don Glen Vliet.

Bluesman Bo Diddley's real name is Ellas Otha Bates. He got his stage name from an African single-string guitar.

Farrokh Bulsara was called "Britain's first Asian pop star." Stage name: Freddie Mercury. (He grew up in India.)

Gary Cooper's real name was Frank James Cooper. His agent (from Gary, Indiana) made him change it.

Former Isley Brothers guitarist Jimmy James is better known as Jimi Hendrix.

Before Herbert Khaury was known as Tiny Tim, he was billed as Larry Love, the Singing Canary.

Paul Hewson's stage name, Bono, is short for Bono Vox, which comes from the Latin *bonavox*, meaning "good voice."

Who are William, Saul, Jeffrey, and Michael? Axl, Slash, Izzy, and Duff of Guns 'N Roses.

Robert Cassotto picked his stage name, Bobby Darin, out of a Bronx phone book.

Bob Dylan used to go by the stage name Elston Gunn.

Ice-T's real name: Tracy Marrow.

Confucius was also called "Master Kong."

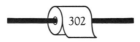

Common Scents

No two humans have the same scent.

According to zoologists, tigers' scent markings smell like buttered popcorn.

On average, older men consider vanilla to be
the most "erotic" smell.

According to scientific tests, the odors that
most commonly turn women off are: barbe-
cued meat, cherries, and men's cologne.

The scents women like best? Pumpkin pie,
lavender, cucumbers, bananas, and...Good 'n'
Plenty candy.

Most people can guess someone's sex
correctly 95 percent of the time just by
smelling his or her breath.

The scent of rosemary seems to improve
long term memory.

Leather actually has a very mild smell—its
recognizable scent comes from the chemicals
used in the tanning process.

A 1947 ad for Barbasol Lotion Deodorant
referred to body odor as "Athletic Aroma."

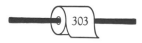

Bath Time

The holes in your sink and bathtub that prevent overflow are called "porcelators."

According to British tabloids, Queen Elizabeth II has a rubber ducky that wears an inflatable crown.

The wife of Emperor Nero kept 500 female donkeys to supply milk for her baths.

The only body part that King Louis XIV of France washed was his nose.

England's Queen Elizabeth I refused to wash her face for the last 10 years of her life.

Before 1950, Americans bathed about once a week. Most Americans now bathe daily.

In AD 300, there were more than 900 public baths in Rome.

Woody Allen won't use a shower or bathtub if the drain is in the middle.

In ancient Egypt, the poor bathed by rubbing themselves with castor oil; the upper class used olive oil.

On an average day in the United States, someone will drown in a bathtub.

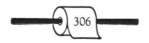

Sauerkraut

The dish that we call sauerkraut originated in China more than 2,000 years ago. It's still popular there today, is called *suan cai*, and is made from shredded cabbage fermented in rice wine.

Sauerkraut means "sour cabbage" in German.

At least one scientific study has found that sauerkraut is as effective as Viagra at increasing sexual function.

During World War I, when America was fighting Germany, U.S. sauerkraut makers renamed the dish "liberty cabbage."

The Reuben, a grilled sandwich that includes sauerkraut, corned beef, swiss cheese, and Russian dressing on rye, has a feminine counterpart: the Rachel—the only difference is that the Rachel uses pastrami instead of corned beef.

At the annual Sauerkraut Cooking Contest in Phelps, New York, contestants have been known to make everything from sauerkraut fudge and salsa to sauerkraut key lime pie.

Sauerkraut can be a remedy against a hangover. The chemicals in the dish help to relieve headaches, neutralize the effects of alcoholic intoxication on the stomach, and clean the liver.

People, Statistically

The world's population grew from one billion to two billion between 1804 and 1927—a span of 123 years. But it took only 12 years (from 1987 to 1999) for the population to grow from five billion to six billion.

About 854 million of the world's adults can't read.

Three of every five people in the world are Asian.

At less than five feet tall, the pygmy tribes of India, the Philippines, and Africa are the smallest people in the world. The Watusi of Africa are the tallest: most of the men are over seven feet tall.

There are about 50,000 full-blooded Aborigines in Australia.

Worldwide, only one out of 10 adults is college-educated.

In the United States, the average adult male is 5'9" and weighs 155 pounds. The average adult female is 5'3" and weighs 125 pounds.

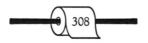

Natural Disasters

The 10 deadliest natural disasters in history are...

1. Yellow River flood: China, 1931
Death toll: between 1,000,000 and 4,000,000

2. Yellow River flood: China, 1887
Death toll: between 900,000 and 2,000,000

3. Shaanxi earthquake: China, 1556
Death toll: 800,000

4. Bhola cyclone: Bangladesh, 1970
Death toll: 500,000

5. India cyclone: India, 1839
Death toll: 300,000

6. Kaifeng flood: China, 1642
Death toll: 300,000

7. Tangshan earthquake: China, 1976
Death toll: 242,000

8. Banqiao dam failure: China, 1975
Death toll: 241,000

9. Indian Ocean tsunami: Indian Ocean, 2004
Death toll: 230,000

10. Aleppo earthquake: Syria, 1138
Death toll: about 230,000

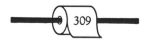

Banned!

Oliver Cromwell banned the eating of pie in England in 1644. He called it "a pagan form of pleasure."

Monty Python's *Life of Brian* was marketed in Sweden as "a film so funny it was banned in Norway."

When it opened in 1959, *Some Like It Hot* was banned in Kansas City because of Marilyn Monroe and Tony Curtis's love scene. And according to some reports, the cross-dressing was "too disturbing for Kansas."

In Fairbanks, Alaska, moose are banned from mating within the city limits.

Italy banned Mickey Mouse in 1935 on the grounds that he frightened children.

In Tajikistan, state law forbids civil servants from having gold teeth.

First video banned by MTV: "Girls on Film" by Duran Duran, which featured topless mud wrestlers.

Sliced bread was banned during World War II. (The slicing machines were melted down so their metal could be used for the war effort.)

France banned all rock concerts in the early 1960s, calling the music "socially subversive."

Prussia's Frederick the Great tried to ban coffee; he insisted people drink alcohol instead. (They drank both.)

In 1933, the government of Syria banned yo-yos, claiming that the toys' up-and-down action caused drought.

The book *Black Beauty* was banned in South Africa in 1955 because the word "black" was in the title.

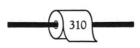

Stars' Common Ground

Russell Crowe, David Duchovny, and David Arquette all knit.

Lucille Ball and Bette Davis were in drama class together.

Charlie Chaplin, Albert Einstein, and Pablo Picasso are left-handed.

Frankie Avalon, Ricky Nelson, and Frank Sinatra have all appeared in John Wayne movies.

Pat Sajak and Big Bird have one, but Clint Eastwood and Jane Fonda don't. What is it? A star on the Hollywood Walk of Fame.

TV's Mr. Rogers and golfer Arnold Palmer were high school friends.

In 1987, Paul Simon the singer and Paul Simon the senator cohosted *Saturday Night Live*.

Robert De Niro and Gene Hackman were both roommates with Dustin Hoffman.

Julie Andrews, Diana Ross, Johnny Cash, and Alice Cooper all appeared on *The Muppet Show*.

More Animal Facts

Forty percent of all mammal species are rodents.

Among mammals, the rule of thumb is...the colder the climate, the shorter the legs.

A musk ox is actually a kind of sheep.

The *Palustris hefneri* species of rabbit is named for *Playboy* mogul Hugh Hefner.

How many wild grizzly bears are left in the lower 48 states? About 1,100. (Before the 1800s, there were about 100,000.)

The largest free-roaming elk herd in the United States is in Oregon's Hells Canyon.

There are no skunks or snakes in Newfoundland, Canada.

According to the National Park Service, more rare animals live in caves than anywhere else.

Cows, camels, reindeer, and cats have all been used to deliver mail.

Squirrels lose at least half the nuts they hide—they forget where they put them.

Koalas sleep 19 to 22 hours a day.

Bond, James Bond

In which film does James Bond play golf with the villain? *Goldfinger*.

Duran Duran's "A View to a Kill" is the only Bond theme song to hit #1 in the United States.

Half the world's population has seen at least one James Bond movie.

In *Live and Let Die*, 46-year-old Roger Moore became the oldest actor to play James Bond.

Mel Gibson turned down the role of James Bond in *Golden Eye*.

Sean Connery started losing his hair at 21. He wore a toupee in his James Bond films.

Ian Fleming planned to kill off Bond at the end of *From Russia with Love*. He changed his mind after fans protested.

Ian Fleming modeled his James Bond character partially with Cary Grant in mind. But when offered the role, Grant turned it down.

According to the novels, James Bond prefers his eggs boiled for exactly 3⅓ minutes.

The white bikini Ursula Andress made famous in *Dr. No* sold at a 2001 auction for $61,500.

Paul McCartney, Nancy Sinatra, and Louis Armstrong all recorded theme songs for James Bond films.

First African American Bond Girl: Trina Parks (as Thumper in *Diamonds Are Forever*).

Ian Fleming offered the role of Dr. No to actor Noel Coward, who replied by telegram: "Dr. No? No! No!!"

The original title of *License to Kill* (1989): *License Revoked*.

Living in America

Each year, 30,000 people in the United States are seriously injured by exercise equipment.

Americans will spend more on cat food this year than on baby food.

How many times will you move in your life? If you're an average American, 11.

A 1995 poll found that 37 percent of Americans thought the Ryder Cup golf competition was a horse race.

Since 1935, the United States has lost 4.7 million farms.

Americans recycle enough paper every day to fill a 15-mile-long train of boxcars.

Approximately 80 percent of 10-year-old girls in the United States will go on a diet this year.

One in every eight Americans lives in California.

There is enough water in American swimming pools to cover the city of San Francisco seven feet deep.

The three biggest party days in the United States: New Year's Eve, Super Bowl Sunday, and Halloween.

Roughly 40 percent of U.S. energy comes from petroleum.

This year, Americans will throw away more than 100 million cell phones.

There are three times as many TV sets in the United States as there are people in the United Kingdom.

Sixty percent of Americans can name the Three Stooges. Seventeen percent can name three Supreme Court justices.

In the United States, people choke on toothpicks more often than on any other object.

Green Things

KERMIT THE FROG. Puppeteer Jim Henson created Kermit in 1955 as the main character on a local television show called *Sam and Friends*. Once he got the job on *Sesame Street*, though, Kermit became a superstar. Today, he's known all over the world by a variety of names: Gustavo in Spain, René the Frog in Latin America, and Kamel in the Middle East.

GRANNY SMITH APPLES. In the late 1860s, a woman named Maria Ann Smith and her husband Thomas owned an orchard outside of Sydney, Australia. The Smiths cultivated apples, and in 1868, they accidentally cross-pollinated a new green apple hybrid that they named Granny Smith, after Maria. Although the Smiths never saw their apple variety become popular in their lifetimes, it eventually traveled beyond their orchard to New Zealand, England, and finally to the United States in the 1970s.

OSIRIS. According to the ancient Egyptians, green was the color of resurrection and immortality. That's why Osiris, the Egyptian god of the afterlife, was often portrayed as having green skin.

THE LIBYAN FLAG. Libya has had a solid green flag since 1977. Why that color? In Islamic culture, green represents the lush paradise Muslims believe awaits them in the afterlife. It was also the color of the banner the prophet Muhammad carried. Many Islamic countries have green on their flags, but Libya's is the only one in the world that's a solid block of color.

JACK IN THE GREEN. In England, May Day parades usually feature this character, a person wearing a costume covered in foliage. The Jack in the Green tradition dates back to the 16th century, when English people dressed themselves up in leaves or flower garlands to celebrate the coming summer with May Day festivals. One

year, a group of chimney sweepers completely covered someone with flowers, leaves, and branches. They called him "Jack in the Green," and over time, he became a recurring character at May Day festivals around the country...and the young sweepers became a regular part of the festivals' entertainment.

The Jack tradition faded in the late 1800s, when England's government made it illegal for children to work as chimney sweepers. The young boys who'd provided so much of the festivals' entertainment could no longer perform. But in the 1980s, Jack in the Green made a comeback. Today, the best-known Jack competition takes place every May 1 in the town of Hastings, where people gather to celebrate Jack and usher in the summer.

THE GACHALA EMERALD. Weighing 858 carats (about half a pound), this is the world's largest uncut emerald. Miners in Colombia pulled it out of the ground in 1967, and today it's on display at the Natural History Museum in Washington, D.C.

BARIUM SALTS. This is the chemical that makes fireworks shoot green sparks.

THE UNITED TASMANIA GROUP. Considered to be the first "green" party in the world, the United Tasmania Group formed in 1972 in Australia. It lasted only five years and had limited success, but many of the United Tasmania Group's candidates moved on to support the Tasmanian Greens and Australian Greens, two mainstream parties still around today.

*　　*　　*

"They'll sell you thousands of greens. Veronese green and emerald green and cadmium green and any sort of green you like; but that particular green...never."

—Pablo Picasso

At the Oscars

Longest Oscar acceptance speech: Greer Garson in 1943, at five and a half minutes.

Jayne Mansfield "popped out of her dress" during the 1957 Oscars.

In 1958, Joanne Woodward accepted an Academy Award in a gown she made herself for $100.

Bing Crosby, the winner of the Oscar for Best Actor in 1944, didn't want to attend the Oscar ceremony. He was golfing when studio assistants found him and made him go.

Only four horror films have been nominated for Best Picture.

First actor to refuse an Oscar: George C. Scott (for *Patton* in 1970).

James Dean was the first actor to receive a posthumous Oscar nomination, in 1955.

Shortest Oscar-winning performance: Anthony Quinn's eight minutes as Paul Gauguin in *Lust for Life* (1956).

Director Alfred Hitchcock never won an Academy Award.

Only seven comedies have won Best Picture Oscars.

Spencer Tracy and Tom Hanks are the only actors to win the Oscar for Best Actor two years in a row.

The only Best Picture nominee based on a TV show: *The Fugitive* (1993).

In 1994, Whoopi Goldberg became the first woman to host the Academy Awards.

The only film for which John Wayne won an Oscar: *True Grit* (1969).

First film to win more than 10 Oscars: *Ben-Hur* (1959).

Agricultural History

In their ancient form, carrots were purple, not orange. The Dutch developed orange carrots in the 1600s.

Ancient Greeks believed that onions were an aphrodisiac.

Romans cultivated asparagus as early as 200 BC.

Tulips aren't native to Holland. They were brought over from Turkey in the 1500s.

Originally, jack-o'-lanterns were made from turnips.

As American as apple pie? Apples are not native to North America; they were brought over from Europe and western Asia.

Chinese gooseberries didn't sell well in the United States until the 1950s and '60s, when grocers renamed them "kiwis." (Calling them "Chinese" had negative associations because of the Cold War.)

Henry Ford was fascinated with soybeans and used them to make automotive paint and parts. (He also grew marijuana, hoping to make new plastics from it.)

The first apple orchard in North America was probably in Boston.

Once upon a time, pumpkins were recommended for removing freckles and curing snake bites.

The sweet potato was once a rare delicacy, believed to be a potent aphrodisiac.

The first vegetables grown in space: potatoes, in 1995.

Shortcake has been around since the 1500s in England, but strawberry shortcake is an American tradition that dates to the mid-1800s, when people held strawberry parties to celebrate the start of summer.

The First Woman to...

...pitch for a men's pro baseball team: Ila Borders of the St. Paul Saints (1997).

...swim the English Channel: Gertrude Ederle (1926). It took her 14 hours, 39 minutes.

...become a professional bullfighter: Conchita Cintron. She began her career in 1934 at age 12.

...compete in the Indianapolis 500: Janet Guthrie (1977).

...have her work published in America: Anne Bradstreet (1650).

...travel into space: the Soviet Union's Valentina V. Tereshkova (1963).

...receive top billing and to headline her own country-music show: Patsy Cline (1962).

...have her artwork displayed at the White House: Georgia O'Keeffe (1997).

...conduct at New York's Metropolitan Opera: Sarah Caldwell (1976).

...lead a jazz band: Sophie Tucker's Five Kings of Syncopation (1914).

Don't Be Scared

Phobatrivaphobia is a fear of trivia about phobias.

Helminthophobia is the fear of worms.

Fear of vegetables is known as lachanophobia.

What is phobophobia? Fear of phobias.

The fear of Fridays is called friggaphobia.

Stenophobia is the fear of narrow spaces.

What is autophobia? Fear of being alone.

What is blennophobia? Fear of slime.

*　　*　　*

FAMOUS FEARS

- Composer Pyotr Tchaikovsky suffered from a paralyzing fear that his head would fall off.
- Queen Elizabeth I of England was afraid of flowers.
- Scientist Nicola Tesla found pearls revolting—and wouldn't allow his female employees to wear them.

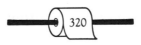

All in a Day's Work

Charles Dickens's son Francis was a Canadian Mountie.

President George W. Bush spent a summer selling sporting goods for Sears.

The kiss between Bill Murray and Scarlett Johansson at the end of *Lost in Translation* was not in the script. It was a last-minute ad-lib by the actors.

Ronald Reagan once appeared in a GE Theater production called *A Turkey for President.*

Dan Aykroyd co-owns a Toronto bar called Crooks. The other owners: several Toronto cops.

Former defense secretary Donald Rumsfeld rarely sat down; he even had a podium in his office that he stood behind.

Young Calvin Coolidge earned spare cash selling apples and popcorn balls at town meetings.

Harrison Ford was offered the part of Mike on *All in the Family*, but turned it down because he felt Archie Bunker was too racist.

Jerry Springer worked on Robert Kennedy's presidential campaign staff.

Bees & Things

One beehive can house as many as 40,000 bees.

Only female mosquitoes bite; they need the blood to feed their eggs. Males' mouthparts aren't equipped to suck blood.

Honeybees have hair on their eyes.

Mosquitoes can hold twice their weight in blood.

A housefly carries as many as 6 million bacteria on its body.

Bee stings are acidic; wasp stings are alkaline.

Mosquitoes aren't attracted to blood. It's the carbon dioxide you breathe out and the lactic acid secreted by glands in your skin that they smell.

Most cicadas have red eyes.

The eggs of some species of mosquitoes can survive in a dried-up state for five years.

An airborne housefly only travels at about 4.3 mph.

A large swarm of desert locusts can consume 20,000 tons of vegetation in one day.

Advertising

First newspaper advertisement: published in the *Boston News-Letter* in 1704, it was looking for a buyer for a Long Island estate.

First commercial jingle: "Have You Tried Wheaties?" for General Mills (1926). It was a last-ditch effort to save the brand, but radio listeners loved the song and singers (the Wheaties Quartet) so much that General Mills decided to keep making the cereal.

In the 1920s and 30s, Burma Shave put up hundreds of humorous billboards along American roads to promote its new brushless shaving cream. Each joke usually consisted of five or six signs that drivers read in succession. One example: Ben met Anna / Made a hit / Neglected beard / Ben-Anna split / Burma Shave.

In the early 1970s, the Coca-Cola jingle "I'd Like to Teach the World to Sing" was a #7 hit in the United States and rose to #1 on the charts in Great Britain.

One of the most influential political ads in history (the "Daisy Ad") featured a little girl plucking flower petals and then a countdown to nuclear war. It aired only once—on Labor Day 1964—but is said to have ensured Lyndon Johnson a victory in that year's presidential election over Barry Goldwater, who had said he'd be willing to use nuclear weapons in Vietnam.

All in the Family

Fidel Castro's daughter Alina defected to the United States in 1993.

Country singers Loretta Lynn and Crystal Gayle are sisters.

Joseph Williams, son of film composer John Williams, was a member of the 1980s band Toto.

Timothy Leary was the godfather of actress Winona Ryder.

Marlon Brando's son Miko was once Michael Jackson's bodyguard.

Of Johann Sebastian Bach's 20 children, 10 died in childhood. Four became composers and musicians.

Wilbur and Orville Wright had two other brothers: Lorin and Reuchlin.

Elton John is Sean Lennon's godfather.

Blues-playing brothers Edgar and Johnny Winter are both albinos.

Four of Mary Todd Lincoln's brothers fought for the Confederacy.

Painter Pierre-Auguste Renoir's son, Jean, was a renowned filmmaker.

Baseball pitcher Barry Zito's uncle is actor Patrick Duffy, who starred in *Dallas*.

Famous Siamese twins Chang and Eng Bunker married two sisters and had 21 children between them.

Kirsten Dunst's production company is called Wooden Spoon Productions...because her grandmother always carried one to keep the grandkids in line.

Harpo Marx once tried to adopt Shirley Temple.

Summer Facts

1816 is often called the "Year Without Summer" because of an abnormally long cold spell in Europe, Canada, and the northeastern United States. That summer, frost killed so many crops that prices for staples like oats and grain rose more than 700 percent, and a June snowstorm dropped a foot of snow on Quebec City, Canada.

Summer school holidays in Australia begin a few weeks before Christmas.

If you stand in front of the Sphinx in Egypt and look west on the summer solstice, the sun will set directly between the two Great Pyramids.

There are more than 10,000 competitors and 300 events in the Summer Olympics.

William Shakespeare's *A Midsummer Night's Dream* takes place on the summer solstice.

Americans take more than 600 million trips between Memorial Day and Labor Day. Of those, 97 percent are within the United States.

During the 19th century, schoolchildren in the United States didn't have a summer break like they do now. Kids at rural schools attended spring and winter terms so they could help out with summer and fall harvests. Urban children typically went to school for 48 weeks a year, with one week off every three months. But in the late 1800s, reformers came up with summer break as a way to put all kids on the same schedule and as a compromise to solve two problems: 1) They felt rural schools were subpar and needed more oversight and structure, and 2) Some researchers worried that too much schooling in childhood without a sufficient break led to insanity later in life.

325

Notable Numbers

Eighty percent of millionaires drive used cars.

About 40 percent of American adults say they "change into something more comfortable" to watch TV.

Seventy percent of Americans have brown hair.

One in 20 people is born with an extra rib.

Americans spend more than 2 billion hours a year mowing their lawns.

Only 55 percent of Americans know that the sun is a star.

Chances you'll die in an accident: one in 77. Chances you'll be murdered: one in 211.

Toast lands butter-side down 62 percent of the time.

*   *   *

DID YOU KNOW?
Bulrushes are papyrus plants...the same stuff the ancient Egyptians used to make paper.

A Mystical Potpourri

There are approximately 3,500 astronomers in the United States...and more than 15,000 astrologers.

Roughly 15 percent of the population of New Orleans practices voodoo.

Mount Horeb, Wisconsin, is known as the "Troll Capital of the World." (There are troll sculptures all over town.)

Between 1520 and 1630, about 30,000 people were reported to French authorities for being werewolves.

Belleville is the "Unidentified Flying Object Capital" of Wisconsin.

Before the advent of Christianity, "witches" in Europe were considered to be spiritual advisers and healers.

The Salem witch trials resulted in the executions of 14 women and six men.

The earliest known images of witches flying on broomsticks date to about 1440, in France.

England's Stonehenge is 1,500 years older than Rome's Colosseum.

There were 736 documented UFO sightings in Canada in 2006.

Earliest documented sighting of the Loch Ness Monster: AD 565.

On an average day, at least one UFO abduction is reported in California.

Two things that might make you become a vampire, according to myth: to be born with red hair or to be promiscuous.

While Warren G. Harding was running for president, his wife, Flossie, visited a clairvoyant. She predicted that he was "a shoo-in" but that he would die in office. (He did.)

Music Milestones

In 1925, *Billboard* magazine stated that the new medium of radio could be good for record sales if songs were not "killed by being radio'd to death."

First platinum single (with 2 million copies sold): "Disco Lady," by Johnnie Taylor (1976).

Bill Haley's "Crazy Man, Crazy" was the first rock 'n' roll single to make the *Billboard* Top 20.

First live musical performance to use an electric light show: a recitation of Alexander Scriabin's *The Poem of Ecstasy* (1908).

First documented use of an electric guitar in a performance: Gage Brewer in Wichita, Kansas, in 1932.

First record to sell a million copies: "Whispering," by jazz artist Paul Whiteman (1920).

First gold rap album (with 500,000 sold): *Run-D.M.C.*, by Run-D.M.C. (1984).

The first record to feature a Moog synthesizer was *Cosmic Sounds by the Zodiac*, released by Elektra Records in 1967.

First rap LP with an "Explicit Lyrics" warning label: 2 Live Crew's *As Nasty as They Wanna Be* (1989).

First song to feature electric guitar distortion: "Don't Worry," by Marty Robbins (1961). It was an accident—the amplifier malfunctioned.

Electric Lady Studios was the first recording studio owned by a major artist—Jimi Hendrix.

The first Fender electric guitar was the 1950 Esquire. Only about 60 were released under that name.

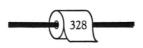

It's True

Ulysses S. Grant suffered from intense migraines that were sometimes mistaken for bouts of drunkenness.

Few photos of Crazy Horse exist because he did not allow his picture to be taken.

After *Dark Side of the Moon,* Pink Floyd planned to do an album that used household objects as instruments. They never released the record, but did record some sounds and used them in their 1975 album *Wish You Were Here.*

Albert Einstein never learned how to drive.

Basketball star Wilt Chamberlain had a superstition about always wearing a rubber band around his wrist.

Reverend Jesse Jackson's PUSH organization launched a campaign against disco music in the 1970s.

Jacqueline Kennedy Onassis was secretly a chain smoker.

Luciano Pavarotti kept a bent nail in his pocket for luck when he was onstage.

Regardless of subject, Roman statesman Cato was said to end all of his speeches with "Carthage must be destroyed."

Albert Einstein slept 10 hours a night.

Favorite game of champion swimmer Michael Phelps: Tiger Woods's PGA Tour golf game on Nintendo Wii.

Patsy Cline didn't like "Walkin' After Midnight," saying it was "just a lil' old pop song." (It went to #2 on the country music charts.)

A Swiss doctor once claimed to have invented a camera that could identify aliens posing as humans.

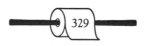

329

Animal Comparisons

Monkeys have tails; apes do not.

Humans and elephants are the only species that recognize and react emotionally to the bones of their own kind.

Caterpillars have more muscles (4,000) than humans (about 640).

There are twice as many kangaroos as people in Australia.

The blond Mangalitza pig has thick fleece like a sheep's.

A dolphin's closest relative on land: the hippopotamus.

From a University of Michigan study: a dog's memory span is five minutes; a cat's is 16 hours.

What do turkeys and turtles have in common? Both have light and dark meat.

Cows have 35,000 taste buds. Pigs have 19,000. Humans have 10,000.

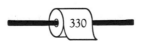

Spaces & Places

The Young Men's Christian Association (YMCA) was founded in London in 1844.

Donald Duck's "official" address: 1313 Webfoot Walk, Duckburg, Calisota.

The Vienna Philharmonic, founded in 1842, has had only "guest" conductors since 1860.

Tin Pan Alley was a real place: West 28th Street between Broadway and Sixth Avenue in New York, where songwriters and music publishers worked.

The Dallas-based "alternative groove funk band" Frognot got their name from a Texas town.

One of Disneyland's original attractions: the "Bathroom of Tomorrow."

The flashing light on top of L.A.'s Capitol Records Tower spells out "Hollywood" in Morse code.

Each copy of the band Black Oak Arkansas' first album (1971) came with a deed to one square inch of land in Arkansas.

There are 142 staircases at Hogwarts of *Harry Potter* fame.

In 1835, Madame Tussaud established her first wax museum on London's Baker Street.

In the 1960s *Batman* TV series, the distance from the Bat Cave to Gotham City was 14 miles.

Nashville nicknames: Music City, USA; Cashville; Nashvegas; and Titan Town.

The Port of Houston ships and receives more foreign freight than any other U.S. port.

First Top-40 radio station: WTIX in New Orleans.

Warriors

During World War I, Charles de Gaulle was wounded several times and was a prisoner of war for three years.

Mickey Marcus is the only soldier buried at West Point who died fighting under a foreign flag. He was a military advisor to Israel in the 1948 Arab-Israeli War.

Adam Swarner of New York was the first Union soldier to die at the prison camp in Andersonville, Georgia.

Before the Civil War began, General Robert E. Lee was offered command of both the Union and Confederate armies.

Baron von Steuben, a Prussian, drilled George Washington's troops at Valley Forge.

Lew Wallace, best-selling author of *Ben-Hur*, was also a Civil War general and U.S. senator.

The architect of the attack on Pearl Harbor, Admiral Isoroku Yamamoto, was a graduate of Harvard.

Wal-Mart's founder, Sam Walton, was an army spy during World War II.

While crossing the Gobi desert, Genghis Khan's troops survived by drinking their horses' blood.

After the American Revolution, John Paul Jones served in the Russian navy.

Between the Red River Rebellion (1869–70) and the North-West Rebellion (1885), the two insurrections he led against Canada's government, Louis Riel (who founded the province of Manitoba) was a teacher in Montana.

To prevent warfare among families, sultans in the Ottoman Empire had the right to kill their brothers.

To the Moon

First man-made object to reach the Moon: *Luna 2*, an unmanned Soviet spacecraft, in 1959.

Earth is 0.02°F hotter during a full moon.

According to astronauts' notes, moon dust smells like exploded firecrackers.

The Royal and Ancient Golf Club's rules committee chastised Alan Shepard for not "replacing his divot" on the Moon.

The last astronaut to walk on the Moon was Eugene Cernan, in 1972.

In 1609, Galileo was the first to discover that the surface of the Moon was pitted, not smooth.

Every song title on the soundtrack to *An American Werewolf in London* has the word "moon" in it.

In 1969, Pan-Am began accepting reservations for flights to the Moon. (The airline went out of business in 1991.)

Seven lunar craters were named for the astronauts on the *Challenger* shuttle.

Many small lunar and Martian craters are named after small towns on Earth.

The *Apollo 11* astronaut who didn't walk on the Moon: Michael Collins.

The Moon is 2,140 miles in diameter. That's less than the width of the continental United States.

The study of the Moon is called selenology, after Selene, the Greek goddess of the Moon.

Distance from Earth to the Moon: about 238,855 miles.

333

Nautical Notes

"Ahoy!" was once a Viking battle cry.

For more than 400 years, pirates were hanged at the Execution Dock in London, on the north bank of the Thames. Today a pub called the Captain Kidd overlooks the original site of the gallows.

In London, in 1700, "frigate" was naval slang for "woman"—specifically a shady one.

Captain James Cook tried to prevent scurvy by feeding his men sauerkraut. It often worked.

In the 1700s, to ease overcrowding in the jails, English convicts were imprisoned in the hulls of old warships moored on the Thames.

"Flotsam" is what floats on the ocean, and "jetsam" is what gets tossed overboard from a ship.

In 1912, the New York Giants and New York Yankees played a charity baseball game to raise money for *Titanic* survivors.

Columbus took his son Diego along on his fourth trip to the New World.

The ironclad Union ship *Monitor*, which sailed during the Civil War, was the first ship to have a flush toilet.

Sea shanties such as "Drunken Sailor" were the only songs the British Royal Navy allowed on ships during the 1800s.

The *Titanic* was running at only 22 knots (about 25 mph) when it hit the iceberg.

What sets the 1908 Olympics apart from all the others? It was the only time that motorized watersports were featured as Olympic events.

Baseball Humor

"It is well to remember that a Martian observing his first baseball game would be quite correct in concluding that the last two words of the national anthem are: PLAY BALL!"
—Herbert H. Paper

"I knew when my career was over. In 1965, my baseball card came out with no picture."
—Bob Uecker

"Things could be worse. Suppose your errors were counted and published every day, like those of a baseball player."
—Unknown

"The place was always cold, and I got the feeling that the fans would have enjoyed baseball more if it had been played with a hockey puck."
—Andre Dawson, on playing in Montreal

"The doctors X-rayed my head and found nothing."
—Dizzy Dean

"What does a mama bear on the pill have in common with the World Series? No Cubs."
—Harry Caray

"I believe in the Church of Baseball. I tried all the major religions and most of the minor ones. I've worshiped Buddha, Allah, Brahma, Vishnu, Siva, trees, mushrooms, and Isadora Duncan. I know things. For instance, there are 108 beads in a Catholic rosary and there are 108 stitches in a baseball. When I learned that, I gave Jesus a chance."
—Ron Shelton (Kevin Costner), *Bull Durham*, 1988

"Hating the New York Yankees is as American as apple pie, unwed mothers, and cheating on your income tax."
—Mike Royko

"Why do we sing 'Take Me Out to the Ball Game' when we're already there?"
—George Carlin

Parks Great & Small

Hot Springs National Park in Arkansas is nicknamed "the American Spa."

Independence National Historical Park covers 45 acres in downtown Philadelphia.

Hovenweep, as in Hovenweep National Monument on the Colorado-Utah border, means "deserted valley."

The world's smallest park: Mill Ends Park in Portland, Oregon, at 452 inches.

First national lakeshore: Pictured Rocks National Lakeshore on Lake Superior.

A 2.5-acre section of New York's Central Park is called Strawberry Fields in honor of John Lennon.

Women's Rights National Historical Park is at Seneca Falls in upstate New York.

The Nez Perce National Historic Park, which celebrates the heritage of the Nez Perce Indians, is made up of 38 different sites spread over four states: Idaho, Washington, Oregon, and Montana.

5 Turning Points: WWII

1. BATTLE FOR THE HAGUE. On May 10, 1940, the Germans invaded the Netherlands, hoping to accomplish two things: 1) capture The Hague, a town in western Holland where most of the country's government was located, and 2) take the country's Queen Wilhemina prisoner. But the Dutch resistance was stronger than Adolf Hitler had anticipated, and by the evening of May 10, they'd forced the Germans to retreat. The Battle for the Hague lasted only one day, but it demoralized German troops and was one of the few early battles that the Nazis lost.

2. THE SOVIET UNION SWITCHES SIDES. When Germany invaded Poland in 1939, the Soviet Union was one of its allies. Hitler and Joseph Stalin had signed a nonaggression pact, but in early 1940, Hitler started planning Operation Barbarossa, a large-scale invasion of the Soviet Union. He launched it the following year—almost 4 million Germans faced more than 3 million Soviets in the largest military operation in history.

Between June and December 1941, the Germans struggled to take control of Moscow. They never succeeded. Instead, over the next three years, the Soviets managed to push the Germans all the way back to Berlin. The Soviet Union also became a key ally of the United States and Great Britain, and Germany, whose army found itself fighting in the east and west, couldn't win a two-front war.

3. GUADALCANAL CAMPAIGN. After the Japanese bombed Pearl Harbor in December 1941, the Americans had to scramble to come up with a response. They launched the Doolittle Raid in early 1942 in an attempt to show the Japanese that their homeland was vulnerable to attack, but that did little to affect the Japanese militarily. For the most part, the Americans and their allies remained on the defensive. That changed in August 1942, when Allied soldiers landed on the Japanese-controlled island of Guadalcanal in the Pacific Ocean and launched the first major attack against Japan.

After six months of fighting, only about 7,000 Allied troops had been killed...compared to more than 30,000 Japanese soldiers. Japan finally retreated from Guadalcanal on February 9, 1943, and the Allies' victory gave them their first strategic advantage in the Pacific.

4. THE P-51 MUSTANG. Many military strategists during World War II believed that whoever had the advantage in the air would win the war. But in the early days, the Germans controlled the skies. Allied fighter planes had barely enough power to fly from air bases in England to the German border. That meant they weren't able to do much to protect the bombers that were attacking Berlin and other cities. German fighters just waited for the Allied bombers to arrive and then decimated them.

That's where the P-51 Mustang came in. Introduced in 1942, this long-range fighter was lighter and faster than previous planes, and went farther on a tank of gas. So it could accompany the bombers on long raids and provide adequate support. Suddenly, the Allies were as much of a threat in the air as the Germans were.

5. THE BATTLE OF THE BULGE. Officially called the "Ardennes Offensive," this was the last major German effort to stop the Allied advance in Europe. Between December 16, 1944, and January 25, 1945, more than 500,000 German troops fought 800,000 British and American soldiers for control of the Ardennes Forest in Belgium. Despite freezing temperatures, low supplies, and a delay in the arrival of fresh troops, the Allies held their ground and eventually were victorious. In the end, the German air force was nearly destroyed, seriously weakening its military overall.

And the "bulge" in the battle's name? That refers to the hump-like shape the Allied line took on as the Germans tried to hem them in on two sides.

*   *   *

"We have only to kick in the door and the whole rotten structure will come crashing down."
—**Adolf Hitler, on Operation Barbarossa**

A Dog's Life

The three most popular dog breeds in the United States: Labrador retriever, golden retriever, and German shepherd.

The average city dog lives three years longer than the average country dog.

A dog can recognize its own urine markings a year after making them.

Dogs have fewer than 2,000 taste buds. (Humans have about 9,000.)

There are 41 references to dogs in the Bible...and most of them are negative.

The five most popular dog commands in the United States: sit, shake, roll over, speak, and lie down.

Scientists have discovered that dogs can "smell" the presence of autism and epilepsy in humans.

Who's the most famous cairn terrier? Toto from *The Wizard of Oz*.

A painting from 79 BC, showing a guide dog leading a blind man, was found in the ruins of Pompeii.

A guide dog's career typically lasts 8 to 10 years.

One in four British vets say they've treated a drunk dog.

Two dogs survived the sinking of the *Titanic*: a Pekingese and a Pomeranian.

The St. Bernard was named for Bernard of Menthon, a medieval monk who built way stations for travelers in the Alps.

A dog's normal body temperature is between 101°F and 102°F.

Alexander Graham Bell tried to teach his dog how to talk.

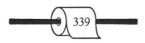
339

More Celebrity Gossip

Dean Martin's vanity license plate was DRUNKY.

J. Edgar Hoover fired FBI agents whose palms were sweaty when they shook hands.

In the 1600s, French women wore high heels to show that they were too rich to walk.

Twenty-five percent of the people at sporting events believe their presence affects the outcome of the game.

Theodore Roosevelt craved attention. It was said he wanted to be "the bride at every wedding...and the corpse at every funeral."

Former heavyweight boxing champion George Foreman has five sons—all named George.

Artist Paul Cézanne taught his parrot to say "Cézanne is a great painter."

Golfer Chi Chi Rodriguez once made his caddie carry him across a river.

Ivan the Terrible blinded Russia's best architect so he couldn't build nicer buildings for other people.

Pro golfer Archie Compston had a second caddie just for his tobacco and pipes.

Vanilla Ice once said, "You can write a book on each of my thoughts."

John Adams—by his own admission—was "puffy, vain, conceited."

Mötley Crüe drummer Tommy Lee once had a Starbucks in his home.

Arnold Schwarzenegger turned down *The Incredible Hulk* TV series because he thought he was too good-looking for the part.

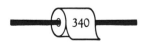

Peculiar Places

McMurdo Station in Antarctica (population: 200) has its own ATM.

Sitka, Alaska, was once part of the Russian empire.

Germany and Italy were united as modern countries in the 1800s.

The towns of Greenwich and Norwich were once ancient salt mines in England. (The Anglo-Saxon word for "saltworks" is *wich*.)

Until 1832, the town of Old Sarum in southern England had two members in Britain's parliament, but nobody lived there. (The land was owned by 11 people who all lived elsewhere.)

The original Guinness Brewery in Dublin, Ireland, has a 6,000-year lease.

Official state rock 'n' roll song of Ohio: "Hang on Sloopy," by the McCoys.

World's steepest street: Baldwin Street in Dunedin, New Zealand, with a 38 percent incline.

The State of Michigan has designated Aretha Franklin's voice a natural resource.

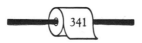

Music Notes

Circus music commonly used to introduce clowns: "Entrance of the Gladiators."

Marni Nixon's singing was dubbed in for Deborah Kerr in *The King and I*, for Natalie Wood in *West Side Story*, and for Audrey Hepburn in *My Fair Lady*.

Alanis Morissette appeared on *Star Search* in 1989, but lost to a singing cowboy.

George Gershwin's last tune: "Love Is Here to Stay," for the 1938 film *The Goldwyn Follies*.

In the 1944 film *To Have or Have Not*, Lauren Bacall's singing was dubbed by Andy Williams.

Led Zeppelin's "Stairway to Heaven" was never released as a single.

Regis Philbin sings "Pennies from Heaven" on *Who Wants to Be a Millionaire: The Album.*

Clint Eastwood did his own singing in the 1969 film *Paint Your Wagon*. Jean Seberg's was dubbed.

The American Film Institute's top two movie songs of all time: "Singin' in the Rain" and "Over the Rainbow."

What song did Hal, the computer in *2001: A Space Odyssey*, learn to sing? "A Bicycle Built for Two."

Dooley Wilson, the piano player Sam in *Casablanca*, couldn't play the piano. He sang "As Time Goes By," but the piano playing was dubbed.

Victor Fleming, the director of *The Wizard of Oz*, nearly cut "Somewhere Over the Rainbow" from the film.

Clint Eastwood wrote the theme songs for *Unforgiven*, *The Bridges of Madison County*, and *Gran Torino*.

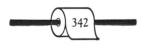

Love, Sweet Love

Arnold Schwarzenegger appeared on TV's *The Dating Game* in 1973.

Maud Gonne, William Butler Yeats's lover, was a founder of the Irish political party Sinn Fein.

Myrna Loy's second husband was car-rental heir John Hertz Jr.

Singer James Brown's wife once tried to get her traffic tickets dismissed because of "diplomatic immunity."

Charles Dickens nicknamed his wife "Dearest Darling Pig."

Golfer Nick Faldo's former girlfriend demolished his Porsche with a 9-iron during their breakup.

On a date with Oprah Winfrey in 1986, Roger Ebert urged her to go national with her talk show. Winfrey credits Ebert with launching her career.

John Lennon's first girlfriend was named Thelma Pickles.

Which celebrity has been married the most times in Las Vegas? Mickey Rooney (eight).

Courteney Cox and David Arquette met on the set of *Scream* (1996).

Rudolph Valentino was arrested for bigamy in 1922. Charges were later dropped.

Each of Tom Cruise's three wives was 11 years younger than the previous one.

Tom Selleck was a bachelor on *The Dating Game* twice. (He wasn't picked either time.)

Comedian Henny Youngman ("Take my wife, please!") was happily married for 59 years.

The ancient Greek temple of Aphrodite, goddess of love, was discovered by an archaeologist named Iris Love.

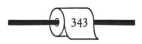

Sports & Leisure

The first permanent concession stand at a baseball stadium was built at Wrigley Field in 1914.

There really is a Southfork Ranch where the TV show *Dallas* was filmed. It's 20 miles north of Dallas, Texas, and hosts nearly 1,400 events a year.

The Opera House in Haskell, Vermont, straddles the U.S.-Canada border. The audience sits in the United States, but the stage is in Canada.

The Ohio State University's stadium holds 101,000 people, almost twice the number of students enrolled there.

It would take you about 200 years to spend a night in every hotel room in Las Vegas.

Oldest surviving Broadway theater: the Lyceum, opened in 1903.

First modern summer Olympic games: Greece, 1896. First winter games: France, 1924.

Philadelphia's Shibe Park opened in 1909; it was the first baseball stadium made out of concrete and steel.

Minnesota's Mall of America is the size of 78 football fields—32 jet airplanes could fit inside it.

John XXIII, who was pope from 1958 to 1963, installed a bowling alley in the Vatican.

In 1959, when Soviet premier Nikita Khrushchev visited Los Angeles, he wanted to go to Disneyland. The city's police chief wouldn't allow it because of "security concerns," which prompted an irate Khrushchev to give a speech wondering if there were nuclear missiles buried beneath the amusement park. (There weren't, and Khrushchev visited a movie studio instead.)

Body Talk

The human body creates and kills 15 million red blood cells every second.

A cough travels at 600 mph.

The fastest-moving muscle in the human body is the one that opens and closes the eyelid.

Your hair grows about 0.5 inch per month, but it grows a little faster in the summer than in the winter.

A human body decomposes four times faster in water than underground.

A bleeding wound will start to clot in less than 10 seconds.

The human brain continues to send electrical wave signals up to 37 hours after death.

It takes four to six months to regrow an entire fingernail.

You burn about 105 calories in one hour of typing.

All your skin weighs twice as much as your brain.

Movie Miscellany

Average cost of a movie ticket in Havana, Cuba: 10¢.

In *Gone With the Wind*, if the dates of the battles were correct, Melanie's pregnancy would have lasted 21 months.

The word "sir" is used 164 times in *A Few Good Men* (1992).

Rod Steiger chewed 263 packs of gum during the shooting of *In the Heat of the Night*.

Who was in both *The Magnificent Seven* and *The Dirty Dozen*? Charles Bronson.

Lawrence of Arabia (1962) is nearly four hours long, but it has no women in speaking roles.

On average, a movie makes about five times more from its video sales than from its ticket sales.

On her eighth birthday, Shirley Temple received 135,000 presents.

Myra Franklin of Cardiff, Wales, saw *The Sound of Music* 940 times.

The biggest U.S. film studio is Universal City in Hollywood, with 34 sound stages on 420 acres.

A two-hour movie uses about two miles of film.

Character most often portrayed on-screen: Sherlock Holmes, with more than 200 films.

Edgar Allan Poe has the most works turned into movies (114) of any American writer.

In 1905, the average movie ticket cost 5¢.

Dirty Harry's badge number is 2211.

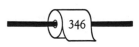

346

And the Winner Is...

Only person nominated for an Oscar, a Golden Globe, a Grammy, and a Nobel Peace Prize: Bono.

Winner of the first Oscar for Best Song: "The Continental," from *The Gay Divorcée* (1934).

Martin "Hezza" Henton won the 2006 World Music Award for "Most Aggressive Harp Player."

Carlos Santana won eight Grammys in 2000, the most ever in a single year.

Solo male performer who's won the most Grammys: composer George Solti, with 31. Female: Alison Krauss, with 26.

Vivien Leigh used her Oscar as a toilet-paper holder.

Roger Clemens has won baseball's Cy Young Award seven times, in three different decades.

The 1961 Grammy winner for Best New Artist: Bob Newhart.

The trophy for Morocco's King Hassan Golf Tournament is a jewel-encrusted dagger.

In 1975, Ellen Burstyn was the first person to win an Oscar (*Alice Doesn't Live Here Anymore*) and a Tony (*Same Time, Next Year*) in the same year.

First baseball player to win the league MVP Award while on a last-place team: Andre Dawson of the Cubs (1987).

College football's Heisman Trophy is named for John William Heisman, an early 20th-century football player and coach.

First Canadian female artist to receive a U.S. gold record: Anne Murray, for "Snowbird" (1970).

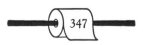

347

The White House, Part 2

Movie screened most often at the White House: *High Noon.*

Warren G. Harding once lost an entire set of White House china in a poker game.

The White House's first Web site debuted in 1994.

The bodies of seven presidents, including Abraham Lincoln and John F. Kennedy, have lain in state in the East Room.

Very few cut flowers were used in the White House during James K. Polk's administration (1845–49) because it was a common belief at the time that flowers gave off unhealthy vapors.

The president, First Lady, and others are carefully tracked within the White House. Signals alert the Secret Service and ushers whenever they enter a room.

Lyndon B. Johnson had a helicopter seat refitted for use as his Oval Office desk chair.

Abigail Adams used to hang laundry in the East Room.

Herbert Hoover held the last New Year's Day reception at the White House in 1932.

John Quincy Adams expanded the White House garden to two acres.

Thomas Jefferson held the first inaugural open house in 1805.

Warren G. Harding had the White House's first radio installed in 1922.

Andrew Jackson bought 20 spittoons for the East Room.

Franklin D. Roosevelt had White House matches stamped "Stolen from the White House."

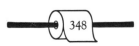

Toon Town

A 30-minute cartoon may contain more than 18,000 drawings.

For *The Lion King*, Disney animators went to Africa to study the movement of wild animals up close.

First animated cartoon character: Gertie the Trained Dinosaur (1910).

SpongeBob SquarePants creator Steve Hillenburg studied marine biology in college.

Walt Disney introduced the character of Goofy in 1932.

Dumbo is the only Disney animated film with a title character who doesn't speak.

Donald Duck made his first screen appearance in 1934 in *The Wise Little Hen*.

Walt Disney's wife convinced him to name his mouse Mickey instead of Mortimer.

First and last time the Roadrunner spoke: in a 1951 Bugs Bunny cartoon called *Operation: Rabbit*.

The full name of *The Simpsons* character Krusty the Klown is Herschel Schmoeckel Krustofski.

According to his "official biography," Popeye is 34 years old, stands 5'6", and weighs 154 pounds.

Bugs Bunny was named for Warner Bros. animator Bugs Hardaway.

Joe Dougherty, the original voice of Porky the Pig, had a real stuttering problem.

Goofy's first on-screen appearance: *Mickey's Revue* (1932).

About a third of *SpongeBob SquarePants* fans are adults.

The Japanese have a word for "obsessed anime fan"—*otaku*.

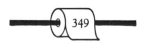

That Old-Time Religion

Saint Peter (AD 1–64) is regarded as the first pope. There have been 264 popes since.

Texas has more churches than any state in the nation—nearly 17,000.

The first Dead Sea scrolls (created around 100 BC) were found in a cave in 1947 by herdsmen searching for a lost goat.

Kawaiaha'o Church in Honolulu was once the official church of the Hawaiian kingdom. Some of its services are still given in the Hawaiian language.

Vlad the Impaler, a 15th-century Romanian prince and one of the inspirations for Dracula, studied for the priesthood.

Pope John Paul II (1978–2005) named nearly 500 new saints, more than were named in the previous 500 years.

Woman with the most appearances on the cover of *Time* magazine: the Virgin Mary.

Robigus is the Roman god of mildew and grain rust.

Sir Isaac Newton was ordained as a priest in the Church of England.

The Aztecs sacrificed up to 15,000 people a year to their sun god.

The religion of India's Todas people forbids crossing bridges.

Ancient Egyptians worshiped more than 2,000 gods.

Verminus was the Roman god who protected cows against worms.

The Romans believed in numerous household gods and spirits, including Cardea, the goddess of hinges, and Forculus, the god of the doors.

Dentistry

In the 18th century, dentists used rubber for fillings.

Peter the Great, tsar of Russia, practiced dentistry on some of his subjects.

The first woman in the United States to become a certified dentist: Lucy Hobbs Taylor, in 1867.

Doc Holliday was indeed a doctor...specifically, a dentist.

In the early 1900s, most Americans did not brush their teeth regularly.

The ancient Greeks thought that telling lies caused toothaches.

Before striking it rich as a writer of Western novels, Zane Grey had a dentistry practice.

Apollonia, the patron saint of dentists, had her teeth pulled for refusing to renounce Christianity.

According to polls, 40 percent of people who move to a new address change their brand of toothpaste at the same time.

A Chinese toothpaste called S.O.D. promises to "brush away senility."

Two jobs where customers expect "friendly" breath: dentists and salespeople.

Sugar was first added to chewing gum in 1869... by a dentist.

Most popular toothbrush color: blue.

Every year, about 2,500 people go to the emergency room with "toothbrush injuries."

Some people are able to pick up AM radio signals through their dental fillings.

Acupuncture uses 388 sites on the body...including 26 just for toothaches.

The First...

...oil well on land owned by the University of Texas was drilled in 1923. The well was dubbed Santa Rita, after the patron saint of the impossible.

...American musical comedy, *The Black Crook*, opened on Broadway in 1866.

...science-fiction novel: *A Journey to the Center of the Earth*, by Jules Verne (1864), according to some scholars.

...American bookseller and publisher: Hezekiah Usher, of Cambridge, Massachusetts, in 1639.

...mention of golf in the United States: an edict banning it from the streets of Albany, New York, in 1659.

...recorded human blood transfusion was performed in 1667 by Jean-Baptiste Denys.

...known musical recording: folk song "Au Clair de la Lune," in 1860.

...museum dedicated to the study of extraterrestrial life: the Alien Museum in Portland, Oregon.

...crossword puzzle collection released: 1924.

...wax figure made by Marie Tussaud was of Jean-Jacques Rousseau, in 1778.

...team to fly to a baseball game: the Marysville Merchants (California), in August 1921.

...rock concert was held in Cleveland, Ohio, in March 1952—the Moondog Coronation Ball.

...novel sold in a vending machine: *Murder on the Orient Express* (1989).

...diet soft drink sold: a type of ginger ale called No-Cal Beverage, in 1952.

...revolving restaurant: atop Seattle's Space Needle (1961).

One-of-a-Kind Animals

No two Holstein cows have the same pattern of spots.

Elephants are the only animals with four leg joints that all bend in the same direction.

The only marsupial native to North America: the opossum.

Every lion has a unique pattern of whiskers.

A type of flea found in Germany lives and breeds almost exclusively in beer mats (those coasters you get in bars).

Flies are the only flying insects that have two wings. All others have four.

The walrus has only two natural predators—orcas and polar bears.

The Chihuahua is the longest-lived breed of dog. Many live to be as old as 18.

Mormotomyia hirsuta is a type of fly that lives only in a crack at the top of Ukazzi Hill in Kenya.

The whistling swan has the most feathers of any bird—about 25,000.

Days & Times

During most of the 19th century, Americans set their watches to as many as a hundred local times. Standard Time was finally devised in 1883 by Sandford Fleming, a Canadian.

The *anno Domini* system of counting the years from the birth of Christ began in 525.

The tip of the hour hand on a wristwatch travels at about 0.00000275 miles per hour.

Mahatma Gandhi observed a day of silence on Mondays.

The first TV commercial: a Bulova watch ticking on the screen for exactly 60 seconds.

February 29, or leap day, was once called Bissextile Day.

According to a medieval system of time units, a "moment" is 1½ minutes.

Hindu holy days begin at sunrise, Jewish holy days at sunset, and Christian holy days at midnight.

Author James Joyce always wore five watches, each set to a different time.

When Britain adopted the Gregorian calendar, October 4, 1582, was followed by October 15.

London's Westminster clock tower (Big Ben) chimes part of Handel's *Messiah* on the quarter-hour.

October almost always begins on the same day of the week as January. The exception: leap year.

The word *February* comes from the Latin *februum*, "to cleanse."

Actress Tuesday Weld was born on a Friday (August 27, 1943). Her real name is Susan.

The Ruling Class

Japan's Emperor Akihito is the 125th ruler in an unbroken line that goes back to the first century BC.

The words *czar* and *kaiser* are both descended from the word *caesar*.

The throne of Ethiopia's Menelik II (1844–1913) was actually an electric chair imported from the United States.

The line of succession to the British throne includes 60 people.

The only English king to die on the battlefield was Richard III, in 1485 during the War of the Roses.

Europe's longest-reigning monarch...so far: Louis XIV of France. He ruled for 72 years, 3 months, and 15 days.

Eleanor of Aquitaine was the only person to serve as queen of both England and France.

Longest-serving monarch: Pepi II, who ruled Egypt for 94 years between 2278 and 2184 BC.

The eldest son of the king or queen of England is automatically the Duke of Cornwall.

The word *khan*, as in Genghis Khan and Kublai Khan, means "ruler."

* * *

Football player who made end zone dances famous: Billy "White Shoes" Johnson, a kick returner who played professional football from 1974 to 1988 and spent most of his career with the Houston Oilers and the Atlanta Falcons.

Huh?

Teddy Roosevelt's "cavalry charge" up San Juan Hill was done on foot.

Russia's "February Revolution" took place in March. The "October Revolution" was in November.

The Battle of Bunker Hill was actually fought one hill over, on Breed's Hill.

The Hundred Years' War lasted 116 years.

In Vietnam, the Vietnam War is called the American War.

Nazi Germany's Thousand Year Reich lasted 147 months.

The town of Waterproof, Louisiana, has been flooded many times.

Virginia extends 95 miles farther to the west than West Virginia.

When the Civil War started, Robert E. Lee owned no slaves. Ulysses S. Grant did.

What do Theodore Roosevelt, John F. Kennedy, and Ronald Reagan have in common? They were all members of the National Rifle Association—and they were all shot with guns.

Random History

A 1935 proposal called for joining the Texas and Oklahoma panhandles in a new state: Texlahoma.

The United States was the first independent country in the New World. Haiti was the second, in 1804.

First country to officially recognize the United States as an independent country: Morocco.

Theodore Roosevelt's 1901 inaugural oath was the only one not sworn on a Bible.

"Hail Columbia," the song played for the vice president's entrance, was once an unofficial U.S. national anthem.

In 1946, the U.S. Marines were called to subdue the Battle of Alcatraz, the deadliest escape attempt in the prison's history. Two guards and three inmates were killed, and 15 others were injured.

What did U.S. presidents John Tyler, Millard Fillmore, and Chester A. Arthur have in common? No vice president.

The U.S. death toll from the 1918 flu pandemic was so high that it created a coffin shortage.

In the early 1900s, the U.S. government wanted to build a canal through Nicaragua. But because a Nicaraguan stamp showed a volcano, the United States chose Panama instead.

First presidential election in which all U.S. women were allowed to vote: 1920. The winner: Warren G. Harding, who'd been a supporter of women's suffrage.

In the 2008 U.S. presidential election, 131 million votes were cast. In the final voting for American Idol that same year, 97 million votes were cast.

On Location

None of the scenes in *Fargo* were actually filmed in Fargo.

The snow scenes in *It's a Wonderful Life* were shot on a movie lot in Southern California during a record heat wave.

Stagecoach was the first of nine films that John Ford filmed in Monument Valley, Utah.

High Noon was shot in 32 days after only 10 days of rehearsal.

The mansion in *Hannibal* is the Biltmore estate in Asheville, North Carolina.

Amadeus was shot entirely in natural light.

The Russian epic *Doctor Zhivago* was filmed in Spain and Finland.

World War II made filming in Europe impossible, so a Welsh mining town had to be created in Malibu, California, for *How Green Was My Valley*.

Oklahoma! was shot in Arizona. (Oklahoma was too well developed when the film was made in 1955.)

Food Origins

VICHYSSOISE. Don't let the French name fool you—this leek-and-potato soup (pronounced *vi-she-swaz*) has an American origin. Louis Diat, the head chef of New York's Ritz-Carlton Hotel, came up with the cold soup in 1917 while looking for something to serve to customers in the sweltering New York summer heat.

FISH STICKS. Clarence Birdseye single-handedly invented the frozen-food industry in the late 1920s when he figured out how to freeze food without ruining its flavor, texture, or nutritional value (you have to freeze it quickly). His curly machines worked best with food that was cut into slender pieces, and one of the first foods he came up with was a knockoff of a French delicacy called *goujonettes de sole*: sole fillets baked or fried in bread crumbs and a light batter. Birdseye switched to cheaper fish (cod), fried it in a heavier batter, and scored a hit.

WISH-BONE SALAD DRESSING. When Phillip Sollomi returned from fighting in World War II in 1945, he opened a restaurant in Kansas City, Missouri. The house specialty: fried chicken. So he named the restaurant "The Wish-bone." In 1948, he started serving his mother's Sicilian salad dressing, which was so popular that he started bottling it and selling it on the side. In 1957, he sold the salad dressing business to the Lipton Tea Company, and today Wish-Bone is the best-selling Italian dressing in the United States.

CORN DOGS. Neil Fletcher wasn't the first person to dip a hot dog in cornmeal batter and deep-fry it, but he did popularize the dish when he began selling it at the Texas State Fair in 1942. Those early dogs were served on plates, though. It wasn't until four years later that Ed Waldmire, a soldier stationed in Amarillo, first put the corn dog on a "stick" (the first ones were actually metal cocktail forks, later replaced by wooden sticks).

O, Canada!

In Canada, milk is sold in plastic bags as well as in jugs.

Lacrosse is the official "national summer sport" of Canada.

Canada has the fourth-lowest population density in the world.

Studies show that the second-most-annoying thing to Canadians is "Someone reading over your shoulder." (First is traffic.)

According to a survey, Canadian teens spend 27.8 percent less time online than adult Canadians.

Canadian performer with the most celebrity impersonators: Shania Twain.

Five percent of Canadians don't know the first two lines of their national anthem. ("O Canada! / Our home and native land!")

In his lifetime, Elvis Presley played only five concerts outside the United States—all in Canada.

Canadian journalist Sandy Gardiner coined the phrase "Beatlemania."

Twelve percent of Canadians admit to having kicked a photocopier in frustration.

The snowmobile was invented in Canada.

Longest street: Yonge Street in Toronto, at 1,178 miles.

A Canadian pilot, Roy Brown, is credited with shooting down Manfred von Richthofen, "the Red Baron."

Canada is the second-largest country in the world. (Russia is first.)

Canadian-born Arthur Irwin invented the baseball fielder's glove in the late 1800s.

Vocabulary Builders

What's an *atluk*? A hole in the ice where seals come up to breathe.

What's a *mondegreen*? A misheard song lyric.

What's the technical name for a *kazoo*? A membranophone.

What's a *quidnunc*? Well? Well? (It's someone who asks too many questions.)

What's a *carriwitchet*? A puzzling question.

What are *ephelides*? Freckles.

What is *punctate pruritus*? The medical term for an itchy spot.

What's a *bibliobibuli*? Someone who reads too much.

What is *nikhedonia*? The feeling of pleasure one gets from anticipating victory.

What's a *pollex*? Your thumb.

What's the scientific name for heavy winter fog containing ice crystals? Pogonip.

What's an *olf*? A unit of indoor odor equal to one day's aroma from a sedentary human.

What's a *mythomaniac*? Someone who lies constantly.

What do you call a nerve cell that has just formed? A neuroblast.

What's an *onychophagiac*? Someone who habitually bites his or her nails.

*   *   *

Studies show: Forty-one percent of Americans say they believe in extraterrestrials who are "much like ourselves."

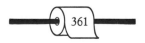

361

On the Farm

Farmers and ranchers provide food and habitat for about 75 percent of America's wildlife.

The McIntosh apple is named for Canadian farmer John McIntosh, who discovered it in 1811.

American farms use the rectilinear grid system, with plots laid out in rectangles. Thomas Jefferson came up with this system in the 18th century.

Cows give more milk when they listen to relaxing music.

Pigs don't sweat—they have no sweat glands. They cool themselves off by wallowing in mud.

Temperature of milk inside a cow: about 100°F.

A cow spends six hours of every day eating...and about eight hours chewing cud.

In Japan, apple farmers use turkeys to guard their orchards against monkeys.

Today, the average yield of a dairy cow is four gallons a day more than it was in the 1700s.

A 1,200-pound horse eats about seven times its own weight per year.

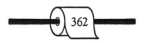

Eyes & Ears

The bottom line on a standard eye chart: PEZOLCFTD.

Ralph Teetor, the man who invented cruise control for cars, was blind.

Baseball player Rogers Hornsby wanted to preserve his eyesight, so he didn't read or watch movies.

Loud noises, aspirin, caffeine, and quinine can all cause tinnitus (ringing in the ears).

The original back cover of the 1973 Wings album *Red Rose Speedway* had a message to Stevie Wonder, written in Braille. (It says, "We love ya baby!")

Roy Orbison refused to perform without his sunglasses.

If a man with normal vision and a color-blind woman have children, the daughters will have normal vision and the sons will be color-blind.

Wearing headphones for an hour can increase the number of bacteria in your ears by 700 percent.

Liu Ch'ung of China (ca. AD 995) had two sets of pupils in each of his eyes.

The opposite of "cross-eyed" is "walleyed."

Leonardo da Vinci made a sketch for contact lenses in the 15th century.

One of David Bowie's pupils is permanently dilated after a friend punched him in the eye as a kid.

Thomas Edison was partially deaf.

Actor Lon Chaney was the son of deaf-mute parents, and thus learned early to pantomime.

Sir Arthur Conan Doyle was also an ophthalmologist.

World Leaders & Politics

Leaders of the First and Second Reichs: Charlemagne and Otto von Bismarck.

As a member of the British Parliament in the early 1700s, Isaac Newton spoke only once. He wanted to open a window.

The writings of Confucius were nearly lost when China's emperor Qin Shi Huang, who unified the country in 221 BC, tried to burn them all.

England nearly went bankrupt after paying the ransom for Richard the Lionheart when he was kidnapped by Austrians in 1192.

Shortly after being exiled from Russia, Leon Trotsky stayed with Diego Rivera and Frida Kahlo in Mexico.

Nuclear scientist J. Robert Oppenheimer was classed as a security risk during the McCarthy era for opposing the nuclear arms race.

When Joseph Stalin became general secretary of the Communist Party in 1922, it was a menial position.

Winston Churchill delivered his famous "Iron Curtain" speech in Missouri in 1946.

David Ben-Gurion, who led Israel through two wars, was actually born in Poland.

Karl Marx and Friedrich Engels wrote *The Communist Manifesto* while in England.

John Hancock, first signer of the Declaration of Independence, was Boston's wealthiest merchant.

The "White Rose" was the name of an anti-Nazi resistance movement in World War II Germany.

Ho Chi Minh based the beginning of Vietnam's declaration of independence on that of the United States.

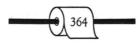
364

Literary Lights

Science-fiction author Isaac Asimov was a claustrophile—he liked small, enclosed spaces.

First person to call Mark Twain the "father of American literature": William Faulkner.

In 1961, when Harper Lee won the Pulitzer Prize for *To Kill a Mockingbird*, she broke out in hives.

First Lady Eleanor Roosevelt was once the editor of a magazine called *Babies, Just Babies*.

Time magazine was originally going to be named *Facts*.

First comic strip artist to win the Pulitzer Prize: Garry Trudeau, for *Doonesbury*, in 1975.

In 1989, baseball pitcher Tom Seaver wrote a crime novel called *Beanball: Murder at the World Series*.

Printing pioneer Johannes Gutenberg was actually a goldsmith by trade.

Karl Marx once worked for the *New York Daily Tribune*.

In 1954, Charles Lindbergh won a Pulitzer for *The Spirit of St. Louis*, his autobiography.

Ulysses S. Grant finished his memoirs on July 19, 1885, and died on July 23; the book sold 300,000 copies.

Elizabeth Barrett Browning wrote her first poem when she was eight years old. She wrote her first epic poem (complete with rhyming couplets) when she was 12.

Winston Churchill worked as a war correspondent in Cuba, India, and South Africa.

Benito Mussolini was a newspaper editor before he came to power.

365

All Mixed Up

Adversaries during the Texas Revolution (1835–36), Stephen F. Austin and Mexican general Santa Anna once belonged to the same freemasonry lodge in Mexico City.

Led Zeppelin's "Houses of the Holy" is on their *Physical Graffiti* album...not *Houses of the Holy*.

Meat Loaf is a vegetarian.

The Lemon Pipers hated their 1968 song "Green Tambourine," but it was their only #1 hit.

The Bank of England was founded by a Scotsman, and the Bank of Scotland by an Englishman.

Chinese herbalists used to prescribe marijuana as a cure for forgetfulness.

Dolly Parton once lost a Dolly Parton look-alike contest.

Sigmund Freud's endorsement of cocaine as a pain reliever resulted in a wave of cocaine addiction in Europe.

The name of the Soviet propaganda newspaper *Pravda* means "Truth" in English.

The *New Yorker* magazine has more subscribers in California than in New York.

One inspiration for Bram Stoker's *Dracula*: vampire bats from Central and South America. They drink a few tablespoons of blood daily.

In the horror film *Trick or Treat*, Ozzy Osbourne plays a televangelist who denounces heavy metal.

In 2004, John Kerry's home-town newspaper, the *Lowell Sun*, endorsed George W. Bush for president...and George W. Bush's hometown newspaper, the *Lone Star Iconoclast*, endorsed John Kerry.

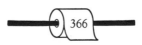

Music Lessons

During the Middle Ages, murdering a traveling musician was not considered to be a serious crime.

The earliest known sheet music for guitars was written by French troubadours around 1100.

First "rock star": Franz Liszt, in the 1840s. Women used to fight over the Hungarian composer's handkerchiefs. They wanted them as souvenirs.

Some Chinese classical music is more than 3,000 years old.

The world's oldest known song, written on a clay tablet, is about 3,400 years old.

In carvings dating to 800, the Norse hero Gunther plays a lute with his toes.

A 3,300-year-old stone carving shows a Hittite poet playing an instrument that looks like a guitar.

First European instrument in China: a harpsichord presented by Jesuit priest Matteo Ricci in 1601.

Klezmer, the name for traditional Jewish music, is from Hebrew words meaning "vessel of music."

In 1931, in Hungary, archaeologists found the remains of a water-driven organ dating to 228.

Until the 1500s, musicians often used bows to play guitars.

Experts say pounding grain was probably the first kind of intentional rhythm created by humans.

The Celts and Romans introduced the bagpipe to Scotland.

Chinese mythology says the founder of music was a scholar named Ling Lun, whose bamboo flutes mimicked birds.

Plant Kingdom

More than 1,000 species of plants live in Death Valley, California.

The scientific name for the tomato: *Lycopersicon lycopersicum*, which means "wolf peach."

Peanuts and peas are members of the same botanical family.

Only one in 10,000 clovers has four leaves.

A saguaro cactus can take up to 75 years to grow a side arm.

Shaggy manes, inky caps, sulfur tufts, and pig's ears are all types of mushrooms.

Invasive exotic plant species infest about 2.6 million acres in U.S. national parks.

The reddish color sometimes seen on snow at California's Lassen Volcanic National Park is a living organism called snow algae.

The world's largest cactus plantation is in Edwards, Mississippi.

During the 18th and 19th centuries, most of the apples grown in the United States were used not for eating but to make hard (alcoholic) cider.

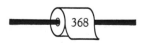

For the Birds, Part 2

An adult turkey has about 3,500 feathers.

The walls of the American goldfinch's nest are so thick that the nest will hold water. As a result, goldfinch nestlings sometimes drown during rainstorms.

King penguin chicks may go five months between meals.

An eagle's bones weigh half as much as its feathers.

The orange-and-black Sri Lanka junglefowl, a kind of pheasant, looks like and is a relative of the chicken.

Mallard ducks have 360-degree vision.

Chickens can't swallow while they are upside down. Gravity is what makes their food pass through their throats.

Puffins can swim faster than they can fly.

Pigeons and doves are in the same biological family, and both are related to the extinct dodo bird.

Gentoo penguins have pink droppings.

Some Middle Eastern farmers breed bald chickens. Why? They do better in the heat.

The Gila woodpecker and gilded flicker are two birds that nest in saguaro cacti.

More than 40 National Park Service sites are designated as "Globally Important Bird Areas."

Rockhopper penguins can travel as far as five feet in a single hop.

About 50 pairs of bald eagles nest in Florida's Everglades National Park.

A hawk can spot a mouse from a mile away.

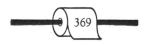

369

Passion for Fashion

Hollywood fashion tip: wearing yellow makes you look bigger on camera; green, smaller.

A Colombian company makes a T-shirt it claims is "stab-proof." Price: $500.

Until the early 20th century, many boys wore dresses up to the age of five.

The green jackets awarded to the Masters golf tournament champions are made of 55 percent wool and 45 percent polyester.

The social status of an ancient Roman was indicated by the stripes on his toga.

Sunglasses became popular in the 1920s when movie stars wore them to shield their eyes from bright camera lights.

The Chinese have been painting their fingernails for more than 5,000 years.

During the 1770s, most people in Europe owned only one or two changes of clothing.

Average number of bathing suits sold in America every second: four.

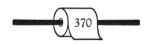

Fall Facts

Technical term for the season: autumn, which comes from the French word *automne*. People started calling autumn "fall" during the 16th century.

John Keats wrote the poem "To Autumn" in 1819.

Retailers in the United States sell about $2 billion worth of candy at Halloween.

Leaves change color in the fall because, as the days get shorter and there's less sunlight, trees stop producing chlorophyll, the chemical that gives them their green color. The bright oranges, yellows, and other colors of fall leaves have been part of the plants all along, but they've been covered up by all the chlorophyll. When the trees stop making that green chemical, the other colors come to the forefront.

Best conditions for fall leaves: a dry late summer, sunny fall days, and autumn nights with temperatures of about 40°F.

*　　*　　*

"Delicious autumn! My very soul is wedded to it, and if I were a bird I would fly about the earth seeking the successive autumns."
　　　　　　　　　—George Eliot

371

Came, Saw, Conquered

When Julius Caesar said, "Veni, vidi, vici" ("I came, I saw, I conquered"), he was referring to Turkey.

The Cuna, Guaymí, and Chocó Indians of Panama wore gold breastplates, prompting the Spanish myth about El Dorado, the "lost city of gold."

Abel Tasman discovered Tasmania, New Zealand, and Fiji, but didn't notice Australia until a later voyage.

In 1498, Christopher Columbus declared that the earth was pear-shaped, not round.

Technically, it was lookout Rodrigo de Triana who first sighted America, not Columbus.

Dublin, Ireland, was founded by the Vikings.

Nobody knows exactly where Columbus landed when he "discovered" America—probably somewhere in the Bahamas.

The term "Silk Road" is a translation from the German *Seidenstrasse*, which was first used by German geographer Ferdinand von Richthofen in 1877.

Polynesian explorers used stars, wind, wave patterns, and seagulls to navigate their way across the Pacific Ocean.

Julius Caesar made history in 49 BC by crossing the Rubicon—Roman armies were forbidden from crossing the river in northern Italy and entering the territory of Gaul. Caesar's crossing made an armed conflict inevitable, but today, no one's sure where the actual crossing took place.

International Law

In Switzerland, it's illegal to flush a toilet or urinate standing up after 10:00 p.m.

In the town of Summerside on Canada's Prince Edward Island, it's illegal to borrow or lend water.

In Cuba, you can be jailed for three days if your house burns down.

It's against the law in Madagascar for pregnant women to eat eels or wear hats.

In Paraguay, dueling is perfectly legal...if both parties are registered blood donors.

Speeding-ticket fines in Finland are based on the driver's income.

Canadian law prohibits anyone from boarding a plane while it's in flight.

Law requires that farmers in England provide their pigs with toys.

Roger Tullgren, a man from Sweden, gets disability benefits for his "heavy metal music addiction."

In Glasgow, Scotland, it's a crime for a man to hug a store mannequin.

Gold Rush

The first gold nugget found in the United States weighed 17 pounds and was discovered in North Carolina in 1799.

About one of out every billion rocks in the earth's crust is gold.

You have a better chance of finding gold than of winning the lottery.

When gold was discovered in California in 1848, the area was still officially Mexican territory.

World's largest consumer of gold: India—936 tons a year, enough to make a gold ring for every Indian citizen.

Every year in the United States, 17 tons of gold are used to make wedding rings.

There's about $137 billion worth of gold at Fort Knox, and about $147 billion in New York's Federal Reserve Bank.

A bar of gold the size of a matchbox can be flattened into a sheet the size of a tennis court.

A typical gold bar weighs about 25 pounds.

Common prices for everyday goods in 1849 California gold-mining towns: $30–40 for a pound of flour and up to $100 for a glass of water.

The average human body contains about 0.2 milligram of gold.

About 90 percent of the gold used throughout history was mined after 1848, when gold was discovered in California.

World's largest gold nugget: a 60-pounder found in Australia.

The Aztec word for gold is *teocuitlatl*…"excrement of the gods."

Family Matters

More than 350 sets of brothers have played baseball at the major-league level, but only nine sets of twins have.

William the Conqueror was illegitimate—his father had an affair with a tanner's daughter.

Only father and son to hit back-to-back home runs in major-league baseball: Ken Griffey Sr. and Ken Griffey Jr.

The woman who modeled for Grant Wood's *American Gothic* painting was Wood's sister.

The last king of the ancient Egyptian empire was Ptolemy XV, son of Cleopatra.

Anne Frank's *The Diary of a Young Girl* was published by her father after her death.

Robert F. Kennedy's 11th child, Rory Elizabeth, was born six months after his death.

Abandoned at birth as stillborn, Pablo Picasso was revived by his uncle.

The Wright brothers were practically inseparable, and neither ever married.

Polish king Augustus the Strong fathered more than 300 children, but had only one legitimate son.

After he murdered his son, Ivan the Terrible had himself rechristened as a monk to atone for his crime.

Michelangelo's father didn't want him to become an artist.

To ensure an heir, England's King Henry VIII had six wives. But none of his children had children.

At her witchcraft trial, Joan of Arc was also charged with disobeying her parents.

Also Known As, Part 2

William Sydney Porter wrote under the pen name of O. Henry while in prison.

In 1993, the town of Ismay, Montana, unofficially changed its name to Joe, Montana.

Washington Irving sometimes went by the pen name Geoffrey Crayon.

Mata Hari was actually a Dutch woman named Margaretha Geertruida Zelle.

Ben Franklin used the pen name Richard Saunders to publish *Poor Richard's Almanack*.

Frederick Douglass named himself after a character in a Sir Walter Scott poem.

Cleo and Caesar were the early stage names of Cher and Sonny Bono.

Rolihlahla Mandela's schoolteacher renamed him Nelson for Horatio Nelson.

During World War II, the Pittsburgh Steelers and Philadelphia Eagles played together as the Steagles.

Outlaw Robert LeRoy Parker got his alias from his occupation (butcher) and his mentor, Mike Cassidy. The alias: Butch Cassidy.

Hard Times

In ancient Sparta, weak babies were left to die on hillsides or sent away to become slaves.

At the time of feminist Susan B. Anthony's death in 1906, only four states (Wyoming, Colorado, Idaho, and Utah) had given women the right to vote.

Henry Ford's newspaper, the *Dearborn Independent*, was violently anti-Semitic...but after Jews boycotted and sued, Ford closed the paper and issued an apology.

In 1725, Dick Syme, the official whipper in East Hampton, New York, was paid three shillings for each person he whipped.

In 1619, a Dutch ship brought the first slaves to North America.

In ancient Rome, women were expected to cover their heads when walking outdoors.

"Sold down the river" entered the American language around 1837. It referred to sales of slaves along the Mississippi.

In 1790, Thomas Halford, a British convict, was found guilty of stealing three pounds of potatoes and was sentenced to 2,000 lashes.

In 1892, Italy raised the minimum age for a girl to be married to 12.

The last country in the Americas to abolish slavery was Cuba (1886).

Sir Thomas More was executed when he refused to acknowledge King Henry VIII as the supreme head of the Church of England.

At the height of its power, Sparta had 25,000 citizens and 500,000 slaves.

In ancient Greece, women didn't start counting their age until they were married.

Cats

If your cat snores while sleeping or rolls over on his back to expose his belly, it means he trusts you.

Chocolate and avocados can be lethal to parrots.

Cat urine glows under a black light.

In the 12th century, the British government passed a law saying every farmer had to own at least one cat...for rodent control.

Cats lose almost as much fluid through grooming as they do through urination.

Studies show: most cats dislike men with long, dark beards.

Cats sleep an average of 16 hours a day.

Top five male cat names in the United States: Tiger, Tigger, Max, Smokey, and Sam.

Cats also have "whiskers" on the backs of their forelegs.

Most people who are allergic to cats aren't allergic to cat fur or dander. They're actually allergic to sebum, a fatty substance secreted by glands under the cat's skin.

Ninety-five percent of cat owners admit that they talk to their cats daily.

Top three cat breeds in the United States: Persian, Maine Coon, and Exotic.

Most cats consume 28 times their weight in food annually.

Cats have three blood types: A, B, and AB. Most cats are type A.

Twenty percent of cats are "left-pawed," meaning they favor that side. Forty percent are "right-pawed," and the rest are ambidextrous.

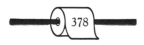

Facts of War, Part 2

During World War I, the Battle of the Somme resulted in more than a million casualties...and advanced the Allies just seven miles.

In 1928, the world powers outlawed war under the Kellogg-Briand Pact. (It didn't work.)

The youngest known soldier to die in the Civil War was 12.

Of the 25 million military casualties during World War II, more than 10 million were from the Soviet Union.

Since the United Nations was founded in 1945, there have been an average of 2.2 wars per year.

Of the last 3,500 years, only 230 years saw no major wars.

The two largest military budgets in 2008: the United States ($651 billion) and China ($70 billion).

In the War of 1812, the United States burned down Toronto, and the British burned down Washington, D.C.

In Britain, rationing didn't end until 1954, nine years after the end of World War II.

When the Civil War ended, some 40,000 former slaves became cowboys.

During World War II, the United States never declared war on two Axis powers: Thailand and Finland.

After the southern states seceded, prompting the Civil War, they created their own constitution...which banned the international slave trade.

Only Communist country attacked by the Warsaw Pact (an agreement among the Soviet Union and its allies to protect each other): Czechoslovakia.

Born in Canada

Pamela Anderson
Dan Aykroyd
Raymond Burr
Neve Campbell
John Candy
Jim Carrey
Michael Cera
David Cronenberg
Michael J. Fox
Victor Garber
Tom Green
Graham Greene
Corey Haim
Monty Hall
Natasha Henstridge
Joshua Jackson
Margot Kidder
Diana Krall
Eugene Levy
Evangeline Lilly
Norm MacDonald
Howie Mandel

Rachel McAdams
Eric McCormack
Joni Mitchell
Rick Moranis
Alanis Morrisette
Mike Myers
Catherine O'Hara
Sandra Oh
Anna Paquin
Ellen Page
Mary Pickford
Christopher Plummer
Sarah Polley
Jason Priestley
Gloria Reuben
Ryan Reynolds
Seth Rogen
William Shatner
Norma Shearer
Donald Sutherland
Alan Thicke
Fay Wray

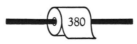

Underwear Origins

CORSET. This is an Old French term for "little body," from the Latin *corpus*, or "body." The garment has its origins in ancient Greece and Rome, where women sometimes wrapped broad bands around their bodies. By the 17th century, it had evolved into a tight inner bodice, sometimes of leather, stiffened with whalebone, wooden splints, or steel, and worn by both men and women. By 1900, the corset was again primarily a female garment, and was modified to conform to the natural lines of a woman's body.

TANK TOP. The term became popular around 1968, deriving from "tank suit," a one-piece "bathing costume" for men (and later, women) in the 1920s. The tank suit was so called because it was worn in a pool, or "swimming tank." The tank top became a fashion staple (on the outside) in the 1970s.

DRAWERS. This old-fashioned term for underwear was originally a men's garment, adopted by 18th-century women to wear under hoopskirts. Before the Civil War, American men's underwear were made of wool flannel. Most were knee-length with a simple button overlap in front and a drawstring at the waist. The word "drawers" dates from 1567 and indicates a garment that is pulled, or "drawn," on, from the Norse *draga*, "to draw."

NEGLIGEE. From the French *négliger*, "to neglect," although in this case the meaning is closer to "to let go." This sense originates with 18th-century women who, during rest periods after lunch, put on a lightweight, loose-fitting garment that released them temporarily from the tight-fitting dresses of the time. The modern negligee was popularized by a 1941 photo of Rita Hayworth in *Life* magazine. After World War II, it became a much-sought-after item of lingerie.

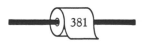

American Food

Top three condiments in the United States: salsa, ketchup, and mustard.

More than 1.5 million Americans are allergic to peanuts.

The three foods Americans say they hate the most: tofu, liver, and yogurt.

In the colonies, pumpkins were used to make pie crusts, not the filling.

Only about one-fourth of all American adults eat three meals a day.

U.S. town with the highest annual per-capita consumption of Spaghetti-Os: Grand Rapids, Michigan.

The average American eats about 67 pickles per year.

Sixty percent of American men say they can eat a hot dog in five bites or less.

The average American eats 200 sandwiches a year.

According to Hormel, Hawaiians eat the most Spam per capita annually.

Americans eat twice as much meat as Europeans do.

About 70 Oscar Mayer bologna sandwiches are eaten every second in America.

Five most popular lunches in U.S. schools: pizza, chicken nuggets, tacos, burritos, and hamburgers.

Most popular sandwich to serve American kids for lunch: peanut butter and jelly.

Thin Mints account for 25 percent of the Girl Scout cookies sold in the United States.

In 1714, the favorite nonalcoholic drink of American colonists was cocoa.

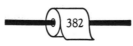

Index

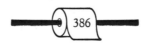

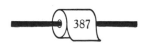

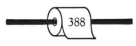

J

Jackson, Andrew, 127,
182, 291, 348
Jackson, Jesse, 329
Jackson, Michael, 20,
234, 324
Jackson (siblings), 30
jails, 105
Jakobs, Josef, 133
Japan, 83, 100
Jaws (movie), 236
jazz, 125
Jefferson, Thomas, 11,
21, 51, 119, 127, 231,
257, 348, 362
jelly beans, 119, 147
jellyfish, 92–3
Jemima, Aunt, 258
Jemison, Mae, 93
Jeremiah Johnson (movie),
31
jerky (beef), 91
Jerry Maguire (movie),
248
Jessup, Violet, 116
jesters, 89
Jetsons, The (TV show),
90
Joan of Arc, 375
jobs, 137, 321
Jobs, Steve, 156
Joel, Billy, 156
John Paul II, Pope, 350
John, Elton, 136, 324
Johnson, Andrew, 27,
348

Johnson, Billy "White
Shoes," 355
Johnson, Dwayne "The
Rock," 115
Johnson, Jack, 11
Johnson, Lyndon B., 27,
119, 182, 214, 323,
348
Jolie-Pitt (siblings), 30
Jonas brothers, 30
Jones, James Earl, 111
Jones, Jim, 133
Jonestown Massacre, 133
Joplin, Janis, 43
Jordan, Michael, 52, 63
*Journey to the Center of
the Earth* (Verne), 352
Joy of Cooking, The
(Rombauer), 91
Joyce, James, 98, 354
Judaism, 102
July Fourth (holiday), 85
jump rope, 174
Juneteenth, 281

K

kamikaze, 123
kangaroos, 330
kazoo, 361
Keaton, Buster, 121
Keats, John, 371
Kelloggs, 126
Kelly, Gene, 79
Kennedy, John F., 71,
348, 356
Kennedy (siblings), 30

Kermit the Frog, 315
Kerouac, Jack, 136
Kerry, John, 145, 366
ketchup, 119, 140
keyboards, 125
Khan, Chaka, 91
Khan, Genghis, 355
Khan, Kublai, 355
Khrushchev, Nikita, 344
King, B. B., 20
King, Martin Luther, Jr.,
43, 72, 100, 133
King, Stephen, 31
kings, 104
Kirk, Captain, 107
Kirkwood, Joe, 21
KISS (band), 32, 87
Kissin' Cousins (movie),
111
kite flying, 36
Kiwis (birds), 77
Klem, Bill, 14
klezmer (music), 367
Knight, Gladys, 136
Know-Nothing Party,
134
Kool-Aid, 133
Koufax, Sandy, 112
Krauss, Alison, 347
kryptonite, 90
Kuhn, Maggie, 136
Kyoto, Japan, 106

L

labor, 137
Labor Day, 325

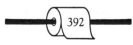

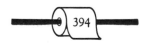

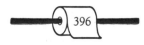

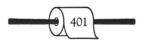

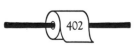